Praise for
Socialized! and Mark Fidelman

"In *Socialized!* Mark Fidelman demonstrates how businesses are able to significantly increase their revenue by becoming a social business both internally and externally."

—Erik Qualman, best-selling author, *Digital Leader* and *Socialnomics*

"Exceptionally well written and engaging....If your goal is to make your business number one in your industry, then this is the book you'll want to own."

—Deepak Chopra, *NY Times* best-selling author

"Fidelman's brilliant insight into the importance of adapting the corporate social sphere, offers real-world, tactical guidelines to establishing a community around your brand. If you want to build an engaged audience, *Socialized!* is the roadmap. This book is a must-read for anyone on my team!"   —Matt Michelsen, CEO, Backplane

"This is not another social media book but the first book that provides organizations with the 'secret sauce' to become a social business. From Fidelman's own experiences to those of his expert sources, there's an impressive portfolio of case studies to learn from and implement immediately to help your business take advantage of all that social has to offer."

—Jeff Schick, VP Social Business, IBM

"For too long the command and control management philosophy has ruled most corporations. That model is over. Fidelman demonstrates why a social business is replacing that leadership model and how new technologies enable a much more adaptable leadership instead."   —Jon Ferrara, CEO, Nimble

"In a world where customers are more vocal than ever, and word of mouth can make or break a business, Fidelman delivers a sound roadmap to guide businesses through the social media gauntlet. As a result of reading *Socialized!*, forward-thinking leaders will have the practical strategies they need to engage with customers that are more loyal than ever, and the opportunity to surpass the competition."

—Becky Carroll, author of *The Hidden Power of Your Customers:*
Four Keys to Growing Business From Existing Customers

"Whether communicating externally or internally, every company needs to harness social, or they're behind. In *Socialized!* Mark Fidelman draws on the practices of innovative companies like SAP to provide a blueprint for the social enterprise. Read this book."   —Oliver Bussman, CIO, SAP

"*Socialized!* is an imminently readable, practical, and modern guide to social business. The playbook section alone is worth the price, and then some. Mark Fidelman has added an important piece to the corporate social transformation puzzle."

—Jay Baer, president, Convince & Convert
and co-author of *The NOW Revolution*

"Social transformation in business is a strategic core element for market relevance and sustainable growth. Fidelman's expert advice is essential for all executives looking to transform their business to a social enterprise. As the chief customer officer for an award-winning social enterprise, I consider Fidelman's thought leadership to be among the very best in industry."

—Vala Afshar, Chief Customer Officer, Enterasys Networks

"Just as I was starting to free up time by tuning out every so-called 'social media guru,' Mark Fidelman comes along with something truly pioneering! *Socialized!* cuts through all the yammer to create the definitive guide for social in the enterprise. You'll never have to suffer through another mind-numbing social strategy meeting because it's all here in this book."

—Steve Faktor, author of *Econovation* and founder of IdeaFaktory

"Mark Fidelman is a brilliant innovator and peerless connector. His social business insights will give you a competitive advantage in this dynamic era."

—Tristan Bishop, Director of Digital Strategy, Symantec

"Standing out from the flood of excellent books on social media for the enterprise, Fidelman's *Socialized!*, from his first-hand experience, offers not only a compelling case that any leader can understand but also an explicit path for socializing a business so that it can stay relevant and sought-after."

—Kare Anderson, author, *Moving From
Me to We, Forbes* columnist, "Connected & Quotable"

"Fidelman's ability to simplify key concepts like the Digital Village, Darwin's Funnel, and the Digital Network, gives the reader a unique and important understanding of the power of Social Business. You'll be sorry if you don't read this book before your competitors do."

—Dr. Natalie Petouhoff, speaker, author,
and social business and social media ROI expert

SOCIALIZED!

SOCIALIZED!

HOW THE MOST SUCCESSFUL
BUSINESSES HARNESS
THE POWER OF SOCIAL

MARK FIDELMAN

bibliomotion
books + media

First published by Bibliomotion, Inc.

33 Manchester Road
Brookline, MA 02446
Tel: 617-934-2427
www.bibliomotion.com

Printed in the United States of America

Library of Congress Cataloging-in-Publication Data

Fidelman, Mark.
  Socialized! : how the most successful businesses harness the power of social / Mark
Fidelman.
     p. cm.
  ISBN 978-1-937134-43-3 (hardcover : alk. paper) — ISBN 978-1-937134-44-0 (ebook) —
ISBN 978-1-937134-45-7 (enhanced ebook)
  1. Business networks—Computer network resources.   2. Social media—Marketing.
3. Strategic planning.   4. Online social networks.   5. Business enterprises—
Computer networks.   I. Title.
  HD69.S8F56 2013
  658.8'72—dc23
                         2012038922

For my loving wife Kelly and my amazing son and daughter

Contents

Introduction

"Don't be a star, be a galaxy."
—*Peter Gloor*

This is a book about how to create a highly adaptive, competitive business by harnessing new business strategies, social and mobile technologies, and emboldened communities. An adaptive business is the only business that will survive the new challenges ahead, challenges caused by a massive shift of power from corporations and traditional media to customers and influencers. My team and I have found convincing evidence in our research that companies that don't make the transition to adaptive, social business will face overwhelming challenges that they are ill prepared to overcome. Too often, we've witnessed organizations fail to understand and act on these shifts, and surrender to their competitors and creditors.

We want to change that. We've created a game plan for leaders of organizations that want to learn how to address these new challenges, and we are providing the playbook for seizing opportunities that weren't available before. Through research and personal experience, we've discovered how to gain a long-term competitive advantage by combining new social and mobile technologies with the right culture to create a powerful growth machine that automatically adjusts to changing market conditions and unexpected black swan events. If this sounds too good to be true, then recognize that the transition to social business is not an easy one, for there are still quite a few entrenched interests that must be moved aside or moved out.

But also recognize that the companies that have made the transition to social business are becoming more innovative. Their power to innovate is exponentially larger than that of companies in a presocial state, because they've learned how to create environments where employees, customers, and partners feel encouraged to share ideas, improve them, and then implement the best ones in record time. They've evolved beyond traditional business; according to the PulsePoint Group in collaboration with the Economist Intelligence Unit, social businesses bring products to market 65 percent faster. The study also reported that 57 percent of social businesses are now letting customers, employees, and partners either suggest new ideas or participate in vetting them.

It's hard not to notice that these companies are leaping ahead of their competition and are laying the foundation for future products that will seize their competitors' market share. They've taken advantage of all the new opportunities that have been handed to them in the form of social technologies and the network effect. Indeed, these agile social companies are building out their networks while their competitors fall further and further behind. The longer a company waits to begin the transformation to social business, the harder it is to catch up.

Community Is King

There's a certain power in digital networks and communities that few understand; even fewer realize how game-changing these tools will become. Matt Michelsen, CEO of Backplane, understands, and he's creating powerful communities for the world's most popular brands that will make them nearly invincible.

In July 2012, Michelsen's Backplane took Lady Gaga's LittleMonsters .com community out of private beta and released it to the world. It was a momentous event for those who understood its importance. Yet it wasn't the fact that the site quickly received more than a million unique visitors from all around the world and it wasn't that those people were spending an outstanding average of thirteen minutes on the site: what mattered was that the business world had taken a great leap forward, and Backplane viewed itself as the vehicle for this giant stride into the future.

Up until now, brands have embraced an opportunistic view of customer acquisition and community building, mostly by building their presence on Facebook, Twitter, Google+, and other social networks, hoping to engage their target audience on platforms with billions of people. But our research revealed that these platforms are like giant digital carnivals, where participants move quickly between unrelated discussions, merchandise vendors, and sideshow curiosities. Most are distracted by every stray prompt, unable to maintain a consistent focus on any one thing.

But as Backplane has discovered, the communities people associate themselves with become parts of their identity. They don't want these pieces of their identity scattered across a vast digital landscape where identity is fractured—there's no meaning in that. People want to join purpose-driven communities that reflect their values and beliefs and they don't want to be interrupted by requests to join Farmville or weird pictures of someone's cats.

That's why, after realizing that brands are giving away too much power to those broad platforms, each of which has its own set of interests, we came to the conclusion that brands must build a stronger voice and participation with their customer base. That means having a larger controlling share in what we term their "digital brand networks," or communities of people who identify with the brand. That means taking back some control over how the brand connects with and understands its customers.

What these brands desperately need are new strategies and tools to understand their customers in a digital world. The analog world, where customers buy a product and then disappear—without the brand ever learning anything more about those customers or how they use the product—is fading. The businesses that understand the trend toward social business, and are able to properly adapt to and prosper from it, will be the winners in the next decade. We agree with Michelsen when he says that one of the best ways for brands to thrive in a digital world is to build and run their own communities. These communities are going to become the lifeblood of every organization in the future. The brands that understand how to nurture communities and provide the right nutrients to them will discover how powerful they can be.

Imagine having a community of motivated customers, influencers, and brand advocates helping you succeed. Imagine encountering seemingly insurmountable challenges that are swatted away by an unpaid workforce that has aligned its interests with your organization's. Your loss is their loss, so they will endeavor to help you. Indeed, a robust organization surrounded by an engaged community is ready for any challenge.

Unfortunately, most companies are not even thinking about a small leap forward, much less a large one. They are stuck in a reactive world, waiting for something to hit the fan before taking action. That strategy is no longer justifiable in a digital world where 60 percent of social-network-fueled customers expect brands to respond quickly to their requests or risk losing them as customers, according to an Arnold Worldwide survey. The stakes are high, and brands need to take a leap forward and engage their customers in a more meaningful way, free from the countless distractions found on general-purpose platforms, and then they must measure and adapt to the needs of those customers.

Why This Book Should Matter to You

Over the past few years, there have been a lot of books written on the subject of social media. These books focus on the importance of social networks, how to be remarkable, the importance of content marketing, or the wisdom of crowds. These are great books and we've all learned from them. *Socialized!* is different: we explain in a global context how the best companies are using social and mobile technologies, the cloud, and data analytics to become highly competitive growth machines. We describe not only the game plan, we provide the plays from the playbooks these highly adaptive organizations are using.

Some people, like me, refer to these organizations as *social businesses.* That is, they are businesses that have learned the philosophy and strategy of using social technologies to create more adaptive businesses. Think of a new kind of business that's agile enough to capture new opportunities, can change shape when confronted with threats, and can call on vibrant communities to support its initiatives. According to the PulsePoint Group and the Economist Intelligence Unit, businesses that have adapted toward a social model are experiencing four times greater business impact than companies that have not.

How do your organization's leaders answer these questions: Can our organization quickly find subject matter experts inside and outside our organization to help solve business challenges? Does our organization allow any employee, at any time, to engage customers on social networks, as long as the employee is trained properly? Does our business generate substantial ideas, revenue, and intelligence from our communities? Are employees actively engaged on internal social networks (we call them digital villages) to help the organization execute on opportunities for growth? If our business was attacked by a malicious social media campaign, would we be able to withstand it?

If your leaders (or you) can't come up with practical answers to these questions, this book will serve as your guide. The cost of being left behind is much greater than ever before, and it's no longer simply a matter of following what other businesses have done to be successful. In some respects, you are in a race against your competitors for the hearts and minds of customers and industry influencers. My team and I believe the advantages gained by executing on the models laid out in *Socialized!* will increase the effectiveness of your organization, its leaders, and the communities it participates in. Certainly we've found in our research that those individuals who've decided to take the journey toward social business have been promoted, are paid more, and have become visible players in their company and industry.

We also believe that organizations that make the journey will become highly competitive just a few years from now. The executives we interviewed at companies that have made the transformation to social business are experiencing higher-than-industry-average growth. But we are not so naïve as to think that simply investing in social business will correct a flawed product or a bad corporate strategy. We strongly believe, however, that a social business model will reveal to the organization that its product and strategy are flawed. For one of the primary benefits of social business is real-time, dynamic feedback from employees, customers, and partners.

In most cases, the adaptive abilities of the social businesses we reviewed produced powerful competitive advantages and superior returns in capital. Of course the real question is, how did they do it and, even more importantly, how can you do it?

Socialized! resolves these critical questions and many more. My primary purpose as an author has been to uncover the strategies and secrets of the businesses that are harnessing the power of social technologies. So my team and I interviewed more than one hundred of the world's most social executives and thought leaders as well as the customers who bought products from them. These are people like David Sacks, CEO of Yammer (now Microsoft); SAP's CIO Oliver Bussmann; Bayer's CIO Kurt De Ruwe; Google's vice president of enterprise, Amit Singh; Jeff Schick, IBM's vice president of social software; Jonathan Becher, CMO of SAP; Maria Klawe, president of Harvey Mudd; Cindy McKenzie, SVP, Information Technology of Fox Entertainment; Andrew McAfee of MIT; Chris Anderson, curator of TED Conferences; and Bill Davidson, Senior Vice President of Global Marketing of Qualcomm. We also talked to many social business experts like Dion Hinchcliffe, Jason Falls, Brian Solis, Jacob Morgan, Ray Wang, and others to understand their perspectives on social business. Finally, we worked with some of the most innovative small and medium-sized companies to understand how social business is working for them.

All of the people we interviewed provided surprising and unique views of what it means to become a social business. Our goal was to investigate how each of the companies made the social business journey as well as to learn the strategies and lessons the leaders who ran or advised the companies learned along the way. We wanted to understand each of their perspectives and what advice they'd give their peers.

As we reflected on the research, we realized that a major roadblock to becoming a social business remained, despite the successes, despite the higher revenues, despite the reduced costs, despite the opportunity to be highly competitive. In short, too many executives want to remain in an era that's already gone, though they haven't yet comprehended the loss. They're like the oblivious Bruce Willis character in the movie *The Sixth Sense,* except that the ghosts that haunt them are business models that want to be set free, but no one knows how. And too many boards of directors, while acknowledging the need for change, don't understand how to make the transitions efficiently and effectively. What we desperately needed was a new playbook for the social era and all of its challenges and opportunities. That is why my team and I decided to write this book.

1

Adapt or Die

As the world socializes and mobilizes, a fifth age of modern business is underway. Rarely in history has a new age opened up so many possibilities across every industry and discipline. In less than five years, the balance of power has shifted from seller to buyer, from big media to the influential individual, from industry trade associations to thriving digital communities.

Now is the single greatest time in history to be in business.

This fifth age of business has created a new set of rules that enables organizations to compete in the economy as equals. Being large no longer ensures a competitive advantage. In fact, being large may be a deficit in the new business environment.

Worse, few executives are aware of the massive transformation that is in motion. Most are stuck in an old management mind-set of command and control that emphasizes "Do as I say" and not "I want to hear your opinion." As a result, they are ill prepared for the colossal challenges that confront them now.

The leaders who will succeed in this fifth age are those who welcome feedback, leverage the wisdom of crowds, create pull, and foster workplace environments that promote innovation. The skills needed to succeed today are not being taught in the workplace, high schools, or colleges, as they were in previous ages. Instead, they are learned through experimentation, which yields both big mistakes and stunning successes.

Certainly, the goal of leadership remains the same: to grow and nurture people so that they are capable of achieving business objectives through shared missions and measurable performance. But the crucial ingredients for success are advancing beyond the old leadership model, to new ones that are more strategic and yield far greater results. As we'll cover in chapter 6, "Introducing the New Social Business Playbook," there are a variety of new competencies these leaders must acquire to remain effective in the future.

But to understand where we are, we must first look at where we came from. We must understand that in each age, businesses and their leaders have had to adapt to technological and market forces. To survive in this new age, because of the increased speed of change, we must learn how to evolve our companies into highly adaptive organizations or be relegated to the ash-heap of history's failed organizations.

The Five Modern Ages of Business Technology

Before we can understand the future of business, we must review the past. I've broken up the business ages into periods of time that I find significant and that show why social business is the next natural evolution of business. I also introduce each business age with a formula which I feel best represents the age in short form. Let's begin.

The Industrial Age and Emerging
Communication Technology (1850–1910)
Telegraph + Railroad = Smaller World

The first instant message, "What hath God wrought," was sent by telegraph May 24, 1844, from Washington D.C. to a B&O Railroad depot in Baltimore, Maryland. The irony of sending a message via the new telegraph technology to a railroad depot, which operated using the old method of delivering messages, probably escaped the sender, Samuel Morse. Until the telegraph, messages were carried by horseback, train, or human courier, which could take days, weeks, or months, depending on the distance. Inadequate infrastructure and delayed communication were the norm, so commerce was conducted primarily by local buyers and sellers in a closed social network consisting of skilled craftspeople, merchants, and farmers.

Shortly after that first telegraph message, an explosion of new technologies and discoveries added to an emerging infrastructure that powered what we now call the Second Industrial Revolution. The railroad was extended across the United States and Europe, delivering people and cargo at far reduced rates. By 1865, a considerable eighty-three thousand miles of telegraph wire enabled instantaneous communication between industry and customer. Almost in parallel, electrical power was harnessed and large deposits of oil and coal were discovered, and these led in turn to the invention of the telephone, lightbulb, automobile, typewriter, and phonograph, and to the electrification of factories.

As infrastructure improved, each subsequent invention brought people closer together, making the world a little smaller. Buyers and sellers were able to reach beyond their local towns to buy goods (but not yet services) from more distant towns and cities far more quickly and at a reasonable cost.

The industrial age also spawned the large business enterprise. Before then, many of the largest organizations were run by the government. In fact, the government-run army provided the blueprint for businesses to scale operations into much larger enterprises. The command-and-control leadership model, with a small number of leaders giving orders to a multitude of followers, provided an effective hierarchical structure for businesses to adopt. It was so effective that it remains the primary leadership model for organizations even today.

At the time, of course, the modern concept of "knowledge management" in business had not been introduced. Knowledge was passed from one individual to another in the form of apprenticeship or on-the-job training. Because specialized knowledge was rarely written down and shared among a wider group, the ability to distribute information about best practices or to build on the ideas of others was limited.

During the industrial age, the relationship between business leaders and their employees was often a highly abusive and contentious one. Most employees of big business were subjected to appalling factory conditions, and labor conflict was intense. The culture in most of the companies was that of a dysfunctional family: everyone was just trying to survive.

Despite the cultural challenges, the American economy was dramatically transformed during this period. The infrastructure created during the industrial age fueled American manufacturing to increase its economic output from $3 billion in 1869 to an estimated $13 billion in 1910. The central vehicle of this rise in economic productivity was the industrial enterprise. The industrial enterprise dominated in this era because it best leveraged the transportation, management, and communication tools of the day.

The Mass Production Age and Broadcast Communication (1910–1950)
Radio + Telephone + TV = Broadcast Messaging to the Masses

The first Model T cars took more than fourteen hours to assemble. By introducing mass production methods, Henry Ford reduced assembly time to one hour and thirty-three minutes. Remarkably, Ford's company undercut its competitors by reducing the price of the Model T from $1000 to $360. As the knowledge of mass production methods slowly trickled out to the rest of the business world, other manufacturing organizations followed suit and began to manufacture products less expensively, thus opening up their availability to a bigger buying audience.

Even more important for its impact on the organization, and arguably Ford's greatest achievement, was his massive publicity machine. Because of the company's increased automobile output, Ford needed to sell more cars. So he targeted every major newspaper (the primary means of large-scale information dissemination) in the country, generating stories and placing ads about Ford cars. Remember, in the early twentieth century, there were no billboards, no radio, no television, and very few advertising slogans.

The company also encouraged some of the first branded communities in the form of local motor clubs, which sprang up around the country to help new Ford drivers find things like traversable roads, places to stay overnight, and a difficult-to-find energy source—gasoline.

By 1934, more than 60 percent of American households and more than

1.5 million cars were equipped with radios. As a result, businesses were able to advertise to prospective customers over the airwaves within a small geographic region. Although it was a one-way transmission, this was the first time the voice of the business could be broadcast across great distances to influence buyer behavior.

By 1940, the telephone had become standard equipment both in the home and business. The number of calls per person rose rapidly—doubling between 1940 and 1960 and doubling again between 1960 and 1980, then doubling yet again between 1980 and 2000. The telephone extended an individual's social network by connecting people over vast distances; people were no longer limited to in-person discussions, but could hold two-way conversations with loved ones, friends, and business-people across town, in adjacent cities, or in the rural countryside. This enabled business to be conducted in real time without the need for travel.

Even with the Great Depression, U.S. gross domestic product rose from $33 billion in 1910 to $293 billion in 1950. Lower costs, due to the integration of mass production and mass marketing, permitted the enterprise to reduce the cost of goods as well as the cost of information about markets and suppliers. This allowed organizations to significantly increase production and reach more prospective customers, achieving ever greater economies of scale.

The companies that prevailed in this era were the ones that took advantage of cost savings where they were greatest. These technology-enabled companies produced and marketed goods in huge volumes for distribution to large, geographically dispersed markets.

The Strategic Management and Telecommunications Age (1950–1990)
Management = Social Networks – Digital

The age of mass production and broadcast communication required that the company's outside suppliers and partners be as efficient as the company factory itself. This necessitated an examination of business management, or, as Alfred D. Chandler labeled it, the visible hand, and how to evolve to a better management model. Chandler was best known for his book *The Visible Hand: The Managerial Revolution in American Business*, in which he observed that companies in the United States created a "managerial class" because they had to manage the increasingly complex and interdependent business ecosystem created in the previous age. The ability to achieve greater efficacy through coordination explained the need for focus on management and business strategy.[1]

The consequences of the visible hand were most pronounced during World War II. The Germans were seen as the better engineers by far; they produced the first jets and the first unmanned rocket missiles, and they needed fewer troops to match their opponents on the battlefield. Yet the Allies, led by the United States, won the war. Their victory was due primarily to the guiding visible hand of leadership. At the time, under American leadership, companies produced more war-related supplies and goods than their opponents combined. And these companies were able to transport war materials to their armies around the world, from Asia to Africa to Europe to Russia. For the most part, this success stemmed from the ability of Allied military and supply management to make context-sensitive decisions on their own or, at minimum, to formulate the options available to their commanders.

Immediately following the war, business borrowed much of its management philosophy from the Allied military. Management was seen as strategic and as a way to organize workers of diverse skills and talent. These new strategic businesses started to define objectives and create strategies to attain them, find people to run the organizations according to the new management principles, and outline metrics that defined success. Management had become both a strategic and a social function, for it created internal social networks that enabled employees to do their jobs and receive feedback from their managers on performance.

This new management layer was built on the technical foundation of the previous age, and the strategic business was able to do much more with less. The companies that developed these strategic management hierarchies and philosophies succeeded in maintaining what we call a "sustainable competitive advantage." They tended to outperform and steal market share from their competitors while better surviving downturns in the economy. Over time, the management-led, strategic businesses went on to dominate their respective industries.

Strategic businesses like General Motors and IBM thrived in this age because they not only leveraged existing technologies, they produced a management structure and communication system that was able to maximize material output at a lower cost while remaining responsive to market changes.

The Information Age (1990–2010)
Success = (content + commerce)/Internet

Every successful endeavor tends to have unintended consequences, and the first consequence of the age of the strategic business was a stifling of innovation. Management became rigid and its decisions centralized, and an emphasis on efficient processes ruled. While command was no longer restricted to the top of organizations, middle management still specified and dictated work activities to frontline employees.

Management saw employee adaptations of the strategic plan as violations and made great efforts to stomp them out. Management also forced customers and partners to adapt their buying habits to the processes created by the organization. With both company insiders and outsiders, the communication was controlled and dictated by management, who sat behind a wall of bureaucracy that made them deaf to the needs of employees, customers, and partners. The result asphyxiated innovation by employees and quelled feedback from customers, both key sources of intelligence. The result, companies told customers what was best for them.

The late Peter F. Drucker, an influential management consultant, is credited with coining the term "knowledge worker," which is how we define individuals today who are valued for their ability to act on and communicate with knowledge within a specific subject area and apply that toward their enterprise. Drucker aptly explained that knowledge was associated not only with a person's intelligence and education, but also with his social skills and social being.

Drucker's knowledge worker became a reality in the information age. This age is defined by the ability of all individuals to consume and transfer information freely without many of the restrictions of the previous ages. It was made possible by the personal computer, which, when connected to the Internet, allowed unprecedented levels of knowledge transfer from one person to another or from one person to many. Reaching critical mass in the early 1990s, these new channels of communication were exploited by companies via e-mail and their websites, opening up a wide range of business opportunities.

And it didn't take long for early-adopting businesses to understand the vast potential of the information superhighway. They quickly put up virtual billboards and product sheets to sell their goods. Innovative entrepreneurs created new companies like Netscape, Yahoo!, and Google to help users navigate and find information on this ever-expanding network. Soon, companies realized they needed a presence on the Internet, because that's where prospective customers were searching for their goods and services.

The benefits for business emerged quickly because a broad range of offline activities migrated online. Anything that could be digitized was digitized. Anything that could be done electronically was done electronically. More and more consumers downloaded music, arranged travel, bought software, and mapped routes online, forever altering the way business is done. Indeed, who still places classified ads in print newspapers, develops film, or researches information in hardcover encyclopedias? What companies rely on fax machines or postal letters anymore?

As more and more written, audio, and video content was added online, companies and individuals began to learn from each other, building on ideas from both sources to produce products, services, or process-improvement innovations.

By the end of 2010, mobile phones and tablets were accessing the web, making Internet activities available anywhere. Many of these activities were either free or were less expensive than the aforementioned traditional means and the quality was much higher. Mobile app stores emerged, offering real-time access to mobile applications that can do virtually anything imaginable in a digital context.

The information age marked a significant change in business that few recognize even today: investments in financial capital and human capital are no longer the primary predictors of the performance of new organizations. As Facebook, Twitter, Google, LinkedIn, and others have shown, the technology advances of the information age enabled organizations with limited capital to compete with large companies that have vast financial resources.

The Social Age (2010–Unknown)
Social Business = Internal Social + External Social +
Social Culture

Some might argue that we're still in the information age, but I disagree. While the information age produced a lot of information and allowed businesses to capitalize on it, the prevailing model was based on the idea of creating and manipulating information. Soon, however, people were overwhelmed with content and turned to their social networks to prioritize and make sense of relevant information. Businesses learned that in order to get their message across they needed to integrate and work within these social networks to remain competitive. Few understood that these same social network concepts could be applied within their organizations to increase employee productivity, spur innovation, improve customer service and company morale, streamline project management, and offer hundreds of other benefits.

As of this writing, in mid-2012, Facebook has 526 million daily users,[2] who upload 300 million photos every day; the site accounts for 20 percent of all page views on the Internet. On Twitter, there are 465 million accounts tweeting 175 million times a day (36 percent of users tweet at least once a day). LinkedIn boasts more than 150 million users in more than 200 countries, with 75 percent of the Fortune 100 and 22 million Americans using it for job sourcing activities.[3] YouTube boasts 4 billion views a day (up from 2 billion just 2 years ago!), with more content being uploaded to the site in 30 days than all of the major TV networks created in the past 60 years.

The good news is that most businesses are engaging with consumers using one or more of these social networks—but some are far better than others in connecting with customers and extracting ideas. We'll cover who and how later in this book.

In the workplace, 58 percent of employees prefer companies that use social platforms effectively, 60 percent of employees believe social platforms enhance innovation, 61 percent believe social platforms help them collaborate better, and 39 percent are more likely to recommend their company's products and services[4] if the company has a social platform. Unsurprisingly, 56 percent of college students who encounter a company that bans access to social media will either not accept a job offer there or will find a way to circumvent the restriction.

It's clear that there is a benefit to deploying a social platform to support these employees' needs. What's less clear, and what we're going to illustrate in this book, is why your organization must develop social business internally to become more adaptive to the rapidly evolving business landscape. And by embracing social business, your entire organization will become smarter and more effective. This is critical to the long-term success of your business.

The picture gets exponentially more interesting when you add mobile devices to the equation. In 2011, global mobile traffic grew 2.3 times, more than doubling for the fourth year in a row. Incredibly, mobile data traffic was eight times the size of the entire global Internet in 2000. Even though smartphones represent only 12 percent of the 4.8 billion[5] global handsets today, they represent 82 percent of total global handset traffic. The typical smartphone generates 35 times more mobile data traffic than the non-smartphone.

Imagine the amount of mobile data produced when the rest of the 88 percent buy smartphones. That's a lot of data being produced and consumed by customers and employees. Are today's organizations prepared for that? Most still haven't optimized their websites for mobile viewers.

Cisco estimates that "global mobile data traffic will increase 18-fold between 2011 and 2016 with a compound annual growth rate (CAGR) of 78 percent reaching 10.8 exabytes per month by 2016." (See Figure 1–1.)

To put that in perspective, the University of California, Berkeley, estimated that by the end of 1999, the total sum of human-produced information (including all audio, video recordings, and text/books) was about 12 exabytes of data.[6]

What does that mean for business? How can businesses better understand this trend, and how can they take advantage of it? We'll cover this in chapters 4 through 6.

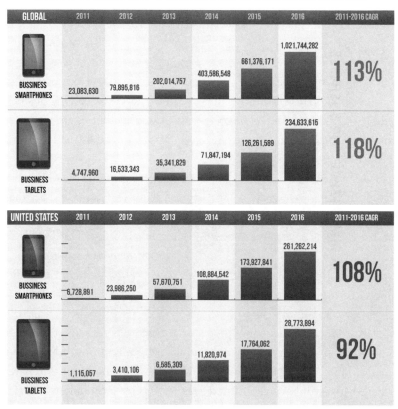

CISCO'S MOBILE VISUAL NETWORKING INDEX[7]

GLOBAL	2011	2012	2013	2014	2015	2016	2011-2016 CAGR
BUSSINESS SMARTPHONES	23,083,630	79,895,816	202,014,757	403,586,548	661,376,171	1,021,744,282	113%
BUSSINESS TABLETS	4,747,960	16,533,343	35,341,829	71,847,194	126,261,589	234,633,615	118%

UNITED STATES	2011	2012	2013	2014	2015	2016	2011-2016 CAGR
BUSSINESS SMARTPHONES	6,728,891	23,986,250	57,670,751	108,884,542	173,927,841	261,262,214	108%
BUSSINESS TABLETS	1,115,057	3,410,106	6,585,309	11,820,974	17,764,062	28,773,894	92%

Cisco's Mobile Visual Networking Index

FIGURE 1–1

SUMMARIZING THE BUSINESS AGES

	Industrial	Mass (1910 – 1950)	Strategic (1950 – 1990)	Information (1990 – 2010)	Social (2010 – Unknown)
Highest performing Compay Characteristics	Standard Oil Company Carnegie Steel	Ford Motor Company	General Motors IBM	Microsoft Google Yahoo	IBM Salesforce.com Starbucks
Social Technologies that shaped the age	Telegraph	Radio TV Telephone Newspaper	Radio TV Telephone Newspaper	Fax Machine Internet Mobile phones	Internet Social Networks Smartphones, Tablets & apps
Business Age Success Formula	Telegraph + Railroad = Smaller World	Radio + Telephone + TV = Broadcast Messaging to the Masses	Management = Social Networks – Digital	Success = (content + commerce)/Internet	Social Business = Internal Social + External Social + Social Culture

FIGURE 1–2

It's Now or Never

The pace of technological and business change is so rapid today that if you were to do a SWOT (strengths, weaknesses, opportunities, and threats) analysis on your organization, your list of opportunities and threats would surely dwarf the strengths and weaknesses. There are simply too many disruptions occurring right now to sit back and do nothing.

History is littered with innumerable organizations that failed to adapt to changing market conditions. Industry leaders Polaroid, Kodak, Commodore International, F.W. Woolworth Company, Montgomery Ward, Tower Records, Tribune Media, Circuit City, Blockbuster Inc., and Borders Group did not adequately respond to changing market conditions and either filed for bankruptcy or went out of business. Each had a different reason for its demise, but each failed to adapt to circumstances despite having superior financial and human capital.

To make matters worse, the business dynamics in play today are far more difficult to navigate. Organizations could afford to be less adaptive in the industrial, mass production and communication, strategic, and to some extent, the information ages. Back then the speed of change was slower, customers had little broadcast influence, and executives became powerful by building walled gardens around themselves. Today, market dynamics are incredibly fluid, dissatisfied customers can disrupt any business on the planet, and executives who build shrines to themselves are far less powerful.

So what type of organization will best meet the challenges of the social age? A successful business in the social age understands and rapidly adapts to change. Its culture is open to failure, but seeks to learn from it. Its philosophy of applying social principles to every department, partner, and supplier knocks down information silos and increases the likelihood of innovative breakthroughs.

Today's businesses will succeed tomorrow because they have developed advanced organizational cultures—cultures with higher emotional IQs, cultures that promote and encourage people to find solutions to the organization's problems. Because individual employees can't handle or make sense of all of the information being driven to the organization, businesses must recognize that their success depends on creating a cultural framework that harnesses the wisdom of the organization. Such a framework must include collaboration and social technologies that make it easy to capture, store, and share organizational intelligence.

No single organization today could build a child's bicycle. Instead, one company might employ individuals with the knowledge to design and build bicycles, depending on partners and suppliers (metal workers, rubber manufacturers, and so on) to help build the product. Within that business ecosystem, and within every step of building a bicycle, there are innovation opportunities to improve the assembly process, lower the cost, and increase the value of the bicycle. There are also myriad opportunities to improve the design and function of the bicycle itself. Yet the ecosystem, and each workplace within it, offers few technological solutions to quickly harness that knowledge, organize it, add valuable insight to the overall project, and build the improved bicycle. Worse, the old command-and-control leadership model prevents most individuals and companies from sharing with each other. They still live with the mindset that information is power and therefore must be hoarded.

Some argue that we should focus more on developing the skills of people and not on the technology to support them, but that is completely false. Technology can be used to influence people's behavior—it always has. Consider human harnessing of fire and the invention of the wheel, the automobile, the airplane, and the computer: each has changed human behavior and opened up incredible possibilities. Of course, the relationship between people and technology is symbiotic, as Peter Drucker concluded: "Neither technology nor people determine the other, but each shapes the other." Today we need to structure our businesses to be more intelligent by developing cultures that encourage sharing, collaboration, engagement, and, yes, failure. That culture needs to be supported by a technological infrastructure that organizes its intelligence to create an environment in which the organization is smarter than any one individual. In such organizations, the engine of productivity becomes more powerful the more it's used. These organizations become exceptionally adaptive organisms that rapidly take root and grow, while pruning back the dead branches.

We call this social business.

Yet most organizations are severely unprepared to handle the changes essential to transform them into social businesses. Indeed, most don't recognize the situation they're in or that their previous situation has changed. They are still playing by the old rules, believing they still apply.

But a few companies have recognized that a tectonic shift is occurring. Some are preparing for it; others, like IBM, are already there. IBM has taken the social business journey and has become one of the most adaptive businesses on the planet.

My team and I interviewed more than one hundred social business executives to uncover the strategies, tactics, and secrets to becoming a successful social business. We've taken that information and created an action plan for you to follow. In subsequent chapters, you'll learn about creating a digital village and a digital network, as well as how to use a Darwin's Funnel to help adapt to market and competitive forces.

The rest of *Socialized!* functions as both a game plan and a playbook for making your business the most competitive and adaptive in your industry. This book is designed to help you build a social business that empowers employees, partners, and suppliers to become more innovative and more effective at attracting customers; a social business that quickly adapts to change and creates superior market returns; a social business that fosters a higher organizational EQ (emotional intelligence), which means that employees will make better decisions.

I am going to make sense of the world of social business for you and tell you where it's going, how to prepare, how to leverage the intelligence of your organization, and how to create a culture that supports it.

That is the promise and the purpose of this book.

Let's get started.

2

Welcome to the Social Business Revolution

In late 2011, Netflix, an on-demand video service that streams movies and television programs over the Internet or ships DVDs via mail, announced it was going to divide its offerings in two. No longer could you get both DVD mail delivery and streaming movies in one package, you now had to purchase two separate subscriptions. Appalled, Netflix customers swiftly took to their laptops and mobile devices to voice their displeasure on social media. In all, eighty thousand negative comments were recorded on Netflix blogs, Twitter, and Facebook, and within months the company had lost eight hundred thousand customers and two-thirds of its market value.

Netflix CEO Reed Hastings was shocked by the response, going as far as to blame the reaction to the service split on the angry mood of the country, likening it to the reactions by the Occupy Wall Street movement. Curiously, when Hastings was asked whether the idea to divide the company had been presented to customers before it was publicly announced, he assumed it had been. He believed Netflix had presented the possibility to focus groups but didn't remember if he'd been given the results.

No matter what you think of Hastings' response, in our current social age, focus groups are no longer tenable. Organizations that rely on traditional arm's-length relationships with customers and who try to dictate the relationship rather than participate in it will find it increasingly difficult to succeed. The increased use of social technologies over the past few years has forever changed the relationship between customer and brand. Now, individuals can create viral videos that reach millions, blog posts that embarrass corporations, and Facebook pages that organize citizens to oust dictators. Netflix was significantly hurt by social media's effects because it wasn't prepared.

Shortly after the public uproar around the announced changes, Hastings wisely offered a public mea culpa. He didn't issue a press release and he didn't use a public relations agency or company spokesperson to deliver the message, he used one of the tools his customers were using—a blog. In a blog post titled "An Explanation and Some Reflections," Hastings delivered what most believed was a very sincere apology. Not everyone believed it was enough, but it did temper the hostile response. It also gave his customers a chance to vent (there were nearly twenty-eight thousand comments as of the publication of this book) and to communicate directly with Hastings. For some this was enough, for others the damage was too severe.

Several months later, when asked about the social media fiasco at the company's April 2012 quarterly analyst briefing, Hastings explained that Netflix still had not recovered from the backlash: "Again, Mark, the brand recovery is partway complete. We had said it would probably take three years, with the bulk of the recovery in the first year. That still seems to us to be the correct model. So, we're feeling good about the progress we've made. We do—we are conscious that it's tender and that we have to be extremely diligent and thoughtful in the way that we act as we build back our brand reputation." Ouch! As you can see, not being tuned in can hurt a company for years.

This book is, in part, about how to prepare your organization for these near death experience black swan events. It's also about how to create the opposite effect, customer advocacy. But first, we need to make the case for social business.

Building the Case for Social Business

In a February 2012 study, the PulsePoint Group, along with the Economist Intelligence Unit, discovered that organizations that fully adopt

SOCIALIZED!

BENEFITS OF SOCIAL ENGAGEMENT

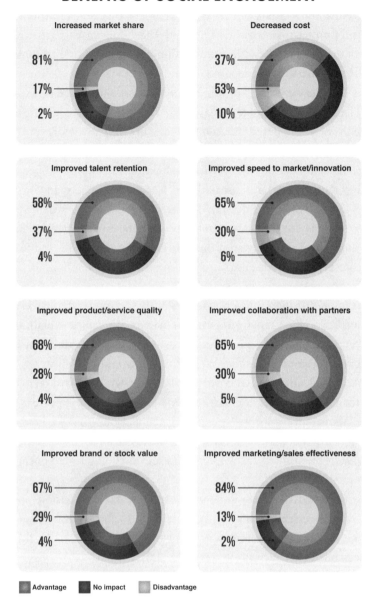

FIGURE 2–1

social business initiatives experience business impact four times greater than companies that do not. More than three hundred executives were surveyed for their perspectives on the benefits of social engagement, and many of the benefits they cited are highlighted in Figure 2–1.

Following are some additional highlights from the study:

• The top two areas where executives thought social engagement had real value were improved marketing and sales effectiveness (84 percent) and increased sales and market share (81 percent).

• Top-performing organizations are more focused on ideas and action over the next two years. Big-return companies crowdsource new products (57 percent) or let customers participate in developing ideas—they are predicting that a significant portion of new products will be derived from social engagement insights.

Indeed, if this data proves one thing, it is the importance of becoming social. Even the most ardent critic of social business would have a hard time finding alternate explanations for the social successes found in this study and countless others. But as with any strategic transformation, there will be cynics and there will be opponents. Rather than fear the conflict, understand that businesses have not only transformed their organizations, they have increased their effectiveness, market value, and sales revenue. You have many models to follow; you also have this book as a guide. I've frequently led the organizations I've worked for through a social business transformation, and I have advised many others during theirs. The age of social business has just begun; it's time you get started.

Social Business Obstacles

Why haven't more companies jumped on the social bandwagon? As Capgemini's managing director and global head of practices Didier Bonnet told me, "One of the key findings in our research was that one of the main barriers to achieving a successful social transformation—77 percent of the time—was lack of skills, culture, and technology. Specifically, most companies demonstrated a lack of social media skills, a lack of advanced-mobility application skills, the wrong technologies, the wrong culture, and a social business guide to use all of them holistically. It seems most companies want to take advantage of the benefits of social business, but lack a road map to follow in becoming one.

Andy McAfee, MIT's principal research scientist for digital business, who collaborated with Bonnet on the research, concluded that, "analog companies eventually are going to get swept aside by digital companies. It's my firmest belief about the future of business." McAfee believes organizations need to overcome the barriers or risk becoming extinct.

While Bonnet and McAfee were careful to avoid the "s"-word—"social"—in our discussions, because for most executives it still equates to happy hour, social technologies are an important aspect of their research. Bonnet explains, "It's becoming a powerful and common word, so we're not fighting it anymore." Indeed, executives continue to be terrified that their employees will waste time on social activities. They needn't be. As we'll demonstrate, employees with access to social tools become more productive.

The most social organizations are leveraging social tools internally and externally to evolve into social businesses. They are creating vibrant communities and connections with external and internal stakeholders that are transforming the way they conduct business. Externally, they don't rely on third party channels like public relations agencies, digital agencies, news media, television, radio, Google Adwords, traffic from Google and Bing search, and other third-party sources to deliver customers to them. Similarly, internally they have thrown out the old model of top-down information flows, with little information flowing back to the top.

These social organizations have changed their structures and hierarchies in ways that will continue to push them to become more adaptive and responsive to their stakeholders' needs and preferences.

The Command-and-Control Management Obstacle

The problem with a command-and-control management structure in a large enterprise is that it makes the executives and other top-level management several times removed from their own customers, and often from the knowledge workers who are directly involved with their customers. As David Sirota, Louis A. Mischkind, and Michael Irwin Meltzer concluded in their influential article, "Why Employees Are Losing Motivation," published in Harvard Business School's online magazine *Working Knowledge*, this strict hierarchy also demotivates employees. In their research they determined that, "A command-and-control style is a sure-fire path to demotivation"—employees whose voices are not being heard, or even acknowledged, eventually become demoralized and thus less effective.

So why are most organizations still led by this management model? It's about control, it's about accountability, and it's about a predictable, well-structured organization in which everyone knows his place. The tools for unleashing the power of the crowd and connecting directly with customers were not around sixty years ago when command and control was first implemented. Until now, command and control for large organizations was the most effective way to govern an organization. But today's tools change that.

We now have tools that allow decision making to be decentralized; all the important decisions need no longer be confined to the executive suite. For an organization to be competitive in today's social age, *every knowledge worker will need to play an active, intelligent, and independent part in the decision-making process.* We can no longer rely on the heralded genius decision maker to make pronouncements, with the rest of us adapting to the consequences. Organizations must become knowledge organizations, in which the ability of every knowledge worker is included to produce better decisions. Most beneficially, with each contribution, knowledge worker participation in the decision-making process increases the decision-making effectiveness of each knowledge worker.

Social Business As a Competitive Differentiator

In MIT/Capgemini's research and in my personal experience building social businesses, five key competitive advantages are consistently revealed across each of the organizations. These benefits were seen almost as soon as the organization began to roll out its business and

cultural transformation. While not limited to five, the following benefits
certainly stood out consistently. We'll cover how to build each in subsequent chapters.

1. The Company's Innovation Culture Went from Weak to Strong

Does your product or service trigger a yawn or a smile? Are you making products that resonate with your target market? Do you have a list of
hundreds or, better, thousands of customers who will buy anything you
create? Instead of conducting expensive and generally worthless focus
groups, these social businesses, through their social platforms, utilized
the collective intelligence of employees, partners, suppliers, and customers to give input on new and existing products.

2. They Are Building a Vibrant Community of Customers

We are currently at a significant turning point in communication—just
as we were once at the brink of the telephone revolution, the e-mail revolution, and the Internet revolution, each of which helped businesses better communicate with their customers. But now the revolution is about
building online communities to connect with customers and foster loyalty, trust, and engagement. The companies that have made the transformation are taking advantage of digital communities, acting as both
supporter and beneficiary.

Companies that are ignoring communities will soon find their customers moving to better neighborhoods.

3. They Gain a Competitive Advantage by Engaging Customers Through Mobile Devices

MIT's Andy McAfee gives just one example of how mobile is becoming a competitive differentiator: "We saw two companies in the same
sector—insurance in this case—create mobile applications but with two

completely different outcomes. The first company tried to simply repli-cate information found on their website. But the other company took an end-to-end approach and was able to get their prospect to sign a contract on the spot because he had access to all the back office information."

Social businesses are adopting mobile business strategies that fit their own set of business use cases to keep up with the way customers are mak-ing purchases.

4. They Gain Global Synergies While Remaining Locally Responsive by Integrating Digital Information

"With the introduction of location based intelligence technologies like Qualcomm's Gimbal, businesses will be able to target specific offers to pro-spective customers within a pre-detemrined radius. We saw some really good examples of initiatives in hotels and entertainment companies, for instance, where they integrated customer data from their CRM system, with data from social media, with location-based mobile data to start rec-ommending offers," McAfee explained to me, referring to a best-in-class example of how companies can integrate data for increased sales.

I've been struck by how few companies understand the power of inte-grating data on a single technology platform. We've all experienced a customer service call where we have to dial in our personal information only to have the data disappear once a live agent jumps on the phone. This is but a small example of the overall problem that most companies have. But the social businesses that understand the importance of data integration are now melding all of the bits of information they have about their customers to create better experiences and sales opportunities.

5. Social Businesses Have a Social Platform for a Common View of Customers and Products

The MIT and Capgemini report states:

> The most fundamental technology need for digital transforma-tion is a digital platform of integrated data and processes. Large

successful companies often operate in silos, each with their own systems, data definitions, and business processes. Generating a common view of customers or products can be very difficult. Without the common view, advanced approaches to customer engagement or process optimization cannot occur.

The big takeaway from the report and my own experience can be summed up as follows: while social interactions are fundamentally a human function, organizations need a digital platform (like SharePoint, with Yammer; Salesforce.com; IBM Connections; SocialText; or Jive) to facilitate social interactions on a global scale.

The technology enables the social interaction, but the social interaction shapes how the technology is used. Each feeds off the other until the organization becomes more effective. Now that's a competitive differentiator.

People Are More Loyal to Socially Engaged Businesses

Another study, conducted by Constant Contact and research firm Chadwick Martin Bailey, examined the behavior of 1,491 consumers ages eighteen and older throughout the United States. The study revealed that 60 percent of brand followers are more likely to recommend a brand to a friend after following the brand on Twitter, and 50 percent of brand followers are more likely to buy from that brand. That study mirrored a Facebook study that revealed that 56 percent of consumers will most likely recommend a brand to a friend after "Liking" that brand on Facebook. Furthermore, 51 percent of consumers are more likely to buy a product from that brand. It's easy to draw the conclusion that engaging your prospective and current customers will pay off.

But, the study suggests, 79 percent of those surveyed follow fewer than ten brands, and a whopping 75 percent of Twitter users don't follow brands at all. Now, depending on how you interpret the data, that can mean either opportunity or difficulty: opportunity in the form of a rich open field of Twitter users who want to engage with your brand or difficulty if most Twitter users don't want to hear from brands. I believe it's the former, and here's why: most brands act as if Twitter and Facebook are just additional advertising channels. They aren't. Twitter, Facebook, Google+, and other social networks are about engaging people with similar interests and sharing relevant content. If your brand is just another commercial interruption, people will either tune you out or unfollow you.

Interestingly, the survey respondents gave several reasons for following brands on Twitter. Here are the top five:

- 64 percent: I am a customer of the company
- 61 percent: To be the first to know information about the brand
- 48 percent: To receive discounts and promotions
- 36 percent: To gain access to exclusive content
- 28 percent: To receive content/information to retweet and share with others

The data suggests that your customers want a one-on-one relationship with brands. They want exclusive access and content that matters to them. Remarkably, the study indicates, 84 percent of a brand's followers read tweets posted by the brands, but only 23 percent tweet about the brands they follow. There's also opportunity to increase that number. We'll cover how to do that in chapter 6, "Introducing the New Social Business Playbook."

Mobile Engagement Increases Customer Loyalty

While customers are proliferating on social networks, they are increasingly turning to mobile devices as direct conduits to your business. A May 2012 survey by VIPdesk and Banyan Branch titled *Engaging and Retaining Customers Through Social Media and Mobile-Enabled Loyalty Programs* revealed that mobile communication and social media are significantly influencing the way consumers interact with the brands with which they do business. These are two powerful forces that enable brands to communicate and engage directly with their customers. That's the best way to build loyalty.

The research also revealed that:

• 27 percent of customer loyalty program members prefer to utilize a mobile device to access program features. I believe this has more to do with being able to use the member benefits at a specific location and also ease of access. I also suspect this number will increase as more apps generate increased awareness about the utility of mobile access to brands.

• 32 percent of customer loyalty programs reward members with points or other currency for participating in social media and/or online discussions about their brand. As we all know, frequent flyer points, credit card award point programs, and other award programs significantly impact behavior. As long as the awards are attainable and easy to redeem, they can be powerful motivators.

• While only 17 percent of customer loyalty programs offer members a mobile application to use when redeeming rewards, another 30 percent have a mobile app currently in development, meaning that 47 percent of loyalty programs have a mobile app in place or will soon.

While loyalty programs have traditionally been limited to retail, credit card companies, and travel programs, there are innovative business-to-business (B2B) companies that are using mobile devices to increase customer loyalty. For example, the office supply giant Staples uses mobile technology[1] to augment its customer service and loyalty efforts. The program, at m.staples.com, is specifically targeted toward small business owners. Staples' mobile site includes product ratings and reviews, a loyalty program, an ink and toner finder, a store locator, store inventory lookup, and enhanced on-site search, including an auto-suggest feature. And this is just the beginning; key to the company's mobile strategy is its "virtual supply closet." Staples' director of mobile strategy, Prat Vemana, explained, "The idea is that we know your purchase history with us, and in addition we allow you to build your own lists of supplies. Then, you either can order on the go or bring your list to the store on your device."

Staples is also taking advantage of the social aspects of the mobile app. When customers are within a mile of a Staples retail store (ascertained by the mobile device's GPS), the app will automatically serve a time-based coupon to them. Vemana went on to say, "Mobile for us is a channel of innovation. It's an opportunity for us to learn what customers are using, what they want, and to quickly implement solutions and keep moving. Certainly there is more to come."

Coca-Cola was an early innovator in social media and is becoming one in mobile. In July 2012, the company partnered with Foursquare (a mobile platform that allows you to "check in" to physical locations) to promote a $100,000 grant it was giving away to America's favorite national park. Cleverly, Coke offered an extra incentive for park lovers to visit their favorite parks. Online, Coke gave each visitor a single vote, but a Foursquare check-in (confirmed by Foursquare's app) at a park received one hundred votes. To make the campaign even more successful, Coke used social media to enhance the campaign by asking its forty million–plus Facebook fans to visit a dedicated campaign page where they could download the app, learn more about the national parks, and tweet about the campaign.

While a connection to revenue may not be immediately clear, Coke is tying its brand to causes that appear altruistic. For a lot of people, that matters.

The bottom line is that your business needs to engage with customers on social networks and mobile devices. With social, you need to be part of the discussion and to be seen as a contributor. With mobile technologies, you need to create apps that build loyalty while making it easy to do business with you. Even small companies can leverage mobile business platforms like Facebook, Google Places, or Yelp to create a connection with their customers. Doing so will significantly increase customer loyalty to the business. Now, who doesn't want that?

Social Business Maps: Mapping the Strategy for the Rest of the Business

So far, we have discussed some of the obstacles to and opportunities inherent in becoming a social business. In this section, we'll outline how to start or accelerate your transformation. It's important to develop a shared vision and a set of realistic objectives that connect to your organization's strategy. You also need to recognize that buying a social platform is just one ingredient to the success of the plan. Dedicating appropriate people, resources, and funding are critical, as is the support of the executive team.

Below are six steps to building a case for becoming a social business. These are nearly identical to the steps I used at the companies I led through a social business transformation, but include some new steps I've discovered through our executive interviews.

Step 1: The Seven People You Need to Help Build a Social Business

In every new business endeavor, you need a team that supports but challenges the organization to be better. Finding the right team can make the difference between success and failure. Based on my experience and our research, here are seven people whom you should recruit to help you with your social business transformation:

THE CHAMPION

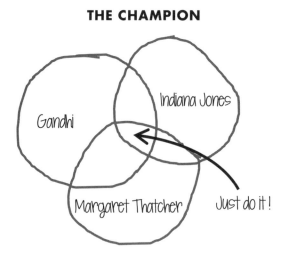

FIGURE 2-2

This individual has the vision, passion, patience, and tenacity to lead and succeed at creating a strategic enterprise transformation. She wants to make things happen and feels comfortable managing the effort. The champion is typically the person rallying the rest of her coworkers to the cause.

THE EXECUTIVE SPONSOR

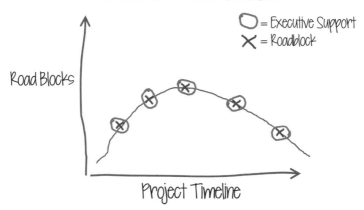

FIGURE 2–3

This is your promoter, your funding source, and your roadblock remover. Without her, a transformation to a social business would be extremely painful and would likely fail. When adversaries understand that she is in your corner, they will be less likely to attack or passively resist your plan.

THE DEVIL'S ADVOCATE

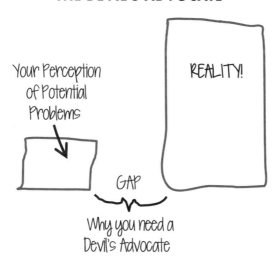

FIGURE 2-4

This is the person who will poke holes in your strategy, plan, and assumptions. He identifies the gaps in your plan, asks the difficult questions no one else will, and is not afraid to challenge you. You want this person—he is looking out for your best interests.

THE EXECUTOR

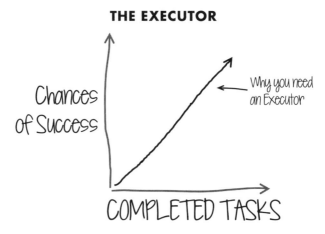

FIGURE 2–5

This individual politely harasses people into accomplishing tasks on time and under budget. He's a relentless taskmaster who enjoys crossing things off his list. You need this person: he will execute on the strategy you've set in motion.

THE QUANT

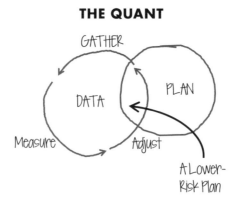

FIGURE 2-6

This person is your data analytics wiz. She is constantly analyzing the data to determine how the early social initiatives are performing, both internally and externally. She's a master at spreadsheets and social monitoring. She seeks to provide data on actual performance versus expectations.

THE SOCIAL BUTTERFLY

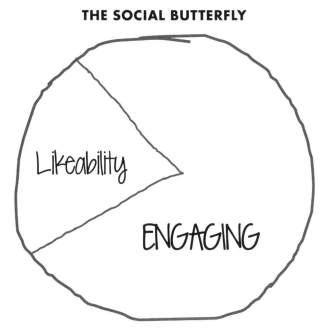

FIGURE 2–7

You need an early adopter of social media both internally and externally. This person already has a lot of followers or has a personality that attracts people in droves. Gregarious, fun, smart, and engaging, this person will be the one everyone else emulates once the business transformation is complete.

THE COMMUNITY MANAGER

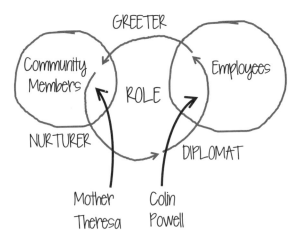

FIGURE 2–8

The community manager ensures the internal and external digital communities are running smoothly. He is a diplomat, a questioner, a nurturer. He likes to keep the community healthy and happy. You need the community manager to create communities that make people want to join and hang out.

Step 2: Define the Vision

Why are you undertaking a social business transformation? Who are the beneficiaries? What culture will you need to support the vision? How will becoming a social business improve your customer, partner, supplier, and employee relationships? Your vision needs to answer these questions while inspiring the organization's stakeholders. You want people to think, "Wow, I want to work there" or, "I want to do business with that company."

It's best to involve key stakeholders (this may be the entire company) in the vision-setting process. With stakeholder input, you'll find executing the social business plan much easier.

Step 3: Diagnose and Assess the Gaps

Once you've defined the vision, it's time to ascertain the gaps between where you want to be and where you are as an organization. Do you have the right people on board, those mentioned in the first step? Are your executives committed to the change, or are some of them on the fence? Do you have a budget adequate to support the new vision? Do you have the right technologies?

Internally, conduct an online survey that includes questions about the culture, technologies, and attitudes toward becoming a social business. You're looking for potential issues that will need to be addressed based on the defined vision. Externally, use social listening tools like those from Radian6 (a Salesforce.com company), Lithium.com, or Crimson Hexagon to gather and assess what people are saying about your products, your company, and your competition. Are you being mentioned more or less than your competition? Is the sentiment about your brand positive or negative?

Once you've identified all of the foreseeable gaps and issues, create a risk-assessment plan that balances potential risks against projected gains in productivity, collaboration, and innovation. Then prioritize the gaps and start to develop strategies to attack them. Don't get too far ahead of yourself, however, because your vision and plan may change based on the next few steps.

Step 4: Set Clear and Reasonable Social Business Goals

Now that you've set the vision and assessed the gaps, set clear and attainable annual goals with quarterly milestones. These goals might include share of voice online, adoption levels of the social software platform, engagement levels with key industry influencers, revenue and cost-reduction goals, customer Net Promoter scoring trends, and so on.

Goals convert the vision and strategic plan into sharp, tangible outcomes for the business to achieve. I like to define SMART goals, which are specific, measurable, achievable, resourced, and time bound. SMART goals are *specific* enough to be understood by those executing them. Tools are put in place to properly *measure* results. Based on your diagnostic assessment, the goals must be *achievable,* and the necessary *resources* must be available to complete them in a well-defined *time* frame.

With each goal, be sure that your objectives align not only with your social business vision, but with your corporate strategy as well. Create quarterly milestones and checkpoints to confirm that your social business transformation is on track.

Now take a moment to assess the plan you've created up to this point. Do you need to revisit the vision? Is it still achievable? Should you reassess and reprioritize the gap strategies?

Step 5: Create a Purpose for Your Organization to Rally Around

Most executives support the need for goals, but few communicate goals in a way that motivates people to take action. Think about why you're undertaking a social business transformation. How will stakeholders be positively impacted? Will salespeople be able to sell more products more easily? Will Marketing have greater reach and impact? Will Customer Support receive higher Net Promoter scores? Why should any of them support your project?

Give your employees a reason to believe, one that creates passion, and watch them rally behind you. Enlist the seven people in step 1 to help to spread the word. They will be your best internal evangelists and principal supporters. You and they must make continuous investments to communicate the vision, goals, and intentions to align all activities to that transformation plan.

"Communication is everything," Amber Naslund, coauthor of *The Now Revolution,* told us. "I know that's not unique to social business, but it is *so* fundamentally important when it comes to making any kind of significant shift in business model, operations, and culture."

Step 6: Build the Business Case Plan and Present It

A good business case depends on understanding the needs of those you're making the case to. What is it that persuades the decision makers in your company? How many of their decisions are based on the bottom line, ROI, savings, operations, productivity, alignment to corporate strategy, and market share?

The first step in building the business case for becoming a social enterprise is understanding the overall mission of the company and how social business can enhance it. If your industry is heavily regulated (financial, pharmaceutical, etc.) be sure to factor the disclosure and privacy considerations into your case.

Then, align and link the social business plan's strategy and goals to the corporate mission. Be sure to cover in detail how social benefits like transparency, increased innovation, reductions in information silos, one-to-one relationships with customers, reduced marketing expenditures, increased revenue, and so on will improve the corporate mission and support the overall corporate strategy. In this step you're creating content that speaks the same language as your executives.

Next, create the gap and competitive analysis and illustrate your prioritized plan to overcome the gaps; show that by doing so, you'll make the organization more competitive. This is also a risk analysis, where you're demonstrating how you plan to mitigate potential issues that arise and the steps you will take, if necessary, to adjust or, worst case, shut down the project. This last point is to show how objectively and practically you're viewing the situation.

In the end, you've created a social business map, one that provides a before-and-after view, a plan to eliminate the gaps, and a path to the finish line. I recommend that you present the plan in Microsoft's Power-Point or Apple's Keynote, but use visual images with only a few words on each slide.[2] Save the details (if anyone wants to read them) for the strategic plan that you've written out to execute later.

Important point: The process of organizing and packaging your accumulated information into a social business plan to win funding should resemble the plans that have won funding previously. In other words, find the individuals whose plans have won funding in the past and ask them to review your social business plan. It's best to choose plans that have been seen as successful enterprise-wide.

I could write a whole book on strategy maps, and this is just a brief overview. Use your best judgment on how deep you need to go in order to convince your organization's executive team.

Tips for a Great Presentation and to Receive Plan Approval

There have been a few times when I have purposely or inadvertently stepped on a few of my peers' toes when presenting an enterprise-wide strategic initiative. I've learned the hard way that research and the support of stakeholders are crucial to the approval of the plan. I've also picked up a few pointers, which I've outlined below:

• Your business case should be concise, jargon free, and easy to read. Illustrate it throughout with practical examples drawn from real cases and include reflective exercises at the end of each section to help reinforce the conclusions.

• I learned the following tactic from Brian Solis, author of *The End of Business As Usual*: "Instead of trying to deliver static strategies, just turn on the research element of listening; not just monitoring but truly listening, almost as if you were in business intelligence, and converting all of that data into actionable insights—all through the lens of matching them against business objectives, business priorities, and stated business opportunities and challenges." In other words, use a social listening tool and record over a short period of time everything that is being said about the company and its competition. Then, provide a short narrative on your insights about the data.

• If your organization is risk averse, consider starting with a small pilot (this may be a good strategy regardless). Tie the success of the pilot to a hypothesis that predicts the outcome within a defined time period (three, six, or twelve months). "Even executives who are risk averse are more likely to approve a program that they know has concrete dimensions," Amber Naslund told me.

• Define a set of key performance indicators (KPIs) by which success will be measured. These are different from the goals discussed in step 4, as they relate to the success of the plan's rollout only. Some that I've used are: percentage of employees who adopt the social platform, number of articles written, number of comments, number of employee profiles created on the social platform, level of e-mail reduction, number of connections made (or followers), and actual versus planned budget.

• Create an executive dashboard using the KPIs and send it to all of the key stakeholders on a weekly basis. Fellow *Forbes* contributor Christine Crandell shared with me her own experience with using KPIs in making social business cases to enterprises: "Keep in mind that most CEOs will not understand that they must transform into a social business in order to remain competitive, you will need to present some key indicators to support your business case. Then reinforce the plan by showing how you will keep them informed of progress."

• If your organization is complaining about lost business due to competition, take the time to create a detailed assessment of your competitors' internal and external social business practices. Gather social stats, technologies used, success stories, and indicators of consumer sentiment. Present what you've learned using side-by-side comparisons (competitors and your organization). Show lost opportunities, quantifying them with a dollar value wherever possible.

Social Business Is Like Owning a Risk Insurance Policy

Let's go back to the Netflix story presented at the beginning of this chapter, to explore whether the outcome might have been different had Netflix been a social business. We can't know for certain whether CEO Reed Hastings would have made a different decision regarding the split if he'd had authentic customer feedback. We can, however, examine the situation hypothetically from a perspective based on public information. At the time, it didn't appear Netflix had a social team in place; if there was a team, it was asleep at the keyboard. Witness the eleven thousand comments left on their Facebook page, and the single "Thank you for your comments" response.[3]

First, let's examine the situation from an internal perspective. Public information shows that Netflix had around twenty-five hundred employees, that they were not using social software, and that the culture appeared[4] to be somewhat Machiavellian. That is, no one sticks his neck out, but it could be financially rewarding to work there, and there was a lot of freedom to live or die by job performance.

Let's dive for a moment into the hypothetical. What could have been done to change the circumstances and subsequent disastrous outcome? Culture issues aside (we'll review these in the next chapter), had the information about Hastings' plan to revise the pricing model been given to employees, odds are that Hastings would have been alerted to the potential damaging effects of the announcement.

Even better, the most innovative employees would have given Hastings advice about how to accomplish his goal without undermining their customers' confidence. Some employees might have said, for example: "Let's show the DVD trend data to our customers to demonstrate that DVD distribution is rapidly declining and that we need to phase out the program over time. Then, we'll test the split product message with a few top users first to determine whether this idea is viable."

Once an idea is on the social platform, other employees can comment and vote on the idea to lend support for it or to suggest it be dropped entirely. Surely, a better decision would have been made if these things had happened.[5]

Externally, Netflix could have asked its best users and influencers about their reaction to the move. I realize these "fans" may have simply provided Netflix the answer they thought Netflix wanted to hear, but stay with me for a second. Let's imagine Netflix asked five hundred of its top users and fifty of the industry's thought leaders for their opinions. If opinion was overwhelmingly negative, the company could have gone back to the drawing board to change course. Had it been positive, and Netflix went ahead with its decision to split the service, there would not have been the extremely negative reaction to Hastings' decision because most of the five hundred users and fifty influencers would have backed him up, given their acceptance of the plan. People will defend and support a decision they were involved in. To be sure, after the negative reaction from the rest of its customers started, the five hundred and fifty would have worked to mitigate the reaction and perhaps tilted it the other way.

Only Netflix executives and employees could in hindsight determine whether being a social business would have avoided this mishap. But as a strategy, this would pass the litmus tests. If Netflix had been a social business, we'd expect the odds of avoiding such a disaster to increase significantly, because we'd expect the intelligence of the crowd to help shape the decision to one that has the greatest impact and the lowest risk.

Throughout the rest of this book I will explain how to prepare for and mitigate such company misfortunes. I'll show that when companies like Netflix become social businesses they are more in tune with their employees, customers, and partners, which presents more opportunity and less risk. I will explain how the best companies in the world are leveraging social, and show how you can learn from their successes and failures. Finally, I will give you my playbook, most of which has never been published. Some of the plays have emerged from our interviews, but most derive from my accumulated experience in building and executing on social business.

Each chapter represents a building block to achieving a more social, more agile, more adaptive business. When implemented, each block improves the probability of success. My team and I are indebted to the many executives we interviewed for much of what follows. We drew upon their work and observations to improve upon this book's overall value. The future of business is more social, more mobile, and more intelligent. Those who embrace the concepts in this book will have a greater capacity to adapt to changing business conditions and be more resilient when disaster strikes. I equate it to natural systems, like Darwin's

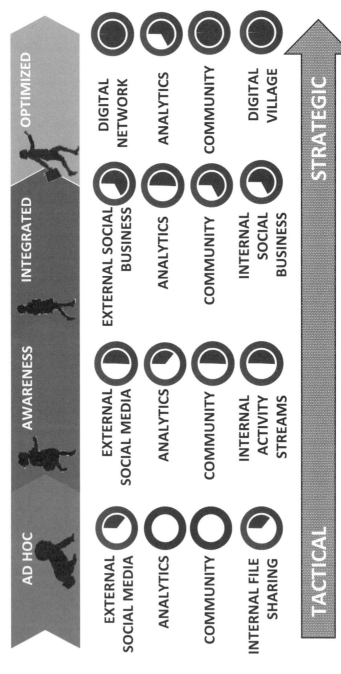

SOCIAL BUSINESS MATURITY MODEL

FIGURE 2–9

model of the evolution, that have worked over millions of years. Your social business transformation won't be easy, and it's more of an evolution than a revolution. But once the transformation is in place you'll see what I see, how businesses large and small can be hypercompetitive in a fast-changing world.

But first, we must have the right culture...

3
Culture Matters

All work and no play…If I were a conspiracy theorist, I'd say that the government has socially engineered our culture to emphasize work and deemphasize play. It's all a big trick to collect more tax dollars. Just look at the differences in work and play from only twenty years ago. When I was in first grade, I could wander around my neighborhood with my friends until nightfall. There wasn't anyone in law enforcement concerned with my "well-being" or safety, and my parents were not setting up playdates. When I was growing up we just played. No dates, no parental discussions about how the kids got along during the "date," and no parents asking for follow-up dates. Kids just worked things out among themselves without much of a hierarchy. It was a time when people's lives revolved more around their home life and less around their work. Yet today, we plan every second of our kids' lives.

When I was a kid, my father, who worked in technology, went to work at 8:45 A.M. and was home by 5:15 P.M. At work, his boss told him what to do and he expected my dad to follow his orders. Information flowed top to bottom through written memos, formal meetings, and telephone calls. There wasn't any play and there certainly wasn't any knowledge flowing back up to the top. This was your typical command-and-control culture.

Today, in most high-performing organizations the situation is beginning to flip—people play at work and they work all day. While some lament the impact on the family, others applaud the effect it's had on employee satisfaction. These high-performing organizations like

Google, Microsoft, and Southwest Airlines have evolved their cultures to support a more trusting, more transparent, less hierarchical environment that is making the companies more innovative, agile, and efficient.

What these companies have discovered, in their different ways, is the reality of proficiency without control. This democratized view of leadership has upended the deeply held belief that a commanding leadership is the source of all competence. Why, after all, do we insist on employees following our orders, and why do we call it insubordination if they question them? We expect employees to become more competent simply by listening to those above them. I suspect that this often-used principle of modern leadership—the reliance on command and control—is one of the primary motivators of skepticism about social business, which focuses on socializing employees, breaking down information silos, and empowering employees to take action, make mistakes, and learn from them. The idea that employees can socialize, collaborate, and act without management participation strikes many executives as barbarous, objectionable, and an affront to everything they learned in business.

Yet the companies that are leading in today's world recognize the benefits of an empowered workforce that feels connected to the organization. Empowered employees understand not only how to make great products but more importantly how to create cultures that continue to make great products well into the future. That's where their focus lies—in developing cultures in which innovation is connected to every facet of the business. From product development, customer support, and marketing to employee career development, these empowered workers care less about the financial impacts of failed innovation experiments (while of course learning from them) and more about developing high-performing cultures that drive customer value over time.

In this chapter, we will assess your company's current culture, highlight the cultures with the greatest potential to be social businesses, and then explain how the best companies use their culture to create adaptive organizations. I'll show how these high-performing organizations create enduring cultures that have a high probability of standing the test of time and how they develop cultures that are able to adapt to internal or external disruptions.

Why Culture Is Important to Building
a Social Business

The *Edelman Trust Barometer®* is an annual survey from one of the leading independent global PR firms, and it gauges attitudes about the state of trust in business, government, nongovernmental organizations (NGOs), and media across twenty-three countries. For the first time ever, the 2011 report showed that trust and transparency are more important to corporate reputation than a company's product or service. As we all know, reputation, like trust, is earned, not acquired.

Where the prevailing wisdom preaches control by the commanding executive and a narrative of obedience by the employee, social business stresses a culture of openness and experimentation, and emphasizes the necessity of community. A company's reputation is now more visible than ever, and a few executives in the C-suite can't control it.

To be successful at social business, we need to move toward a new business culture, one informed by purpose, mission, objectives, shared values, and the business environment, both economic and social.

How Do I Know If My Company's
Culture Is Ready?

"Peggy, I'm glad that this is an environment
where you feel free to fail."
—*Don Draper, Mad Men*

I spent a lot of time interviewing executives across North America, Europe, and Asia, and I have found five primary cultures in business today. I have developed a model of these cultures and a corresponding framework that you can use to compare your culture with the five primary types of organizational culture. You can use the framework to determine whether you have an ideal culture for a social business transformation.

Of course, most companies are an amalgamation of these five cultures, and in some cases the culture may vary depending on the business unit. But for our purposes, the five primary cultures will serve as a useful guide in determining how easy or difficult your social business transformation will be.

In order to help you determine which of the five primary organizational cultures your company's culture most resembles, I have created a short survey to guide you. In completing the survey, choose the answer that most aligns with your company.

Question 1: What Is Our Company's Management Style?

1. Our company's management approach can be characterized as opportunistic, risk taking, and innovative. It's generally driven by daredevils who look at the world as their oyster.
2. Our company's management approach can be characterized as supportive, educational, and personal growth–oriented. It's generally driven by nurturing individuals who are trying to help colleagues develop their full potential.
3. Our company's management approach can be characterized as an aggressive, results-oriented, take-no-prisoners style. It's generally driven by highly competitive, sports-oriented individuals.
4. Our company's management approach can be characterized as efficient, process driven, and organized. It's generally driven by efficiency experts who like to break everything down into a sustainable, repeatable process for everyone else to follow.
5. Our company's management approach can be characterized as intimidating, eccentric, and relentlessly in pursuit of success. It's generally driven by the bulldozing types who don't ask but rather tell employees what their opinions should be.

Question 2: What Are Our Primary Cultural Attributes?

1. Our culture resembles an entrepreneurial start-up, where discussions about new ideas, new products, and how we're going to

change the world occur regularly. Risk taking is encouraged and failure is seen as acceptable.

2. Our culture resembles a large extended family, where people are not afraid to share information, support each other's goals, and help other employees, even if there's no personal advantage to them.

3. Our culture resembles a professional sports team, where the company must win at all costs. Employees are highly competitive and are often compared with one another in order to create optimal results.

4. Our culture resembles a military unit, where employees are governed by rules and procedures and are expected to listen and follow instructions given by their leaders.

5. Our culture resembles a fraternity, where the loudest and most threatening people determine the company's next move. Employees are generally depleted and just go along to get along.

Question 3: What Are Our Criteria for Success?

1. The company defines success as having the most unique and innovative products on the market. We create products that people love to use.

2. The company defines success based on employee and customer satisfaction. We might also include the contributions we've made to the surrounding community.

3. The company defines success as being the market share leader and the most respected company in our industry.

4. The company defines success as being the most efficient and low-cost producer of goods in our industry. Delivering a low-cost product on time and under budget is seen as the pinnacle of success.

5. The company defines success as generating more revenue than it did in the previous quarter and by how often the company is referred to in the press.

Question 4: Which Philosophy Dominates Our Quality Strategies?

1. Our approach to quality can best be described as surprise and delight; the little things matter, as do continuous improvement and challenging the status quo.
2. Our approach to quality can best be described as providing a great work environment so that we develop enthusiastic and satisfied customers 100 percent of the time.
3. Our approach to quality can best be described as a focus on the supply chain in order to get our products to customers quickly, inexpensively, and efficiently. We measure everything and involve our partners and suppliers in the process.
4. Our approach to quality can best be described as process driven. We like to detect errors and solve problems with tools, and we have strict procedures to ensure a quality product.
5. Our approach to quality can best be described as wanting to deliver a cool product that enhances our customers' image. We strive to make our customers look good by using our products.

Question 5: What Is Our Cultural Approach to Strategy?

1. The company's strategic approach tends to focus on developing products and services out of the best ideas. "Ideas worth creating" may be the mantra of our organization.
2. The company's strategic approach involves high levels of collaboration, openness, and individual buy-in. Nearly everyone gets a say before the strategy is approved.
3. The company's strategic approach can best be described as a win-at-all-costs approach. Our company stresses destroying the competition, hitting stretch goals, and may call our customers names like "muppets."
4. The company's strategic approach stresses a defensive posture, where risk taking and bold ideas are frowned upon. Employees tend to follow a strict set of quarterly or annual objectives. Doing

anything outside of their positional objectives might be seen as insubordination; at best, it's a waste of time.

5. The company's strategic approach is frequently tactical. The company is controlled more by intuition and feeling, and long-term planning means what we're going to focus on for the month.

Which Culture Type Are You?

There are two things you must do to determine which culture you are most like and how easy or difficult it will be to transform your organization into a social business. First, determine which of the answers (1–5) you chose most often. For example, if you selected answer 2 three times, answer 1 one time, and answer 4 one time, then you are most like profile 2 (see profiles below). Next, add up all of the answers you chose and divide by 5 (e.g., 2+2+2+1+4 = 11 then divide by 5 = 2.2). Generally, the lower the number is, the easier it's going to be to transform successfully into a social business. From our experience, any number lower than 3 (out of a total 5) is a good candidate to become a social business.

For the best results, get your colleagues to take the test with you and compare and debate the results.

The Five Primary Culture Types

Our research revealed five primary corporate culture types. Each are explained below. See if you can identify which one your business most resembles.

Profile 1: Innovative Culture (16 percent of companies surveyed)

This culture type is an ideal candidate for a social business transformation. Organizations with innovative cultures typically encourage new ideas and feedback, and operate with a great deal of transparency.

- **Leadership attributes:** Visionary, entrepreneurial, risk taking
- **Culture style:** Start-up culture
- **Ten-words-or-less mission statement:** We create experiences that surprise and delight

Representative companies: IBM, Amazon, Facebook

Profile 2: Community Culture (21 percent of companies surveyed)

This culture type is another ideal candidate for a social business transformation. The culture emphasizes the success of the people in the work environment, teamwork, and compassion for the customer. Decisions are usually consensus driven and transparency is typically high. Individualism may not be encouraged or appreciated, which may cause some minor issues during a social business transformation.

- **Leadership attributes:** Coaching, supportive, consensus driven
- **Culture style:** High EQ (emotional intelligence) workplace
- **Ten-words-or-less mission statement:** We treat employees, customers, and suppliers with respect and dignity

Representative companies: Zappos, Starbucks, Google, Southwest Airlines

Profile 3: Execution Culture (22 percent of the companies surveyed)

This culture type may be less able to make the transition to a social business without considerable effort from leadership and perhaps outside consultants. The culture emphasizes results over collaboration, and leaders like to be leading conversations and not taking much input from the front lines. This competitive culture usually means people are accustomed to hoarding information rather than sharing it.

- **Leadership attributes:** Competitive, demanding, challenging
- **Culture Style:** Performance based
- **Ten-words-or-less mission statement:** We want to be the market leaders for our industry

Representative companies: General Electric, General Motors, Home Depot

Profile 4: Command-and-Control Culture (27 percent of companies surveyed)

This culture type is very structured, and process governs the way people work, therefore it is very unlikely that the company can be transformed into a social business without significant changes. A premium is placed on efficiency, coordination, and following procedures. The leadership governs the company like the military runs its operations. This command-and-control culture typically means top-down information control with little tolerance for contrarian views from the front lines.

- **Leadership attributes:** Hierarchical, expert at process and coordination
- **Culture style:** Efficiency and cost control
- **Ten-words-or-less mission statement:** We deliver quality products, on time and under budget

Representative companies: Oracle, Northrup Grumman, U.S. Postal Service

Profile 5: Adolescent Culture (15 percent of companies surveyed)

This culture type thrives on delivering products that their customers think are stylish. The culture reminds most people of a fraternity or sorority. Leadership is known to be brash, immature, and tactical. Information is usually force-fed to the masses while contrarian views are shouted down by management. At times, the culture can seem playful and fun, but there always seems to be some ulterior motive at work. This culture type is not an ideal candidate to become a social business.

- **Leadership attributes:** Impetuous, short-sighted, self-centered
- **Culture style:** If it's cool, we'll make it
- **Ten-words-or-less mission statement:** We make products that make our customers look popular

Representative companies: The majority of start-up businesses and some large family-run organizations.

Culture is the primary factor in the success of a social enterprise. Creating the right culture is essential to implementing and maintaining both internal and external social business. As the *Edelman Trust Barometer*® data suggest, companies are increasingly being judged by their customers on trust and transparency. Without the right culture, it will be progressively more difficult to meet customer demand in these areas.

In our research, we saw that the companies excelling in social business have culture profiles that fit numbers one or two. Some type three, four, and five cultures have made attempts at social business transformation, yet many have failed. We'll cover the reasons for that below. The best social business cultures have made great efforts to maintain and promote their cultures as a strategy for maximizing employee collaboration and retention, which ended up increasing customer satisfaction.

We also found that the organizations struggling with social adoption didn't have technology issues, they had cultural impediments. Before a company attempts to become a social business, it should take the time to foster the right culture. Otherwise, the chances of success are exceedingly low.

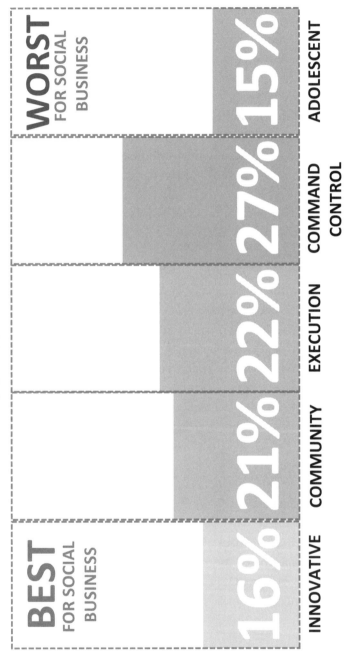

TYPES OF BUSINESS CULTURE

BEST FOR SOCIAL BUSINESS

16% INNOVATIVE

21% COMMUNITY

22% EXECUTION

27% COMMAND CONTROL

WORST FOR SOCIAL BUSINESS

15% ADOLESCENT

FIGURE 3-1

How Do We Change the Culture?

Rome wasn't built in a day, and a social business can't be either. *Transforming into a social business means changing your very business culture, but culture change doesn't happen overnight.* Realizing a new business culture requires a new strategy. It takes time, persuasion, resources, planning, teamwork, and measurable goals. And the venture is filled with obstacles, fears, skeptics, cynics, growing pains, resistance, and mistakes along the way.

In the rest of this chapter, I'll show you how a well-known, real-life enterprise was deeply impacted by its culture, then rose from the dead and successfully transformed its culture to one that supports a social business. We'll also see how the company was able to create a positive shift in its business culture, which led to an enormous increase in market valuation.

We'll discuss how, by using a set of cultural rules and an action plan, you can take the necessary steps to create a social business–ready culture. We'll discuss what you need to do in order to facilitate change. And I'll show you the crucial success factors in changing culture, such as agreeing to a set of objectives, getting buy-in, applying peer pressure, and getting your leadership to support the plan. I'll help you define tangible and measurable activities that facilitate the shift to a social business culture.

IBM: Success Defined by Culture

The 1960s were considered one of IBM's golden decades. For many people, IBM was the gold standard in American ingenuity. The culture at IBM was shaped by Thomas Watson, Jr., who summarized the culture by comparing it to a wild duck: "We are convinced that any business needs its wild ducks. And in IBM we try not to tame them." IBM's technical culture started what many refer to as "geek culture," represented by the countless employees who wore black-rimmed glasses and pocket protectors, and carried slide rules.

IBM started the 1960s as a technology leader and ended it as a global empire. That dominance continued through the 1970s and into the early '80s when, on August 12, 1981, IBM launched its first consumer computer, the IBM 5150. IBM's 5150 was introduced in response to the company's fear of being left behind by computer makers Apple, Commodore, and Texas Instruments. As former IBM executive Jack Sams recalled, "The worry was that we were losing our customers' hearts and minds. So the order came down from on high: 'Give me a machine to win back the hearts and minds.'"

The effort was led by IBM's Don Estridge, considered to be one of the key people who "invented the enterprise." Estridge is notable in several ways because he changed IBM's deeply ingrained culture with a small team of fourteen people and a vision. Whereas before 1981 almost every part of an IBM product contained IBM parts and software, Estridge was able to convince IBM leadership to use third-party hardware and software in order to keep the costs of the PC down. This decision infuriated the "not invented here" crowd, but ultimately he was able to change the culture to accept the new business practice.

If that wasn't enough of a culture shock, Estridge decided to make the PC "open" and to allow third-party manufacturers and developers to build on the platform that IBM had created. In effect, this allowed companies to create new versions of the PC adapted to their specific needs. That decision, of course, resulted in sales that far outpaced IBM's chief rival, Apple. Prior to the release of the IBM PC, Estridge's team estimated they'd sell 250,000 units over three years. They were way off the mark. In fact, almost one million IBM PCs were sold by 1985.

IBM's cultural decision to be open also led to the rise of powerhouses Microsoft and Intel, which paved the way for PC Compatible machines. Hundreds of billions of dollars are estimated to have been generated in market value outside of IBM. In a 1982 interview with *PC Magazine*, Estridge summed up the decision by saying: "We didn't think we could introduce a product that could out-BASIC Microsoft's BASIC. We could have tried to out-BASIC Microsoft and out-VisiCalc VisiCorp and out-Peachtree Peachtree—but you just can't do that."

The openness IBM displayed in its products did not, however, translate to its organizational philosophy, and by the end of the decade IBM was clearly in trouble. Under CEO John Akers the company culture became very conservative and failed to recognize and capitalize on its early computer networks, online services like Prodigy, which characterize the Internet today, and other inventions that may have kept the growth engine going. Worse, the company that helped make the PC popular was now being undermined by it. IBM's sales of mainframes plummeted as a result of the PC's ubiquity.

Now purchasing decisions were being made by individuals and business units, which is not where IBM had long-standing customer relationships. The company was unable to connect with the new decision makers and, as a result, earnings tumbled to $3 billion in 1989, whereas it had been at least $5 billion annually since the early 1980s.

The situation got worse in the early 1990s. IBM's attempt at maintaining a vertically integrated focus instead of a segmented approach to the market—where leaders Microsoft (operating system and desktop software), Oracle (databases), Hewlett Packard (printers), and Seagate (disk drives) had gained a superior foothold—caused the company to suffer even greater losses. From 1991 to 1993, IBM lost a staggering $15.8 billion, because it failed to recognize the best-of-breed trend. Thus, the three-decade-long super-growth engine was immobilized, and hundreds of thousands of IBM employees lost their jobs, including CEO John Akers.

What caused a company that had three decades of stellar growth to suddenly collapse? Why, under Akers' leadership, was the company slow to counter prevailing trends? Why weren't frontline sales people able to successfully communicate to executives that the market had changed? How did IBM lose its "wild ducks" mentality and become less innovative? Did IBM lose touch with its customers? Was its messaging off?

The issue, in my estimation, was the corporate culture created by Akers. His command-and-control approach meant that the company's vision came from the executive suite, and there was no Steve Jobs with a sixth sense about what the market needed. Think of IBM's much-delayed

PS/2 (second-generation PC) launch, which had to be forced grudgingly into the UNIX world. Akers was loath to consider outside viewpoints and was generally unwilling to hear contrarian opinions.

According to an IBM research and development (R&D) insider named Denos Gazis, a very famous study by Jim Utterback and Bill Abernathy was circulating around IBM:

> [The pair] asked the managers of an R&D organization to rank the effectiveness of various departments. They observed that the departments that were ranked the highest were managed by people who were able to invite, sift, and promote the ideas of the people they managed. Many managers with excellent technical ability were ranked low because they tended to smother their people's ideas in their eagerness to promote their own.

Apparently Akers didn't get the memo or chose to ignore it. But it underscored the primary problem at IBM, one that I believe precipitated its decline. That is, in a world of rapid innovation, command-and-control cultures don't cut it. In IBM's case, executives were loath to reduce investment in their mainframe cash cow and shift that R&D budget to PCs, fearing that if they made the wrong decision heads would roll. It's easy to blame their flawed thinking, but let's look at it from their perspective.

Most executives of large organizations (even today) that have a successful product are under tremendous pressure to defend the "cash cow." This sounds like good advice, but it's a daunting obstacle to innovation. History is littered with companies like Blockbuster, Borders, Polaroid, and many others that became extremely successful and then failed because they refused to cannibalize their own products, even after understanding that market trends were working against them. From an executive's perspective, it's safer to defend a proven product than to risk the company on an untried product. That tendency is more pronounced in a command-and-control culture, given that most of the decisions are made by a handful of people. Because if they're wrong, they have only themselves to blame.

To illustrate this issue at IBM, Denos Gazis wrote at the time:

> One of the most notable failures was our inability to convince our divisions to capitalize on the development of the 801 minicomputer. We tried very hard, but the success of IBM in its current line of products was an insurmountable barrier. We instigated a special task force to examine the merits of the 801 architecture. The task force concluded that dollar for dollar the 801 architecture was at least three times more effective than any other architecture, even if it had to emulate the instruction set of those other architectures. But still, we were unable to convince the divisions to take the 801 computer on for commercialization. One of the statements I remember from an IBM executive at the time was: "I have all the Fortune 500 companies in my pocket with our line of products. Why do I need yet another kind of computer?"

Instead of embracing a more open culture, where information and feedback were encouraged, IBM's culture frowned upon it. Instead of adapting to new market trends, IBM believed that it was infallible. Instead of leading with innovation, IBM waited for customers to pay for it first. This change in culture set it up for a fall, and fall it did.

I'm told that Akers inherited a lot of the command-and-control culture, but clearly he did nothing to change it. He may have even made it worse. What's also clear is that the wrong culture can significantly impact an organization's survival. IBM did survive. It did so by slowly adapting to market trends while reverting to its strengths.

Modern IBM and Social Business Culture

About fifteen years ago, around 1996, a team within IBM called WebAhead decided to place the entire IBM corporate directory of employees (around three hundred thousand people) on the web. According to John Rooney, CIO of technical strategy at IBM, this was a seminal moment in IBM's cultural transformation toward social business. This level of accessibility not only made it easier to find colleagues, it exposed employees to web technologies.

Rooney explains:

The WebAhead team was always looking at best practices on the web. They looked at patterns that were developing and thought about how to apply those patterns in our corporate environment. Introducing the corporate directory on the web is one of our first examples, we then deployed instant messaging to IBM in the late '90s and web meeting technology later. I think of that as an example of what shaped our culture. Our culture then became primed for social business.

Another seminal event that helped shape the new IBM culture was the launch of BlueIQ, led by Gina Poole, then IBM's vice president of social and web marketing. Poole led a team to create a center of competence for social initiatives and collaboration, and their model was to train volunteers from some of IBM's departments to become more social and collaborative.

And that's when the magic started to happen. Jennifer Okimoto, associate partner of IBM's Global Center of Competence, told me, "Then amongst that volunteer community, at the center of competence, they began to share their approaches, their lessons, their success stories, and success patterns while the rest of us built on their ideas along the way. We learned so much that we're actually building those kinds of centers with clients of ours now."

The success of the BlueIQ community caught the attention of several key executives. Some of these executives started to accelerate the pace of social initiatives by assigning individuals on their core team to specific accounts or relevant communities. They became the "resident experts" who applied social methodologies to meet their department's business objectives. The experts then helped to onboard and train the rest of the team so that they could participate. In its own way, IBM was starting to adapt to the use of social technologies because the company realized how effective they were.

As more employees participated, the company began to see the network effect, which created in turn a bandwagon effect. Employees who were participating in social initiatives saw increasing value as their coworkers joined, and those who weren't participating joined because they didn't want to be left out. As a result, employees were building on the ideas of others and producing better content faster than they could previously. The culture was changing.

As the company shed its old hardware business model and transitioned to one of software and services, IBM benefited from the new culture. It's more collaborative, adaptive culture helped make the transformation easier. Executives had an easier job of connecting strategy to execution, while employees were able to collaborate effortlessly across departments and time zones. Once management understood how agile the company had become, they were able to ask, "What is our business objective here?" and then to say, "Let's create the environment that makes sense for our business to achieve it."

Today, IBM personifies a social business. Its open and adaptive culture grows stronger by the day as it learns by participating and building on the work of others. The benefits are apparent in the financial results as well. If you had invested $10,000 in IBM two years ago, your investment in the summer of 2012 would be worth more than $14,000. That means that in just two years IBM has created more than $60 billion in shareholder value. To put that in perspective, that's more than the total market value of Hewlett Packard.

From IBM vice president Sandy Carter's perspective, IBM's social culture is partially, if not directly, responsible for IBM's success: "Our employees use social computing tools to foster collaboration, disseminate and consume news, develop networks, forge closer relationships, and build credibility. As a result, they're better informed and prepared to take action on behalf of IBM."

Ten Social Business Culture Rules

In our research, we were able to discern ten guiding rules for executives to follow in order to change their company's culture to one that supports a social business. This list is by no means an exhaustive one, but it provides a focus on some key areas.

Rule 1: Let Employees Know It's Okay to Fail

Chances are you will see inappropriate behavior. Typically, because employees know they're being monitored, they are careful not to put inappropriate content in e-mail, social media, or on your social software platform. Occasionally, however, employee-generated content crosses a perceived line, and people get upset. Most people's first reaction is to come down hard on the offending individual, but that reaction can stifle future discussions, especially if the perceived offense was taken out of context. The best response is to politely and privately ask the offender to clarify the information or remove it. That way, employees realize it's okay to push the envelope and that the worst that will happen is a short chat from a manager.

Rule 2: Reinforce Social Media Guidelines

In chapter 6 we discuss why social media guidelines are an important part of any social business initiative. Guidelines are also critical for maintaining the right culture. Employees want to be confident about what's expected of them. They also want to know that there won't be repercussions as long as they follow the guidelines. Be the company that takes this seriously.

Rule 3: Encourage Transparency

Hoarding information should be discouraged in the organization. There are legitimate reasons to keep some information private, but not the information that can help people do their jobs better or provide the chance to build on past successes. A transparent culture nurtures trust, and trust breeds passion.

Rule 4: Hire Great People—Look for a Good Cultural Fit

How many times have we heard this aphorism? It's true that predicting whether someone is a great employee and a good cultural fit can be difficult. You must try anyway. We'll cover several strategies for hiring and developing employees in chapter 7, but know that to create a social business culture, you must have the right people on board.

Rule 5: Create a Cultural Ambassador Program to Help Employees Embrace Social Business

Just as IBM made use of social expert volunteers in the case study above, use social experts as mentors and role models for adopting social tools and practices. Evangelize in your organization and recognize these social ambassadors to subtly let executives know that they represent the future employee. Assign social experts as reverse mentors to senior executives who want to become more social. You need to show the organization that, from top to bottom, social is the new norm.

Rule 6: Let Ideas Float from the Bottom to the Top

Several studies have shown that executives and managers who are better armed with information from the front lines are better able to make optimal strategic decisions. With today's technology, it's never been easier. Choose the platform that makes information sharing easiest for your organization, and then encourage its use. Discourage or remove managers who suppress others' ideas.

Rule 7: Eliminate the "Not Invented Here" Mentality

Even the most innovative companies today do not have a monopoly on great ideas. Encourage partners, suppliers, and customers to provide feedback on your business. And once feedback is offered, respond to every legitimate communication. You must show that some action is being taken for the feedback to keep coming over the long term. Also, have a system in place to implement the best ideas.

Rule 8: Think Globally, Act Locally

Many of the executives we interviewed decried the loss of knowledge transfers within their global workforce. They viewed the vast, untapped

reservoir of skills and experience as an invaluable asset that was difficult to extract. Sharing information in different languages and across
cultural barriers can be taxing, but losing the knowledge is worse. Take
the time to create an information-sharing strategy that leverages new
language-translation technologies and recognizes how different cultures
collaborate.

Rule 9: Have a Clear Vision of Your Social Business

Without a vision, people don't have a road map to follow. Without a road
map, they get lost. Communicate and reinforce your organization's vision
of the social enterprise and how it supports your organization's strategy.
Why are you becoming a social business? What benefits will the organization realize? What social software will you use to support it? What is
expected of employees?

Rule 10: Build in Incentives for Information Sharing

In the past, because of information scarcity, hoarding knowledge led to
power. To move from information scarcity to information abundance you
must create incentives for people to share. Some of the best examples
of this concept are web-based question and answer (Q&A) applications
similar to Quora. Whereas employees in the past had to call an internal
help desk, with Q&A they need only ask a question to the entire company. Those who answer the question are awarded points, which are
used purely for reputation or to spend on prize giveaways.

Culture Is Just the Foundation for Social Business

By itself, culture does not generate performance. The orchestra can't
perform remarkably unless there is a symphony. And to create a sym-

phony, a great many specialists have to contribute—people like composers, singers, conductors, and producers. And of course the orchestra needs its tools, the instruments themselves. All must work in concert, under the same rules and in the same environment, to be effective.

Only the right culture can provide the optimal environment that knowledge workers need in order to be more collaborative. Only the right culture can efficiently convert the specialized knowledge of the knowledge worker into organizational performance.

Building (or changing) the company culture to accommodate a social business can be difficult. But it's a critical component to the success of the organization in order to deliver consistent results over time. Here's why: over time, the number of interactions between employees, partners, suppliers, and customers is practically unlimited. There are countless opportunities to fail and succeed. Culture is the bond throughout the organization that drives an expected interaction between the parties. Culture increases the odds that each customer, partner, and supplier receives the same treatment as he would from the CEO. To put it in perspective, United Airlines and its eighty-six thousand employees probably have millions of interactions with their passengers every day. How does United's leadership team increase the odds of passengers receiving a high standard of service? They must instill the company's values and expectations about service in every passenger-facing employee. That's done by creating a culture that rewards the right behavior.

Seven Steps to Building a Social Business–Friendly Culture

You can copy a competitor's business plan, products, and messaging, but you can't copy its culture. Culture is one of the primary differentiators in any long-term competitive situation, and it's one that can make or break your organization. Therefore, in order to start or strengthen your social business, I've created a seven-step culture-changing plan that I have used professionally and at organizations where I have been charged with culture change. Keep in mind that most of the cultural transformations I've led or participated in have taken upward of a year to complete.

1. Assess your current culture by taking the survey earlier in this chapter. If your culture type meets the minimum requirements to become a social business, then proceed.

2. Define a new (or revised) vision or story for the organization that involves social business but still aligns to the organization's purpose. And, because you're becoming a social business, involve employees by asking for their opinions. That will help create ownership and buy-in. For example, United Airlines' vision statement is: "To be recognized worldwide as the airline of choice." This could be updated to: "We want our employees, passengers, and partners to feel like they are a part of our family." Then, United should ask employees to comment on or offer alternatives to the new vision, what that vision means to them, and how it can be reinforced through action.

3. Reinforce the new culture through peer pressure. A few years ago, I had an employee who liked to crack the occasional off-color joke. Most of the time, at least one person was offended by the joke but never spoke up. I counseled the employee about offending others, but she told me that others didn't complain, so they must like her sense of humor. I knew from her peers that they were indeed offended and wanted her to stop. Instead of coming down harder on her, I moved her desk to a location where she'd be surrounded by people who weren't afraid to express their distaste for her jokes. Within a few days, she got the hint and the problem was solved. You see, we tend to conform to the behavior of the people around us. Which is why changing the current culture can be so difficult. The point here is that peer pressure can be an effective tool to modify behavior to match the new culture. Use it wisely.

4. Reinforce the culture with stories. If your stories are about how people get promoted through information hoarding or how people

get fired for raising negative issues, you'll need to change them. Those types of stories define your culture. If you want to change the culture, start by telling new stories.

5. Introduce a new management structure to support the new social business. If your leadership model is command and control, reorganize the structure so that it is more social business friendly. You still need leaders, but you don't need dictators. The new structure should support a social business philosophy where the best idea wins, not the person with the high-ranking title.

6. Reinforce the culture through systems and processes that focus everyone's attention on the company's vision. If you want to become a more open environment, then ask for feedback from the front lines. If you want people to connect with their peers, then feature an employee every week on video and post it to your social platform. If your decision-making process is linear and siloed, then open up the process for others to weigh in.

7. As a last resort, remove people who are obstacles to the culture change. Becoming a social business is too important to allow a few selfish individuals to put up roadblocks to the process.

Culture change requires a new story. But storytelling can't originate from one source. People are much more willing to support change if they participate in creating it. I've found that when executives open up their vision and invite others to contribute to it, buy-in and commitment to that vision dramatically increase. By organizing culture change workshops and allowing employees to help shape the vision of your social platform, you'll have a better vision that the whole company can get behind.

Measuring Culture Change—The Cultural Health Index

It's one thing to start a culture change, it's another to understand the impact of the tactics being used. I'm a big advocate of creating a cultural health index (CHI)—like your FICO score, it allows the organization to see at a high level how the cultural transformation is working. This can be done by measuring three cultural categories, which are as follows:

- **Perceptions**. Do your employees truly understand the values of the organization? Analytics and sentiment analysis tools deployed on your social software platform can key in on employee attitudes, values, and priorities versus the stated vision of the organization. For example, comparisons can be made between employees and managers, managers and executives, and executives and the board. Differences in perceptions of the culture among these grouped pairs can point out issues that may not be detected by analysis of the aggregate data alone. If you don't yet have this capability, then the traditional survey can be developed and used quarterly to obtain this metric.

- **Behaviors**. Are people making the right decisions based on your set of core values? For instance, if being more transparent is part of your cultural vision, measure the number of social interactions over time that take place on your social software platform. The key here is to pick three or four behavior metrics that align to your vision, make sure you can measure them efficiently, then score them.

- **Employee and customer satisfaction.** How are the cultural changes impacting an organization's most prized assets—customers and employees? I make this simple. For customers, I implement a survey that is sent out automatically and that asks the all-important Net Promoter question ("What is the likelihood that you'd refer us to your friends and do business with us again?"). For employees, I send out e-mails to employees at random or ask people to take an online poll that aggregates the results of an internal satisfaction question ("How likely would you refer a friend or family member to work here?").

I assign weights to these three dimensions to create a weighted average based on their relative importance and the integrity of the data in each category. I am a big advocate of initially measuring monthly and then moving to a quarterly model after ninety days, then surveying on a semi-annual basis thereafter. You don't want to leave culture change to chance; stay on top of it, especially in the early stages.

Creating a new culture, one that facilitates a social business, involves creating realistic expectations in the minds of employees and engaging them in ways that establish trust, shared understanding, and "ownership," which are the foundations for a successful social business transformation. Culture can either make or break your social business. This is not something to gloss over or skip. Take the time to create the right culture. Your company depends on it.

4

Building Your Digital Village: Internal Social Business

"Capital is only one key resource of an organization and is by no means the scarcest one. The scarcest resource is any organization is performing people."

—*Peter Drucker*

Today's hottest growth companies become tomorrow's failures all the time. Many organizations that start with the right product at the right time believe the music will never stop. But of course it does. They become serial optimists and fall victim to what Clay Christensen, author of several popular books, calls the Innovators Dilemma, or they become incumbents who are unwilling to cannibalize their cash cows.

The smart companies, companies like 3M, IBM, Google, Intel, and Starbucks, understand that they need to remain adaptive and focus their attention on creating an innovative culture with internal systems to support it.

Dion Hinchcliffe of the Dachis Group asked the question likely troubling most executives, "How can employees and managers best adapt to today's changing and increasingly social workplace?" This has become a central question as organizations look at social computing as a new primary channel, both among their workers and for their customers and business partners. According to Hinchcliffe:

> While we often see traditional areas within companies—such as corporate communications, human resources, or the intranet team—being tasked with making the initial foray into internal social media, many business leaders I talk with are already looking beyond "old school" functions and trying to *think through the broader implications as organizations become more social.* They are also getting a sense that there is something unique and different about a social workforce.

I demonstrated in chapter 3, "Culture Does Matter," that successful social business starts with transforming your organization *internally.* This is often overlooked as a crucial step toward social business. Yet not only does having an internal social business system make businesses more effective at the external effort, it's often critical for a company's long-term social business success. External social business alone, without an internal social business component, will not transform the business culture.

In this chapter, I will show you how to build the infrastructure for a digital village, or an internal social network, where your employees can go to connect, share, collaborate, and receive help from their colleagues within the company. The village metaphor is appropriate because you're creating an online location that over time will become a rich, vibrant community, a community that is the core of your adaptive business.

I will also demonstrate why some of these internal initiatives to build a digital village have not worked in the past and why they will in the future.

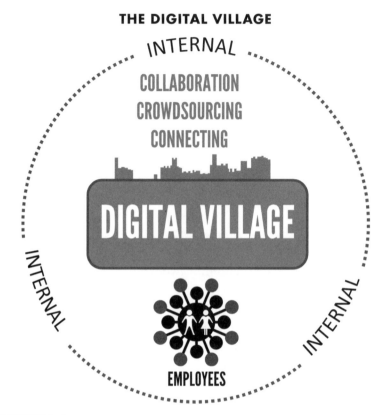

FIGURE 4–1

What Do We Mean by *Internal* Social Business?

The purpose of creating an internal social business is to help employees, customers, and suppliers collaborate, share, and organize information. *Internal social business* refers to social business activity *within* an organization. This includes its employees, management, operations, workflow, technology, platforms, strategy, organization, methodologies, standards, and governance. All of these refer to the internal aspects of a business—people, processes, and policies—that are currently in place.

Internal social business has also been defined as the *updating* of structures, processes, and workflow. Internal social business, the internal aspects of any organization involved with social business, has been referred to by some experts as "enterprise 2.0."

What Executives Need to Know

According to a McKinsey & Company study, the internal value of creating an internal social business (our digital village) is: a 20 percent increase in customer satisfaction, a 20 percent decrease in the time it takes to bring products to market, a 30 percent cost reduction in talent management, and a 30 percent reduction in the time it takes to find knowledge experts. From my experience, this is the short list of benefits. There are many more hidden benefits to becoming an internal social business, and we will discuss these below.

CEOs who give up on social business or cede responsibility to some low-level manager are making a big mistake. Understanding how to derive business value from an organization's employees, and knowing how to replicate the successes again and again, is an important executive skill to master in the new social age.

What is the proper role for corporate leaders when it comes to social business? My team and I learned from our work with hundreds of companies that senior management has a sizable impact on how aggressively and how effectively the company adopts a social business program. In this chapter, we set out eight internal social business requirements that executives can follow to both build and jump-start their companies' internal growth engines. Senior leaders who have implemented these policies, systems, and workflows have created opportunities for growth that were never before possible given the constraints of a command-and-control business model. In our research, we've seen companies surpass the benefits that McKinsey lists above, while preparing the business to be more adaptive for future challenges.

Requirement 1: Get the Right Team and Budget in Place

It's difficult to create a social business with executive support. It's nearly impossible without it. Ramin Mobasseri, eBay's enterprise portals collaboration manager, told me about some of the challenges he had to surmount to get his company moving toward a social business: "I had to go to a number of directors, people who really wanted us to become more social, and ask them to pay for the social platform [eBay uses SharePoint]. They agreed, which was great. Then I created a stakeholder's analysis map of power, support, influence, and need to get the big picture on the rest of the organization." From that analysis, Mobasseri pinpointed and recruited a group of people, including Alan Marks, an eBay executive, to help him push for change throughout the organization.

Don't wait for your mid-level and frontline employees to push for change. Find the right team and change agent to build and carry out a program of change. I've never met an executive who thought social business was not a priority, but I've met many who limit the budget and restrict their involvement to seeing that it happens. Worse, most of them were not monitoring progress against a set of objectives set by the team.

The key here is to get the right team in place to start designing and building your digital village.

Requirement 2: Create a Digital Village Code of Conduct

In any township or city, the citizens are governed by a set of laws and rights. In your digital township, you will create the same—but yours will be better suited to a digital environment. Here are a few useful codes we have observed:

Thou Shall…

a. Read and abide by our Social Computing Policy (covered later in the book)
b. Fill out a digital profile and provide a picture, image, or avatar
c. Endeavor to contribute quality content or participate in quality discussions
d. Be interesting or be invisible
e. Understand that if it's not worth discussing, it shouldn't be posted in the village
f. Provide quality feedback to coworkers when appropriate

g. Use the social platform for all project-related digital content
h. Consider information on the social platform to be confidential and "internal only" unless otherwise noted
i. Not discriminate or harass others under any circumstances
j. Challenge and engage coworkers in honest debate
k. Share expertise, be found, be useful
l. Use common sense

Create your own code of conduct, but remember to update it as the village evolves.

Requirement 3: Realign the Village to Create a Social Environment

We've all worked in organizations where it's not okay to talk to other departments (at least not in a business capacity). In the social organization, these silos are quickly knocked down to make way for cross-department employee communications.

These more socially enabled employees work within a rich feedback system where ideas are enhanced by other employees, questions are answered quickly, and information is shared freely. This leads to employees with greater skills and to better worker retention, which leads to greater economic success.

Conversely, employees working within a closed system get minimal feedback. Such an environment leads to fewer opportunities for employees to develop their skills, which leads to a breakdown in strategy, priorities, and the mission of the organization.

It's difficult to knock down these entrenched interests, though you must. But how? According to my own experience and from talking to dozens of other change agents, the key is to identify the early adopters in each department. Then, after your social technology platform is in place, welcome them to an exclusive, invite-only opportunity to shape the organization's future technology platform.

Most accept the invitation and start collaborating in this exclusive internal community. Shortly thereafter, as you may expect, the rest of the employees begin to wonder why they haven't been invited. But don't take matters into your own hands. Allow the early adopters to invite ten of their associates who they believe can make the community better. Once this early majority is on board, open the invitation process again. Repeat until everyone is on the platform.

Requirement 4: Deploy Social Platforms to Support the Infrastructure of Your Digital Village

According to the leaders we interviewed, the primary social platforms companies are using to support their social strategy are Microsoft's SharePoint, Jive Software, Yammer, SAP Streamwork, IBM's Connections, Salesforce.com with Chatter and Work.com, and Drupal.

It's important to note that while these platforms can enable organizations to be social, they will not replace the need for a coherent social strategy and seamless integration of these tools into current processes. As these solutions evolve, the visionaries expect these platforms to better connect people with information in new and contextual ways.

Jeff Schick, vice president of social software at IBM, expanded on this point: "I see information being embedded or being leveraged within the context of the ways people work to socially augment messaging and real-time communication. Organizations that aggregate and create experiences for their employees in context will be far more effective in multiple dimensions of their business."

The key to choosing the right platform for your organization can be complicated. Here are just a few questions to ask yourself when choosing a platform:

• **Do you know what you need?** The most important step for any organization is probably deciding which social platform is best for its business. There are many factors to consider, but first and foremost I recommend starting with a list of requirements from your key stakeholders. Even if your current needs are modest, try to anticipate what your needs will be based on various success scenarios.

• **Do you have employees working remotely?** While e-mail is an effective communication tool, it's not the best digital solution for collaborating with several people. With a social platform, however, real-time communication and activity streams allow your employees to communicate and follow discussions as they develop. Most of the social platform vendors provide some type of mobile device access, but they vary tremendously. If you have mobile employees, make sure the social platform has the necessary solution to meet your requirements.

• **Do you need to integrate information with your social platform?** Most companies will eventually want to integrate data from their customer relationship management (CRM), enterprise resource planning (ERP), human resources, or other information systems in order to use that data to provide a fuller picture. For example, when coordinating sales activities around a customer request for information (RFI), wouldn't it be nice to see how much that customer has spent with you in the past (ERP), what activities they've completed or the content they've consumed in the past (CRM), and who in the organization has specific knowledge to answer the RFI (social platform)? When this information is combined, it can make your response to the RFI quicker and more effective.

• **Can the system grow and adapt easily to changing needs?** It's important that the platform you are considering be ready for the next major business trend. It's difficult to switch to another platform entirely. It's far easier to modify or add onto the existing platform. Make sure the social platform you choose can easily adapt to your business's evolving needs.

• **How easy is the platform to use?** As we've all learned from the introduction of just about any product from Apple, design matters. Not design for design's sake, but design that enhances the way the product works. Bad design costs your company money because you'll have to spend more on employee training. Take into consideration which social platform is best designed to get people on the platform and keep them there.

• **Have you tested out your platform (with the user in mind)?** It's mind-boggling when enterprises' IT departments implement a new social platform without actually doing any usability testing with their own employees. Usability testing, sometimes referred to as user-interface (UI) testing or user experience (UX) testing, is an important technique for evaluating a social platform by testing it on users before a widespread implementation. Something as simple as a sampling of employees across all departments, with a list of expected tasks relevant to their departmental responsibilities, and recorded for sharing the collective user experience, will save greatly on any adjustments that will likely need to be made to the platform software immediately or in the near future.

To summarize this requirement, the objective is to build the infrastructure for your own digital village. If you're starting from scratch, keep in mind the capabilities your shopkeepers (departments), villagers (employees), and bankers (finance people) need to be successful.

Requirement 5: Leverage the Village's Collective Intelligence

A social business, properly led, creates an environment where people learn from others' ideas, mistakes, and successes. It's a learning venue for teachers and students where observation, participation, and sharing become the norm.

One of the things I observed early on is how quickly employees found experts in these environments. When faced with a particular challenge, employees are able to harness the aggregated knowledge and insights of these experts to solve it.

The best places to observe this phenomenon are at Amazon's Mechanical Turk, 99Designs, and elance.com. What each of these services has in common is the way it has been able to organize its network of generalists (Mechanical Turk), designers (99designs.com), and freelancers (elance .com) to accomplish a specific user task. This, of course, is exactly what your goal should be internally, but don't limit it to your employees. Make sure your partners, suppliers, and consultants are able to participate.

Let me give you an example of the way this works. I submitted a request through 99designs.com to get website concepts for a blog I was launching. I received sixty designs within a week. I then went through the process of rating and commenting on each one to determine the top five. Based on my feedback, those five designs were further refined so that I could choose my favorite. Within ten days I had a state-of-the-art blog design that I was satisfied with.

You might be asking, so how does this work for my business? Let's assume you needed a landing page design for a new product launch. The first design you received from Marketing was decent, but didn't appear compelling enough. By submitting a request on your social platform, you invite teams in Europe, Asia, and Australia to come back with compelling designs they have tested in the past with resounding success. Another team in the United States suggests that you add some social networking buttons to the landing page because they've found that about 5 percent of the site's visitors share that information with their own networks. One of your partners in Canada who is on the social platform notes that he has used a solution called Marketo to uncover which customers have visited the landing page by connecting the IP address and browser cookies to their CRM system. In just a few days, you've made your landing page better by asking the organization to help.

Requirement 6: Invest in Social Media Training and Certification

You need to allocate a significant training budget to educating the employees who want to represent your brand on external social networks. If the training is done properly, and if most of your employees get trained, the payoff potential will be significantly greater than it is for most of your marketing efforts. We discuss ROI further in chapter 8, but for now, imagine an army of employees sensitively pushing your organization's educational content through their networks. Over time, the content they push helps to attract more people to your brand. The point here is that, as in any educational situation, the more people you educate in the village, the greater its capacity to do remarkable things.

Requirement 7: Refocus Human Resources on Human Experience

Employee problems are dysfunctions of the corporation, and, if left uncorrected, become degenerative diseases. But for the social organization, and, above all, for the Human Resources Department, employee problems represent a major source of opportunity.

Here's how. In the social workplace, Human Resources should focus more on developing internal communities within the digital village (via the social platform). HR's role will be to ensure that the platform's user experience, aesthetics, and collaborative elements support the HR mission of employee recruiting, satisfaction, and retainment. If analytics and sentiment about employee discontent are trending, HR can take meaningful steps to stop the trend or learn from it.

As Rachel Happe, cofounder and principal at The Community Roundtable, put it to me, "Internal community management will become the human experience within an organization that parallels the digital user experience. With more interactions happening online, this is a critical competency for companies to establish."

Requirement 8: Feedback, Analytics, and the Digital Village Court

What do you know about your employees? Are they more influenced by executives, their peers, or partners? Do your employees care about the company? Are projects falling behind or are they ahead of schedule? Do employees provide constructive feedback to one another? Which areas in the digital village are being used more than others? Why?

Questions like these can be answered with the right social platform analytics. As a digital village leader, you need to make sure the village remains healthy. To do that, be sure to deploy analytical software that can answer the questions that are most important for your business.

Amber Naslund, coauthor of *The Now Revolution* contends that a superpowerful way to evaluate and illustrate the value of social is to do it inside the organization:

Establish collaboration programs designed to better share knowledge within an organization, or develop a social council that can work across functions to outline strategy and put well-thought guidelines in place before carrying things out to customers or partners. Internal programs have the advantage of more protected trial and error, and the opportunity to explore and ask a lot of questions before scaling something publicly.

One final point about your digital village: at times, you'll see conflict. Early on, there may be a lot of it, and that's okay. I recommend you set up a small committee that meets on an ad hoc basis to resolve any disputes.

Why You Need the Digital Village

The strong communities of the past, where family, businesses, church, school, and courts were all part of a village, have faded in importance in modern society, where we can easily reach beyond the local. In its place, for many people, is the company, which in large part is replacing the old village communities. There are some differences, but also many similarities. Whereas the village was a place you were born into, a company is something you choose to join. The village is the place where you live, shop, and work, while the company is a vehicle for a set of profit objectives. A village came together to solve a societal problem, but the company comes together to solve a customer problem. A village seeks to educate its citizens to increase the benefit to society, while the company educates and trains its workers to be more effective employees.

Why do we want to recreate a village in digital form? Decades ago, the majority of problems that had to be solved were solved by the local community, and this was a very effective method for taking care of one's own. Villages that operate in the physical world are no longer tenable given the mobility of society. It's no longer a given that people will put down roots in neighborhoods that influence what their home looks like, what they do for work, or, indeed, what they think.

Today's society is such that many more people can be successful by choosing how and where they want to work. They no longer are stuck in the town they grew up in; society has evolved its technical infrastructure to the point where knowledge work can be done from almost anywhere. It has also given us the flexibility to join companies located anywhere in the world. But as society's infrastructure has evolved, the concept of the village community has gradually waned. And we're missing out on an important human need to connect and share experiences. Yet it's not going to remain that way for long.

How will the village reemerge? Today, the primary purpose of a corporation is to reduce the expense of bringing together, in a coordinated fashion, a large number of people to accomplish a set of objectives. Most companies do an adequate job of leveraging their employees offline but either don't understand or are afraid to extend the model to an online social platform. That's an egregious mistake.

For much of the last seventy-five years, we understood how a company was supposed to operate. Business leaders went to business school to learn slight variations on the army blueprint model for business operations. The command-and-control leadership model, with a small number of leaders giving orders to a multitude of followers, provided an effective hierarchical structure for businesses to adopt. We assumed all business was conducted the same way. Anything different was considered foolish and frowned upon by board members and Wall Street.

In that hierarchical command-and-control model, information was handled at each level by one person who was tasked to solve problems to his ability. Complex or more difficult problems were sent up a level to people supposedly more skilled and better able to solve the issue. Information was rarely shared or disseminated to other employees so that, if they faced a similar issue, they could solve the problem on their own. Even more challenging, the higher up the command chain you went, the less likely the person was to get the opinions of people below her. Worse, the final decision-making authority was concentrated in the hands of one or two people, typically the CEO and perhaps another top executive. Clearly this model doesn't work in the fast-moving business environment we now operate in.

Why Enterprises Need an Internal Social Business Strategy and Social Platform

Fifty-six years ago, William Whyte, in his 1956 bestseller *The Organization Man*, argued that the popular company ethos of the day represented a dismal type of utopian communalism that stripped its employees in spirit and in body. Companies that bureaucratized their innovative potential by stifling individuals through the emphasis of meaningless process over substantive thought. Today, many businesses still suffer from this prejudice.

But as I have argued, this business philosophy is no longer justifiable. Companies must harness the wisdom of individuals while simultaneously dismantling the command and control management apparatus. To ignore this advice will leave you vulnerable to competitors that are more agile, more powerful, more innovative, and, ultimately, more profitable. Here are but a few of the reasons that we encountered in our research that demonstrate the need for internal social business supported by a robust social platform.

- There is now more data than ever and it can't remain in information silos.
- It makes the organization quicker to adapt, respond, and be proactive.
- It allows us to more easily streamline overflow of information.
- It allows us to better work together and collaborate with employees and vendors.
- It offers unique capabilities to address operating challenges and improve operating metrics.
- It improves overall business performance, promoting more effective collaboration between employees and their data sets, and improving employees' ability to share and push forward creative and practical ideas that meet business objectives.
- Decision making is faster, because the right information gets into the right hands quickly.

Some will be shocked to learn that corporations have tried to break down the command-and-control information structure before. In the 1950s, which most of us still think of as the heyday of the bureaucratic corporation, companies were fanatical about making decisions by committee and increasing teamwork. Chroniclers of the rise of the information worker point out that, while corporations were ostensibly committed to gathering worker input and to decisions made by consensus, most executives just paid lip service to the programs while continuing to make decisions on their own.

The consensus among executives at the time was that information quality varied enormously and the pursuit of unanimous agreement produced poor results. Back then, it was difficult, if not unheard of, to circulate ideas and decisions to a diverse population outside of conference rooms. This created two problems that limited the effectiveness of companies to capture and use the expertise located throughout the organization. First, since the information being shared was geographically limited to a single, fixed location, and to people who wanted to get along with one another, the information tended to be of low quality due to the lack of debate and shared experience amongst the team. Second, even if a quality decision and plan was derived, there was no way to circulate it to the rest of the organization for future reference. Thus, the incentive to maintain a culture of information sharing, collaboration, and joint decision making was negligible.

Even if companies found an effective way to model their organizations less on command and control and more on social business principles, there was little incentive to do so. American and European corporations operated similarly, with nearly the same command-and-control structures. Most were operating locally and didn't require a lot of collaboration outside their own headquarters. But as companies moved from the strategic management and business age (1950–1990) into the information age, management's multilayered command-and-control structure became too costly and time consuming for a world that was discovering the value of information sharing via e-mail, fax machines, and the early Internet.

As some companies began to leverage these new technologies in creative ways, others remained resistant for years. They kept information flows concentrated at the top and occasionally pushed it down layer after layer until the frontline employee received it many weeks later, if at all. This structure, paradoxically, decreased the effectiveness of senior leadership because vital information from frontline employees either took months to make its way up the multilayered bureaucracy or was never received at all. This structure drained the ingenuity and passion from employees, even in the most resilient organizations.

But some organizations were leveraging the new technology to create a competitive advantage. They set up the beginnings of an early digital village by putting up static intranet sites and internal shared drives, and they used e-mail to route employee communication. Information was shared more freely and employees were better able to communicate and collaborate with one another.

During the past twenty years or so, digital technologies have evolved to a point at which we can effectively recreate the village as a corporate digital village. Technology can scale down the complexity of a large workforce while accommodating employees wherever they may live or travel. Technology manages to make an organization feel like a small village, where connecting with people is as easy as clicking on a name in the activity stream or obtaining results from a search. Technology provides immediate answers to problems employees, suppliers, and partners have that day. Technology suggests employees follow other employees with similar interests or documents that they may find interesting. *In essence, it's a digital village.*

Employee Benefits: Job Satisfaction, Increased Effectiveness, and a Sense of Community

Many of the business leaders we interviewed felt that the vast reserves of knowledge, experience, and skills within their organizations represented an invaluable asset. Yet most companies aren't doing enough to make use of those reserves. Others have found that being innovative can help.

Wayne Shurts, CIO of Supervalu, described a situation that occurred in early 2012:

We just gave out a few hundred iPads to store managers with some apps that we developed. They received the iPads last week, and began using them immediately. For most people, it's worked. A few had issues or problems, and they used Yammer as much as the help desk to say "I am having a problem." We monitored Yammer and gave an immediate response, faster than using the help desk. Just a week in, we're already seeing great ideas—real ideas—coming from the managers. "I can solve this business problem if...." Some of the ideas for what should be included in the next version are already coming out. The process is much faster than the few months it would have otherwise taken to call a bunch of people and schedule a meeting.

I found from my research and from talking to business leaders that there is a sense that there is something unique and empowering about a social workforce. There's good reason behind that: an internal social business program gives your employees purpose and shape, because they operate and adapt to their surroundings. Internal social business lets you create adaptive environments where the infrastructure, mission, and management strengthen the desired employee behavior.

Equally important, an internal social business program empowers employees to do what is expected of them and what fulfills their own extrinsic and intrinsic motivations for working for the enterprise. As Yammer cofounder Adam Pisoni said: "What internal social business has certainly proven thus far is that you can have more efficient and happier employees."

Benefits to Mid-Level Managers

For managers who don't have a lot of visibility across the enterprise—usually there's visibility a layer up and a layer down and, of course, at one's own layer—the job becomes increasingly easier and work output more efficient. The job is easier because their teams are more capable of doing their jobs more effectively because of the increased information flow. And it's efficient because information that used to take weeks or longer to locate can now be found in seconds.

The manager also benefits from the aggregation of information in one place. No longer does she have to context switch into myriad applications, looking to piece together the story. She simply needs to click on a piece of information, and contextual information is provided by the social platform for her.

Managers need to also understand that by transforming internal business to a social model and showing results, they're more likely to be promoted very quickly in their organizations. Because few organizations have individuals who are knowledgeable and can help lead a business through a social business transformation, forward-thinking people with these skills quickly become the organization's most valuable employees.

Benefits to Knowledge Workers

In the past, your employees haven't really been able to see their impact on the organization. It was invisible. Now their accomplishments are more visible than ever before. That's actually very motivating, and represents an important, if often overlooked, employee and organizational benefit. Within the digital village it's much easier to see your impact and get instant feedback for your participation.

We've seen employees become instant company celebrities because of their participation in the organization's social platform. They obtained that status by simply sharing what they know, answering questions from their coworkers, and developing a reputation as an effective communicator.

We've seen employees find quick work product done by other teams across the globe, work product they would have had to replicate if not for the social platform. We've seen employees learn new skills, meet new friends, and build a network of company followers, which increases their influence.

When you add it all up, everyone feels like he belongs to a community with a shared purpose. And it's all supported by the digital village.

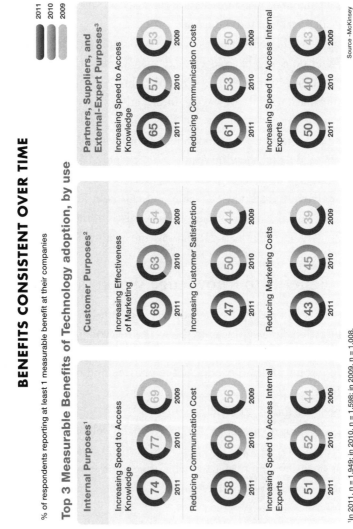

FIGURE 4–2

Organizational Benefits: A More Adaptive Workforce

The benefits internal social business brings to an organization are profound. Consider this account, from my discussion with Jeff Schick, IBM's vice president of social software: "We have over eighty thousand consultants at IBM, they are called Global Business Services (GBS). GBS has a competitive advantage in having specific domain experts that they can leverage for our client's business problems."

The consultants are able to work within a community called the Practitioner Portal, which is an internal, online community where consultants are able to share documents and other information without reinventing the wheel. So if they've built a body of work for one automobile company in Europe and they receive a similar request from a car company in North America, the consultants have a place to find intellectual property or knowledge that they no longer need to recreate. GBS participants also use the community to discover new people, locate experts, and find content that's relevant to projects they may be working on. Schick explains, "When we look at the productivity savings, it's tremendous, and we've been able to quantify that into real cost savings at IBM."

Another example illustrates an issue I believe we can all relate to in our careers. An employee at the Heber facility of Ormat Technologies, a provider of energy technology, recounted a situation in which an open digital village would surely have helped: "We broke more pumps in the last year than any previous year the engineers could remember. Not the inexpensive kind, but the large two hundred–horsepower, $22,000 pumps used in our geothermal power plants; each blew up in a succession of preventable blunders." If that wasn't bad enough, things got worse. The employees complained to management, suggested a solution, and management did nothing about it.

To my knowledge, details of the gross negligence still haven't reached the executives of Ormat. That valuable, actionable information is being stockpiled and kept hidden from everyone else for a variety of selfish reasons, and this fact stands as one of the most important symbols of why organizations, large or small, need to become social businesses.

To fully grasp the situation at Ormat's Heber facility, one first needs to realize that, regrettably, this isn't just circumstance or an isolated incident. Situations like these play out around the world in millions of companies.

The reaction of Ormat's employees, of course, is entirely predictable. Recognizing that things do not change, despite overwhelming
evidence that they should, employees become apathetic. Their apathy
is exacerbated by managers either too worried about delivering bad
news or too stubborn to recognize that their new maintenance and control procedures are destroying pumps. As one Ormat employee who
wished to remain anonymous said, "If our executives knew what we
knew, they'd start firing people. Clearly, our internal communication is
broken."

Colliers International ran into a similar situation, but this time the
account is from the perspective of an executive, Veresh Sita, the CIO:

> When we started out using SharePoint, one of the problems we
> were trying to solve was lack of information sharing; you know, we
> keep joking in our company, if only Colliers knew what Colliers
> knows. We set out on that path, saying, "Okay, we now know what
> we know." By connecting our data with the systems, somebody
> could go into SharePoint using Enterprise Search and just type
> Coca-Cola. It will go into our dual tracking system, it will go into
> our CRM system, and it will go into our people database and bring
> up contextual search results and tell you everything we know about
> Coca-Cola. It will tell me who's got relationships, what deals we've
> done, which companies we've done those deals with, and the nature
> of those deals.

According to Karthik Chakkarapani, formerly of the *American Hospital
Association* (AHA) and now a Senior Principal of Social Business at Sales-
force.com, The real value of an organization's digital transformation comes
not from the initial investment, but from continuously re-envisioning how
capabilities can be extended with digital technology to increase revenue,
cut costs, or gain other benefits.

"We're in the stage where we need to ask, 'How do you manage information now?' For example, a year ago we were talking about how to use
an imaging mobile application for AHA; should we create an app and

those kinds of things?" Chakkarapani said. After a brief discussion, they ended up turning the idea into an enterprise-wide project.

Chakkarapani said, "Okay, can we create an app for annual conferences?" For AHA the answer was yes, which generated an extra $60,000 in new revenues. According to Chakkarapani, the whole idea through execution wouldn't have happened if they hadn't started collaborating on their social platform. For AHA, nearly every other group was able to share their best practices on creating the application, how to sell it, and how to market it. It saved AHA countless hours in understanding the mobile application project. One of the primary reasons for organizing hundreds or thousands of people to work together in a digital environment is that together they can be more effective and intelligent than if they were working separately. Another reason is that how well an individual, an organization, an industry, or a country acquires and applies knowledge will become a key competitive factor. As Peter Drucker once wrote:

> The knowledge society will inevitably become far more competitive than any society we have yet known—for the simple reason that with knowledge being universally accessible, there will be more to build from. There will be no "poor" countries. There will only be ignorant countries. And the same will be true for companies, industries, and organizations of all kinds. It will be true for individuals, too. In fact, developed societies have already become infinitely more competitive for individuals than were the societies of the beginning of this century, let alone earlier ones.

Challenges with Internal Social Business and the Digital Village

Like any new disruptive endeavor, change can be hard. Below we highlight the key roadblocks that we witnessed in our research and personal experience in building a social business.

Poor Technology Integration

A big problem in the enterprise is maintaining multiple social technology tools and determining whether a new tool should be adopted, but not planning adequately for how the technologies provide workflow synergy. My fellow *Forbes* writer Christine Crandell says that many organizations wind up with a hodgepodge of systems that will not do what they need, are not scalable, and don't enable cross-channel social interactions. "I've met so many companies that 'cut and paste' social posts into their help desk/customer service case management systems," Crandell says. "This is clearly a solution that neither scales nor enables cross-channel social interactions to be threaded into a conversation from which context, customer sense, and intent can be understood."

The key to mitigating this potential threat is to follow the guidelines in requirement 4, above, and make sure the technology selection team understands the need for integration. Most of the organizations I discussed this with take the time to map out their business workflows and ask at every step, "Do we need data integration here or not?"

Poor Leadership

Often, it can be difficult to decide which corporate roles are best suited for an internal social business team and which roles just don't mesh. It's a question I am asked frequently: Who is in charge of transforming the organization into a social enterprise?

"Typically [responsibility for social is] kept in the social media committee (a triumvirate of IT, HR, and Legal) but those people aren't very familiar with the business itself. Often there are change champions on the ground but they often don't have budget, influence, or mandate," Dion Hinchcliffe, Executive Vice President, Strategy at Dachis Group says. I advocate placing a senior executive in charge of social business transformation and a chief social strategist in charge of the internal and external social initiatives. Often, these roles are not compatible and need to be split up (we'll cover this in chapter 7, "The Rise of the Social Employee").

In many cases, one of the organization's lines of business jumps in and starts implementing social in its corner of the business so that the group can get things done. While this is a great way to prove the value of a social initiative and typically leads to other departments following suit, social initiatives need to align with the organization's long-term goals and be managed by a leader with the power and budget to manage the overall program.

Without strong leadership and a unified social strategy, your internal social business program has a higher probability of failure.

Difficulty Integrating Business Processes with the Overall Vision

Amber Naslund shared with me that, for businesses that have the requisite mind-set and attitudes, integrated business processes and a unified approach to social across the organization are probably the biggest challenges, especially if the organization has very independent business units. "You can have relatively autonomous social strategies within a business, but they've all got to tie back to the overarching business vision. The paradox, of course, is that the social web is moving at breakneck speed, but that kind of scale and integration of operations takes time and a lot of effort," Naslund says.

Michael Brito, Senior Vice President, Social Business Planning at Edelman, adds that enterprises need to treat their internal social business program not as separate from their social brand initiatives (i.e., external social efforts), but as aligned. "This requires a shift in thinking because aligning external and internal initiatives is not quite the norm for business today," Brito says.

Both Naslund and Brito point out the primary reason why the person (I advocate a chief social strategist) in charge of social strategy needs a seat at the executive table. Like other corporate-wide initiatives (Six Sigma, Balanced Scorecard, etc.), a sound social business initiative requires a sponsor who is accountable for the overall program and its results.

The Culture Isn't Mature Enough to Support It

In the PulsePoint Group's study *The Economics of a Fully Engaged Enterprise*, most of the challenges to a becoming a social organization are what I refer to as cultural issues.

ROADBLOCKS TO DEEPER SOCIAL ENGAGEMENT

45% Innability to prove ROI

33% Legal or regulatory concern

32% An unclear strategy for change

25% Complexity of organization

24% Poor collaboration within organization

23% Lack of employees with appropriate skills

22% Lack of budget

21% Lack of engagement among competitors and peers

16% C-suite does not see need for change

Source: PulsePoint Group Study

FIGURE 4–3

Just as you wouldn't launch a product or develop a service without the appropriate foundation, don't rush into a social business transformation unless the right culture is in place.

How to Give Your Social Transformation the Best Chance for Success

While this book provides best practices for building a social business, there are some subtle, yet powerful tactics you can use to increase the chances for social business success. Here are a few we discovered in our research.

Provide Soft Skills Training

A report from Capgemini and MIT titled *Digital Transformation: A Road-map for Billion-Dollar Organizations,* concluded that one of the main challenges to internal social business in the enterprise is that skills in the current workforce are lacking. I believe that not only are social media skills lacking but also the *soft skills* needed to better build relationships.

The term *soft skills* refers to a person's emotional IQ, or "EQ" (emotional intelligence quotient). Soft skills include personal traits, social graces, communication skills, personal habits, and behavior that other people find attractive. Whereas hard skills (specific, teachable abilities) are the occupational requirements of a job, soft skills are a person's inherent and demonstrated ability to "work with others," that is, relationship skills. Soft skills that are considered attractive and desirable in the workplace (and usually rewarded) are friendliness, authenticity, caring, listening, responsiveness, and active participation.

Those with the better soft skills—I see this today—are more successful with social media and, in turn, with social business. The digital natives growing up today are going to have these soft skills and they're going to be better equipped when they go into an organization to understand how to relate to people outside the company. But what they need to be trained in is how to relate to people *internally* (i.e., their fellow employees, vendors, and other internal stakeholders).

Build Incentives into the Social Initiatives

One of the smartest things Varesh Sita, CIO of Colliers International, did to get most of his nontechnology-focused real estate brokers onto his social business platform was to build in creative incentives. Sita essentially said that if the broker created a profile in SharePoint (Colliers' social business platform), "here's what we're going to do for you. Since SharePoint is integrated with our external Colliers.com website, your profile will automatically show up on Colliers.com if you put it here." In effect, he offered a huge benefit to the brokers simply by getting them to fill out their profile.

Think about how you can encourage users to participate in your own digital village by giving them the proper incentives to do so. In my experience, about 25 percent will participate right away, another 25 percent will participate within the first 120 days, and the rest will straggle in when they can't do their jobs without participating. Don't wait for the late adopters to get comfortable on their own, as that could mean doom for your plan. Build incentives to participate into your social transformation strategy from the outset.

Use Gamification to Drive the Right Behavior

According to a recent Gallup Poll, about a third of all U.S. workers are dissatisfied with either the recognition they receive, their chances for promotion, or the amount of money they earn. Worse, 71 percent of American workers are "not engaged" or are "actively disengaged" in their work.

What motivates people?

Michael Wu, Lithium's principal scientist and author of *The Science of Social,* believes people's behavior has a lot to do with intrinsic motivation:

Dan Pink wrote about autonomy, mastery, and purpose. But there's another and it's called relatedness. Scott Rigby is a researcher for motivation. He found that autonomy, competence, relatedness, and reason are essentially the four intrinsic motivations for people. Relatedness is actually what a lot of people just call social. It's the social facilitation and the social competition.

Wu describes the need for gamification in business tools to create critical mass and engagement: "A lot of times the way we work is heavily dictated by the technology choice that a company makes. It changes the way that people work. I think an important aspect of that is for technology vendors to infuse gamification principles in their technology to drive a social facilitation, a social competition which is related to aspects of motivation."

What this means is that you need a technology platform that supports a reward system (e.g., Bunchball and Badgeville) to create a competitive situation that motivates people to do things they normally wouldn't do. For example, why does consumers' behavior change when they are faced with a decision to use certain credit cards or airlines over others? Even if there is a better, lower-cost option, most people choose to stick with the credit card that offers them the best incentives or the airline that gives them frequent flier miles—they like accumulating the rewards.

The key challenge with gamification is that most motivating factors are specific to the individual. It's difficult to find gamification options that motivate large numbers of people. Moreover, according to Wu, gamification is only a temporary option for most situations. The impact tends to decay over time.

But, for the short term, gamification is a powerful concept for driving desirable user behavior.

When All Else Fails Try Plan B: The Trojan Horse

If the leaders in your organization are resisting the move to create an internal social business, then I understand your situation. I understand the entrenched self-interests, and I am here to help you overcome them. What you need is a Trojan horse, a strategy that delivers a desirable (expected) effect and a covert (unexpected) one by undertaking the following:

• Create a detailed assessment of your competitors' internal and external social business practices. Gather social stats, technologies used, success stories, and consumer sentiment. You are basically gathering information to build a case.

• Present what you've learned using side-by-side comparisons (competitors and your organization). Show lost opportunities, and try to quantify a dollar value.

• If the data is compelling and your executives agree, then ask to pilot an internal social business initiative. Make sure you have the necessary resources to be successful. Then execute.

Like the title suggests, you'll want to subtly roll into the organization a social initiative that you feel has a high probability of success. Pay attention to timing and look for opportunities where your coworkers are complaining about losing data or lack of teamwork or something a small social initiative can solve.

Powerful Result: The Adaptive Growth Engine

Traditional management has failed to deal with a changing business environment and to create a workplace that supports productivity in the new environment. Today, the entire company must be focused on developing new value to customers through continuous innovation and, over time, becoming more effective at it. To become more effective, companies must develop what I refer to as a digital village to host all of the organization's information and data and to provide it to people in contextual ways.

You'll find that combining the digital village with a mature culture to govern it will promote a sustainable growth engine. You need to cultivate: a culture that tolerates frequent failing, but failing fast; an adaptive organization that learns from its mistakes and keeps trying until it gets it right; an engine that is able to efficiently improve and capitalize on the best ideas; a belief that if an employee develops a great idea, that employee will be rewarded; and a holistic system in which, from idea to product shipment, the organization is fine-tuned to deliver on its promises.

In order for a company to create its own adaptive growth engine, it must surrender past management philosophies in exchange for new ones. Growth is no longer the predictable result of a successful business model. It's no longer a linear path: if we do A, B, and C, we get D. Those days are over. Companies need to become more adaptive to external changes that impact their business model and become more skilled at profiting from them. But that requires that the CEO and senior executives support the cultural, technical, and process changes that need to occur internally. They need to stay focused on the big picture, establish the digital village, resist the need to control, and lead the organization through change. Respect the requirements above, and you will build an adaptive growth engine to power your organization into the next decade.

Survey

Here are some questions you should prepare to research and have answers to before implementing an internal social business plan:

- What social technologies or other workflow technologies are already in place within our organization?
- What is the social engagement level of workers internally?
- Are social business processes well defined? Does everyone know her role in them?
- Do we have a social business platform in-house? If not, do we need to get one?
- Have we matched what that social business platform must do for our organization and key groups/departments?
- How will we do user-testing with employees before a widespread launch? How will we make adjustments?
- Are there any departments that might be ideal for a pilot program?

Bulding an internal social business and its supporting Digital Village is a critical aspect of social business success. It's the foundation from which to build on. Therefore, let's summarize and reinforce the key concepts and ideas in this chapter in the form of takeaways:

- Internal social business addresses the challenge of how employees and managers can best adapt to today's changing and increasingly social workplace.
- Internal social business is about being a "social workforce"— brought about by the "empowered employee" through advancements in social technologies and investments in IT.
- The digital village supports an internal social business by providing a digital place where employees can collaborate, share, and communicate.
- Have an integrated, yet distinctive, plan for internal adoption (aside from social media adoption).
- Create environments where desired behavior for internal social business is strengthened by the infrastructure, governance, people and initiatives.

5

Engaging the Digital Network: External Social Business

Earlier in my career I launched and was involved in many marketing campaigns. Most of these campaigns were broadcast via traditional channels like direct mail, e-mail, radio, or television. If we received a 3 percent response rate we were ecstatic. We knew that if we only sent out more mail and e-mail and ran more ads we could expect a predictable return.

That worked until it didn't. The digital age arrived and all of a sudden our old models didn't work anymore. Increasingly, they were less predictable. The old guard still ran ads, still blasted their e-mail list with special offers, and still sent useless junk in the mail, even as most consumers ignored them. When they finally got wise to the new rules, they created blogs and videos and joined social networks but still found themselves applying the old broadcast methodologies to the new medium. No surprise as to the results. They were abysmal.

Their common mistake was to conclude that the old rules applied to the new order, and the only option was to create more of the same and to focus on the top of the funnel. When it didn't work, many declared social media marketing a failure and either gave up entirely or focused on it less. That was a mistake.

Today, most companies have come to the realization that they need to participate in social media in order to generate more leads. They've either heard or experienced that providing relevant, funny, or engaging content can positively impact their revenue. Most of the time, this social media participation is tactical or supports a larger initiative. There are a great many books out there to help you with executing on a social media plan. So this chapter will focus on how to develop an external social business by adapting to changing business opportunities or threats in the market. It's important that you become an external social business rather than just participating in social media.

Today, your brand is the platform. *Think of your brand as the show and not the actor.* It's your ability to create quality content worth spreading. To create that which attracts people to your organization rather than repels them, that which causes some of them to buy products (tickets to the show), that which leaves them with the impression that yours is a company they want to build a long-term relationship with.

Instead of thinking like an actor—"How can I trick the audience into believing that I am X when really I am Y"—think about how you can build an audience by delivering educational, entertaining, or surprising content that gets people excited to receive your next communication.

To put on a sustaining "show" for your target audience, one that keeps them interested and engaged for long periods of time, you must build an infrastructure that supports it. That infrastructure is what we call the *digital network* and it's an extension of the digital village we discussed in the previous chapter. While it's not impossible to build an external social business without a vibrant internal one, without an internal infrastructure to support your external business your chances of success are tremendously reduced. We therefore caution you against making the move to an external social business without first embarking on an internal initiative.

What Is External Social Business and Why Should We Bother?

External Social Business = Your Digital Network

"External" social business speaks to the activities your business conducts that directly affect people *outside* your workforce rather than those within your workforce. The goals of external social business involve maintaining a community of connected consumers who engage with the enterprise, and with each other, to cocreate value for everyone. The key word to remember here is "engaging" (a two-way or multi-way communication) and not business-as-usual "broadcasting" (one-way communication).

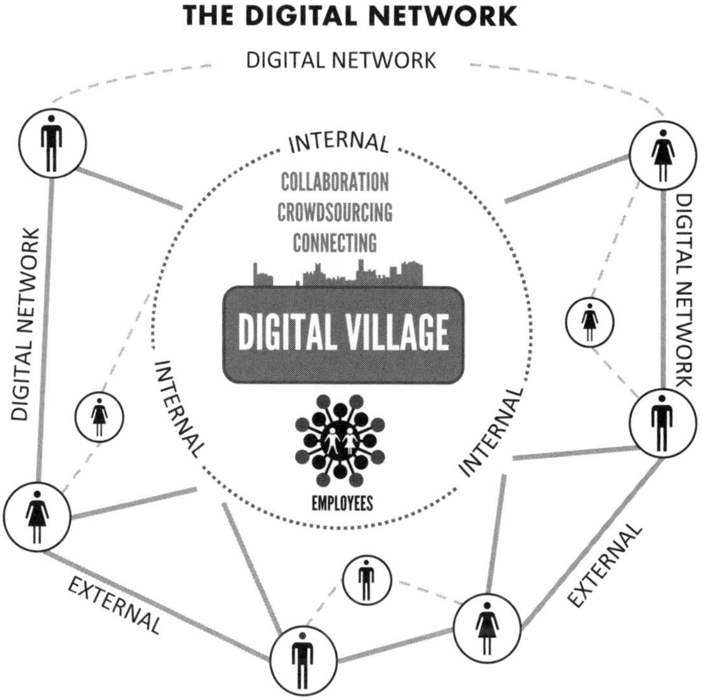

THE DIGITAL NETWORK

FIGURE 5–1

Why Do External Social Business?

The short answer is—it's where your customers are, and it's what they demand of you.

Shashi Bellamkonda, senior director of social media at Network Solutions and an adjunct professor at Georgetown University, put it aptly: "With the emergence of the digital native—who relies on social networks, peer reviews, and online communities to influence her decision making—as the preeminent consumer, *you risk being left behind*. As we move forward, social media is no longer an option; it is an imperative for business success."

Customers already have an augmented voice and greater choice, thanks to social media. They are empowered by their peers and by the content and conversations they share, all of which make them smarter about who they choose to do business with. They are figuring out who is willing to be "social" with them.

According to Bellamkonda, "…the underlying theme of a company's use of social media must be contributing valuable insights and information to the community in ways that encourage participation and develop genuine relationships based on an exchange of ideas." This translates into all aspects of external social business beyond just media, but also into what notable social media author Mari Smith labels as a move from B2C (business-to-consumer) or B2B (business-to-business) relationships toward P2P (person-to-person) relationships.

Examples of external social business include:

- Social media publishing, sharing, and networking
- Customer relationship management (CRM)
- Community management
- Crowdsourcing and collaboration
- Monitoring, listening, and responding to audience feedback
- Contests
- Creating social engagement through social campaigns
- Thought leader engagement

Aren't Social Media and External Social Business the Same Thing?

Actually, social media is just a component of external social business. It's an incredibly important part—an essential part, in fact—but there is much more to external social business than just social media. External social business also includes customer relationship management (CRM), sales, and, of course, non-Internet channels for business relationships with those outside your own workforce.

Who Is Involved with External Social Business?

Usually, external social business at the enterprise has been the domain of the Marketing and PR departments, content publishers, and online community managers. But external social business is fast becoming much more inclusive: not only can most of a company's employees participate as "brand ambassadors," but so can that enterprise's nonemployees, including partners and volunteers.

For example, an enterprise can and should have its R&D department participate in a customer/consumer collaboration and idea-generating program; the power of both the connected consumer and the outside community can play a strong role in shaping the direction for new products and services.

Who Is the Audience?

There are many groups and subgroups that enterprises connect with in external social business—these are not solely existing and prospective customers, but also fellow industry professionals and thought leaders, as well as friends, fans, and followers.

What Are the Tools and Platforms of External Social Business?

Your enterprise likely has already been using most or all of the following technologies already, and most should sound familiar to you, while others may be entirely new. All of them involve paying attention to activity and people outside your enterprise. They can include:

- Corporate blogs
- Your industry's tier-one and tier-two media sites
- Wikis
- Mobile apps
- Your websites
- Social media and networking sites like Twitter, YouTube, LinkedIn, Google+, Facebook, and Pinterest
- Video-sharing sites

- Web portals
- Community platforms and forums
- Facebook, Google+, and LinkedIn Groups

There are a number of professional and enterprise-level platforms and tools for external social business. While this list does not include all the players, you can see how social technologies are applied to different, complementary, and sometimes integrated external aspects of social business.

- Listening/Monitoring: Shoutlet, Radian6 (a Salesforce.com company), Sprout Social, HootSuite, UserVoice, eCairn, SocialBro, Commune. it, Social Mention, Google Alerts, Backtype, Search.Twitter.com, Alterian, Nimble.com

- CRM: Salesforce.com, SugarCRM, Siebel (Oracle)

- Content/Promotional: Buddy Media (now Salesforce.com), Shoutlet, HootSuite, Sprout Social, Vitrue, TweetDeck

- Analytics: BuzzMetrics, Facebook Insights, Google, Omniture, HootSuite, Shoutlet, Crowdbooster, Sprout Social, Socialbro, Mention-Mapp, Tweetmap, Storify, Bit.ly

- Social Networks: LinkedIn, Twitter, Google+, Facebook, Pinterest

The Digital Network Infrastructure

Remember when the news of the day was controlled by a handful of television news networks, newspapers, magazines, and radio stations? These organizations either collaborated to create news stories or put out news that was picked up by the rest. There was very little diversity in news content and thus a national "group think" became the norm.

It's different now because anyone can become a publisher, curator, or commenter of media content. Your customers (and prospective customers) also have much more control over what they watch and, more importantly, with whom they engage. They want you, the brand, to listen to them; if you don't, the consequences can be significant. Today, news can be created, improved, and spread through a variety of platforms and channels, each of which has the potential to reach billions around the world. But how do companies best take advantage of this new reality? Let's start with a table that illustrates the eight major shifts.

TABLE 1–1 EIGHT COMMUNICATION SHIFTS

Shift	Old Model	New Model
• Senior Leadership	• Read magazines, blogs, and websites to get the industry's latest news. Stay hands-off with customers, partners, and suppliers.	• Nurture relationships and discussion with customers, suppliers. Earn trust and build a following.
• Community	• Visit online forums, Facebook fan pages, or groups about products and services.	• Join cause communities.
• Customer Support	• Via phone and e-mail.	• Social media support, crowdsourced support.
• Content	• Static website, e-mail blasts (content is ads).	• Dynamic website, video, infographics, dynamic landing pages (content is king).
• Thought Leadership	• Focused on company.	• Focused on company's digital network.
• Social Engagement	• Trade show contests.	• Online contests, crowdsourced events, social events (mix of offline and online).
• Mobile Content	• Text messages.	• Location-based games, promotions, apps.
• Monitoring, Measuring, Adapting, Repeating	• How many people read the paper or magazine, or watched/listened to the TV or radio program we just advertised in?	• Are people engaging with us no matter where we are?

Let's take a look at these shifts one by one, so that you are better able to change your approach to engaging your organization's customers, suppliers, and partners. This is not another ten-step program for becoming better at social media, it's a look at how the best organizations in the world are shifting from their old models to new models. It's a look at how to lay your company's foundation for becoming more effective and ultimately more adaptive. Let's get started.

Your Digital Network Needs Leadership

A 2012 IBM study concluded that "[a]s CEOs ratchet up the level of openness within their organizations, they are developing collaborative environments where employees are encouraged to speak up, exercise personal initiative, connect with fellow collaborators, and innovate." Learning to be social internally is good preparation; it means learning new ways of communicating with an audience in a digital environment. It's like rehearsing before a big show goes live to the public.

When IBM conducted its study of 1,709 CEOs around the world and found only 16 percent of them participating in social media, I figured we still had a long way to go. But later in the report, the analysis shows that the percentage will likely grow to 57 percent within five years. Why? Because CEOs are beginning to recognize that using e-mail and the phone to get the message out isn't sufficient anymore. They recognize the need to develop relationship with their customers, partners, and suppliers that goes beyond what they can accomplish with traditional media.

I like to cite an example of the billionaire oil man and the millionaire rapper as a fun example of the incredible reach of social media. This conversation would never have occurred in traditional media.

Aubrey Drake Graham, a twenty-five-year-old Canadian rap star who goes by "Drake," is one of the most popular rappers in North America. In 2010, his album *Thank Me Later* did quite well and he became very popular. Eighty-four-year-old T. Boone Pickens is ranked by *Forbes* as the 328th-richest person in America and made his money in Texas selling oil.

Only on a public social media platform like Twitter would you see the following exchange.

BILLIONAIRE AND MILLIONAIRE

Drizzy @Drake 1d
The first million is the hardest.

In reply to Drizzy

T. Boone Pickens
@boonepickens

The first billion is a helluva lot harder RT @ Drake: The first million is the hardest.

13 hours ago via TweetDeck

Drizzy @Drake 1d
@boonepickens just stunted on me heavy

In reply to Drizzy

FIGURE 5–2

Drake, in a moment of self-congratulation, tweeted to his fans that making his "first million is the hardest." Unimpressed, T. Boone Pickens responded: "The first billion is a helluva lot harder." Realizing that Pickens' response just set him straight, Drake replied: "Boone Pickens just stunted me heavy." Where else on the planet would you see an exchange like this one? You wouldn't—which perfectly illustrates the far-reaching potential of social media.

The point here is that, instead of continuing the broadcast paradigm of old media, which doesn't allow for discovery of new discussions or feedback about something said, senior leadership needs to engage in social media for themselves. That way they begin to understand its potential for their own organization and are better able to lead not only by example but intelligently and with experience.

Because a business's purpose is to create a customer, business leadership must be in tune with current and prospective customers to understand their needs. Using social technologies to engage with customers, suppliers, and employees will enable the organization to be more adaptive and agile. The aim of this social engagement is to know and understand the customer so well that the executives can better lead the organization moving forward.

Executives Will Need to Become
Social to Remain at the Top

Picture yourself as an executive in 2017 struggling to make sense of how many of your peers are out of jobs, having failed to become social. Many of them got pushed aside by their more savvy underlings who built up both internal and external social networks. These up-and-comers built large networks that wield tremendous power, have great collective intelligence, and have the ability to influence both employees and customers. Many of the executives who didn't adapt were caught in a type of "vocational innovator's dilemma" where they stubbornly refused to change despite the warning signs.

SAP's CIO, Oliver Bussmann, who, incidentally, in 2012 was the most social CIO in the Fortune 250, believes that future executives must be more open, transparent, and engaging to succeed in the long term. Even longtime social naysayer and competitor Larry Ellison, CEO of Oracle, got on the social bandwagon in mid-2012 with a tweet attacking competitor SAP. He's got a few things to learn, but at least he's diving into the social waters.

Bussmann doesn't just preach—he practices. In 2009, to demonstrate the effectiveness of being more social, he cited an internal scoring system similar to Net Promoter that was used to rate the effectiveness of his department. The IT Department received a 4 out of 10. At the end of 2011, that same score skyrocketed to 7.3. It happened because he worked to adapt the IT Department to the needs of the company.

Externally, Bussmann recommends you first open up accounts on Twitter and Google+ because that's where business-oriented people are found. He suggests you then connect with thought leaders and analysts to better understand what topics the groups are discussing as well as the issues other companies are facing. Listen first, then engage.

When asking, "How can I become more effective as an executive?" the executive needs to also ask, "And how will I do it?" For Bussmann, the answer to both questions is to leverage social technologies, for they are the best way to address the myriad changes in today's more transparent business environment.

In the summer of 2010, there was a community of analysts that began to interact with Bussmann on Twitter. Until those interactions, he didn't recognize that many analysts were convinced that people were looking at the iPad as an enterprise product and not just as a consumer product. Realizing he may have missed an opportunity had he not interacted with the analysts, he soon saw that participation in external social networks was a big deal.

Equipped with this new information, Bussmann's team, in late 2010, quickly created one of the first corporate apps for the iPad. As of June 2012, Bussmann says his internal app store has over forty apps and, using a Sybase (SAP) solution called Afaria, can deploy services to between three thousand and four thousand devices in a month.

In the social age, information means getting timely, accurate facts about the conditions and circumstances the business is competing in. It's critical to remaining competitive that the executive team obtain unfiltered facts. Information also means communicating knowledge that influences perceptions. Perceptions are facts and narratives that keep competitors guessing and your customers tuned in. Every executive who masters both will be much more valuable than the executive who does not. There's no better way to master both than participation in social media.

Building the Digital Network
Through Community

There are not many community platform providers capable of creating an online community that resembles what a brand represents in spirit. But companies like Backplane are developing community platforms that do just that. "There's Facebook, which is the web's largest audience, but it's more of a walled garden. You have Twitter, which is this mass broadcast utility that only blasts out information. Then you have the YouTube layer, which is this discovery apocalypse of more content than any human will ever be able to understand in their life," Sarah Ross, CMO of Backplane, told me. "While these networks are amazing, the big thing that's missing in the social web right now is context and a high-quality content experience."

Where the old model consisted of building communities around a company's product or services, the new model involves finding a cause that will attract the brand's prospective customers. Take Nike as an example. As of late 2011, Nike had fifty million consumers engaged in its active communities around the world. Nike+, the company's highly successful community for runners, was built to give runners a place to connect with other runners. The value to consumers is the ability to track their health statistics and running data, as well as challenge their friends and themselves. But Nike didn't build the community out of sheer altruism, it sells products that tie into the community to make it more rewarding for users.

"Ultimately, we are about connecting with the consumer where they are," says Nike's Global Digital Brand and Innovation Director Jesse Stollak. "We started with the notion that this was about publishing to them with the right message and at the right time. We've quickly evolved to a focus on conversations and engaging them to participate as opposed to using new media in traditional ways."

Nike's engagement involves selling products like the Nike+ GPS App, Nike+ GPS Sportwatch, and the Nike+ Fuelband. Each works to enhance a user's experience with the community by adding data from the physical world. For example, the Fuelband is a device you wear around your wrist that keeps track of your physical activity and provides live readouts on calories, steps taken, and "fuel" used. The fuel is an activity metric that displays charts, and stats motivate the user to exercise more and compete with her friends. This information can be shared with the community, and thus enhances the experience, because people can discuss each other's stats.

The Nike+ community is also very social. For example, in Nike's GPS app, there is a "cheer me on" function that enables the runner's friends on Facebook to provide motivational support. So when the user is running, he hears applause over his music when friends "cheer" him.

To build an effective digital network, you have to realize that people want to connect with you in much more rewarding ways. It's not about listening to a product pitch or liking a brand's video anymore, it's about creating engaging experiences within a community that keep people focused on your brand. Your customers and prospects have more control over the dialogue, and they want more interaction within the communities you engage in or control. The stronger the connection in the community, the stronger the brand.

Community strength, vibrancy, and engagement are some of the new metrics for which brands will be valued in the near future. They indicate a level of trust that will signal to customers whether your brand is worthy of their attention and hard-earned income. Your community will come to represent the essence of your brand and what it stands for. It will also become one of your primary revenue sources.

Your Digital Network Must Have World-Class Customer Support

Self-service support communities are beginning to replace the help desk for internal and external customer support. In fact, these communities are simultaneously reducing costs (fewer support calls) and increasing revenue (SEO lead generation). But only a handful of companies have implemented robust support communities.

Because you don't have the tools today to measure how effective your product/service documentation is for your customers, you need to stock your company full of customer support people. That can be expensive.

And if you're like most customers (including me), you don't bother to check the product documentation because your expectation is that it's light or won't address your specific issue. So you place a call to customer support. And in aggregate, that gets expensive for the organization. In fact, according to our research, it costs $156 per customer, on average.

So why not enable your customers to help solve customer support issues? Why not allow them the opportunity to post video tutorials? Why not give them the tools to better your current documentation and support site? Why not have tools that enable your organization to monitor documentation usage? Reports and dashboards that give you real-time heads-up displays on what users are searching for and not finding? Analytics that display how useful an article is and if the article needs updating?

Increasingly, your customers are expecting more. More information about how your product or service works and more interaction with your brand. But your static documentation doesn't provide that. So they go elsewhere. Maybe even to your competitor's site.

To get a peek at how a company does support communities well, I talked with Barbara Gordon, corporate vice president of customer service and support for Microsoft. When asked about Microsoft's approach to customer support, she said, "We want to give our customers the ability to get resolutions to their issues with the least amount of work possible."

Gordon went on to add, "We are always thinking about how we hold ourselves accountable for increasing customer (support) expectations." She went on to explain how they measure first call-resolution statistics and other key metrics in real time to ensure that Microsoft is meeting their customers' key challenges

Given how open Gordon and other team members are with answering questions and listening to feedback, it appeared to me that Microsoft is constantly checking the pulse of their support communities to ensure they are providing best-in-class customer support.

The key to Microsoft's social support is their MVP Program, its social recognition program for active support users, along with its Questions and Answers page. Throughout most of Microsoft support sites, there is an active social component that enables non-Microsoft employees to provide support for Microsoft customers.

What's amazing is that nonemployees who help Microsoft answer support questions are compensated only in digital support badges and MVP points. These points and badges help the MVPs differentiate themselves from everyone else, and because they post their status on resumes, LinkedIn, and other sites, MVPs have a greater chance of receiving job or consulting offers.

Microsoft has over 4,100 MVPs who are certified to provide support to its customers. According to Toby Richards, Microsoft's general manager of communities and online support, these MVPs are thirty times more active than the average user. In fact, Microsoft considers them a "tremendous asset that provides support in multiple languages across ninety-eight countries."

Using Social Media and Mobile for Support

In a 2012 survey by customer support software vendor Zendesk, 62 percent of consumers have used social media for customer service issues. And 76 percent would be more likely to use social media if they better understood the tools available to them. Expect these statistics to shift to nearly 100 percent in the next few years. Customers will want the quick access to support through social media, and brands will want the visibility of a satisfied customer in return.

In another survey conducted by Zendesk, 56 percent of smartphone users preferred using an organization's customer support app over calling a support center. Seventy-nine percent of smartphone users would view the brand more favorably if they offered a mobile customer support app. The survey also showed that mobile will become an increasingly important channel for customer support.

What both Zendesk surveys tell us is that it's imperative that you set up a social media listening and response team to handle support requests in social media and build mobile apps that use information from your internal and external support knowledge bases.

Companies like Dell have been tuning in to their prospective and current customer conversations about their brand for the past five years. Initially, the program started as a small project, but Michael Dell quickly ramped it up, asking the team, "Why aren't we monitoring everything in the realm about us?"

Content Really Is King

The first thing I say, when asked how a company should start engaging with its digital network, is that it should create content worth spreading, content that makes people think, take action, or share it with their friends. For our purposes, content is information that can be spread through your digital network. For example, content is online videos, blog posts, infographics, images, online contests, and action-oriented tweets.

This advice is usually followed by an objection that sounds something like this: "My industry niche is so boring." Or, in the business-to-business (B2B) space, "people don't want to read about work-related subjects." Your industry niche isn't boring, and I know of a lot of people (myself included) who only read work-related content.

The key is to present the information in creative ways that get it noticed and to make it easy to share with other people. There are at least eight types of content that have consistently worked for me in the past.

1. **Hold online contests.** Even the most boring products can spark interest if you hold a contest about what people are doing with that product. Take, for example, a company that sells birdseed. Not many people are passionate about birdseed, but they are passionate about birds. What better way to generate buzz and excitement with your target audience than to hold a contest where people submit photos of where they are feeding birds? Imagine the variety and interest you'd generate. Surely your birdseed brand would benefit as a result.

2. **Create guides that help other people.** Hubspot is an online marketing automation company based in Boston, Massachusetts. Rather than focusing its blog posts and digital content exclusively

around its product, Hubspot instead creates content and resources for Sales and Marketing departments. *Its content helps marketing and sales people become more effective with or without Hubspot's product.*

3. **Create a questions and answers section on your website.** One of the most powerful things you can do to connect with your digital network is to create a place where people can ask relevant, industry-related questions. Not only does it make people feel better about engaging with your brand, it has a lasting SEO effect as well. Think about how people find your products today. Are they asking these same types of questions in a Google search? Yes, of course they are. And if the answer can be found on your website, then those people will be sent to your website.

   For example, Intuit's Mint.com was able to reduce its support tickets by 75 percent, saw an almost instant 50 percent increase in traffic, and engaged ninety thousand people across fifteen thousand topics because it used GetSatisfaction's support solution, which included a Q&A function.

4. **Create simple yet creative videos to explain your product.** Even commodity products can be seen as exciting to use if you create a video to present it differently. Take Dollar Shave Club as an example. The company produced an edgy, entertaining online video about how they're different than the "other" guys. As of the date of this writing, the number of people who have watched that video is at 4.5 million and counting. As one pundit remarked, "This isn't even a particularly new concept, you can set up automated repeat orders of a lot of things on Amazon. In this case, it was just the right combination of marketing, ease of use, and a decent product. With that, I have a feeling I will be using Dollar Shave Club for a while."

5. **Create helpful blog posts on how to use your product strategically or technically.** The best examples of how to do this can be found at ehow.com, wikihow.com (crowdsourced), and howcast (videos). The key is to visually illustrate how to use or assemble your product, or to present best practices for using your product. Make your posts simple and easy to follow. A great example of how

to do this well was created by my friends at iFixit—they make installing or fixing products extremely easy.

6. **Create infographics that are easily shareable.** Infographics are typically large images that attempt to simplify either large data sets or complex processes. TheOatmeal.com's 15ish Things Worth Knowing About Coffee simplifies the history of coffee, and the image was shared by hundreds of thousands of people because it made a boring subject fun. Infographics can also be interactive. One of my favorites is from Unruly, a social advertising company that created a living spiral infographic. It's a clever ad in disguise for Unruly Media that vaulted them to the top of the list for people who were looking for socially engaging videos or infographics.

7. **Simplify complex products.** Is your product, solution, or service so difficult to understand that only a handful of people can tell you what it does? Unless your product is truly suited for just a handful of people, you need to simplify it through tutorials, how-to videos, or a series of blog posts on the subject. The more succinct the better. CommonCraft does a great job of this with video. For example, watch their video "Social Media and the Workplace."

8. **Curate the best content from around the web.** Museum directors are typically not great artists. If they were, chances are they wouldn't be museum directors. But they do make great curators of art. So if your company isn't ready or doesn't have the right resources to create great content, then design your blog to be an aggregator of great content relevant to what your audience wants. The mantra for this type of blog is "The audience is king, so serve them well."

When I am designing and creating content, I like to make sure it passes the following three-question test: First, will my prospects and customers care about this content? Second, do I need to interview or get an internal expert to support the content's premise? Three, how do I design into the content or content program a method to make it more shareable?

I used to argue with the search engine optimization (SEO) crowd that quality content has much better value than putting out average content in quantity. Experience has proven me right. You need to develop content that draws people to you—and that doesn't repel them.

Be Your Industry's Thought Leader

We cover how to engage thought leaders in chapter 7. In this section I will explain how to become a thought leader in your industry's digital network through an eight-step process.

When I first joined harmon.ie, a small software company that had recently changed its name from Mainsoft, not many people knew about the organization. When I presented at industry events for the company and asked the audience if anyone had heard of us, very few people raised their hands. I knew we had to change the situation quickly.

What makes thought leadership so important in an industry is that if you're one of its leaders, *you get to help set the agenda and decide what's important.* For example, a great thought leader can change the industry discussion from topic A to topic B just by posting a blog post or thought-provoking video. At harmon.ie, we did this constantly by highlighting why executives need to be social and what companies need to know about the future of business.

For your business, you need to identify the areas for which you want to own and control the discussion, then follow these eight steps:

1. **Identify your in-house subject matter experts (SME).** These are people who truly understand your industry and how to make sense of it. If you don't have any (perhaps you're starting a new company or moving into another industry), then learn by researching, listening, and asking questions about your industry.

2. **Become a storyteller.** To be an effective storyteller, you need to be passionate about the subject matter. You need to have the kind of passion that keeps you working on that blog post until 3 a.m. The kind of passion that pushes you to create videos that inspire and teach. The kind that motivates you and your designer to

create an infographic that visualizes a data set instead of posting a data table that everyone ignores.

3. **Find your voice.** If you have passion, you have opinions. My friend Steve Faktor, author of *Econovation*, has one of the most unique voices in the field of innovation and has never been afraid to express himself. Faktor calls it "strong opinion with a touch of satire." It's not something he's developed for the sake of his thought leadership, it's how he communicates in conversation. My point is, don't develop an insincere voice; use your own voice and make it interesting.

4. **Challenge the status quo.** If your industry is dominated by what Geoffrey Moore called an "eight-hundred-pound guerilla" or a large company that owns most of the market share in the industry, then use strong opinions to tell people why your product solves their problems better. Make sure you can back your opinions up with strong data or testimonials from your customers.

5. **Interview industry experts, customers, and pundits.** Assuming you follow the previous steps, one of the fastest ways to establish thought leadership is for you to interview and write about the industry's VIPs. That does three things. One, it establishes you as someone who is connected with industry leaders. Two, it potentially connects you with important people who can impact your business. Three, it makes it more likely that these people will write about your company. This is a very powerful step, and one that is overlooked by most people.

6. **Make sense.** The future belongs to people who can make sense of the noise and not those who produce it. Your customers want quick access to a reliable voice that cuts through the jargon and gives it to them straight. No one has time anymore to do this on their own.

7. **Publish on channels regularly and consistently.** I've seen too many companies post a video one week and a blog post the other. Sometimes the company blog isn't updated for months. What does this communicate to your potential customers? For me, it says "That's a company without a lot going on." It's like the restaurant that never has anyone in it. Eventually, you begin to wonder what's

wrong with the food. The same experience is occurring in your prospects' mind. They're thinking, "This company looks like no one cares—why should I?"

8. **Build a following.** Even if you do everything above religiously for months, you may not have established a thought leadership position. The reasons can be many, but typically it boils down to not having an active network that shares most everything you produce. Are you just a broadcaster of information, or do you respond to comments on your blog, Twitter, or Facebook fan page? Do you expect the network to build on its own or are you reaching out to people in your industry?

Think it's tough for your company to build a following? How about building a following with a company name like Namecheap.com? Yet, through content production, outreach, and responding to people on Twitter, they've managed to attract ninety-five thousand followers. With a following like that, the content they publish has a high probability of being seen by more of their prospective customers.

It's best to also understand why people will or will not share your thought leadership content. I have found that there are four main reasons why people will share your content. The first reason is to help other people. The second is to connect and build relationships with like-minded people. Third is to associate their identity or philosophy with the content. Fourth is to disagree about published content and to add their remarks. It's best to keep these in mind if you want shareable content that will help build thought leadership and a following.

Creating Social Engagement Performances

Before the Internet and social media, businesspeople met at industry events, hotel conference rooms, or office conference rooms to learn about new products, network, or share best practices. If you had an imaginative Marketing Department, they'd throw in something creative on the trade show floor to lure in unsuspecting prospects. Sometimes it worked, other times it failed miserably.

Businesses reached consumers with a variety of in-store promotions, TV advertising, and print and radio buys. For big companies, the spend justified the results. For smaller companies, competing with the big guys was very difficult.

We now sit in front of our big and small screens to share, learn, connect, and collaborate in our digital networks. We still like to meet physically, but it's far more efficient and less expensive to do it remotely. Today, brands need to realize that the traditional methods of reaching their prospects are coming to an end. They need to get creative about how they reach their audience and create remarkable experiences to keep them engaged. I recommend brands design affordable social engagement campaigns designed to connect with people, with the goal of acquiring new followers and, ultimately, new customers.

For business-to-consumer (B2C) organizations, one effective method for creating a campaign is to humanize an issue that your company can solve. Take the BlueCross BlueShield of Minnesota Human Doing social campaign at the Mall of America in Minnesota. A local resident named Scott Jorgenson lived in a glass apartment in the mall for a month. To demonstrate the effectiveness of regular exercise, Jorgenson worked out three to five times each day in ten-minute stints. The twist, however, was that BlueCross allowed its Facebook and Twitter followers to dictate the type of exercise for each session. Jorgenson's blog captured his daily thoughts, and live webcams allowed his audience to observe his every move.

The results after thirty days: Jorgenson's cholesterol dropped from 260 to 150, he lost 29 pounds, his triglycerides plunged from 187 to 42, and his blood pressure fell 10 points. For BlueCross BlueShield, the Human Doing had 2 million social media impressions and received 143,000 votes of public support. On Facebook, it received more than 1.6 million views and 8,000 comments.

As of this writing, we're still seeing the impact of that campaign, as Jorgenson continues to post updates to his fans (he posted updates 120 days, 6 months, and 9 months after the original campaign ended).

Of course, building a glass apartment in a mall is expensive, but the basic ideas from the campaign can be used by large or small companies.

Think about what your business represents. Perhaps you're a deli that makes healthy, vegetarian sandwiches. You might hold a contest where you select a customer to eat one of your sandwiches every day for a month. The audience gets to choose which sandwich that person eats by voting via Twitter, Facebook, Google+, or wherever you have the desire to increase your engagement. After thirty days, the customer reports on how she feels or notes any positive changes she's experienced. The key is to make it social, fun, and interactive, with an eye towards future revenue.

For business-to-business (B2B) companies, the goal is to engage other businesspeople in a cause associated with your brand. One example comes from another friend of mine, Mark Miller of EndUserSharePoint .com. Mark started a "build an app to solve a business challenge on Share-Point" challenge, in which he encouraged developers to create applications and then allowed the public to vote on the best results. In this ongoing campaign, Mark issues a challenge on his website and on Twitter, and developers then spend a week to build and submit their apps. Mark then hosts a live event where judges (I was one) comment and make remarks on the app's ability to solve the business challenge. For the next week, the public votes on the best app and a prize is awarded to the best developer. This ongoing event costs Mark almost nothing—just time and preparation.

Another B2B example from Cisco occurred when the company wanted to launch a new router. Cisco leveraged blogs, Twitter, Facebook, YouTube, videoconferencing, mobile, and games to create a social campaign that had ninety times the attendance and cut more than $100,000 from their traditional launch attempts. Instead of flying executives, customers, and employees in from around the world (they estimated they saved forty-two thousand gallons of gas), they leveraged their numerous social channels to promote the new product. And because the launch was done online instead of offline, Cisco measured more than forty million impressions and saw a thousand blog posts created as a result of the material being online. Cisco said the event cost one-sixth what a traditional launch costs.

LaSandra Brill, Senior Manager of Global Social Media at Cisco noted, "It was classified as one of the top five launches in company history. It was the crossing the chasm point for us in the adoption phase of social media and helped us get over the hump of internal acceptance."

For both B2C and B2B campaigns, make sure you promote the campaigns before, during, and after launch for the best results. Leverage the thought leader network that you've established (chapter 5) to give the campaign even more of a lift. Successful campaigns take a lot of planning, preparation, and work, but there's never before been a more powerful promotional technique to create short- and long-term profits. It's important that you are monitoring and measuring your social campaign in real time so that if it begins to take off, you can double down on it to maximize short-term profits.

Meanwhile, in most cases, the campaign benefits will be realized over the mid- to long term, and may come not only in the form of increased revenue, but in a larger community, more followers, or more brand awareness, all of which lead to more opportunities to sell products.

Finally, one thing I consistently emphasize is the need for sales and marketing alignment around your social campaigns. Integrating sales and marketing into the campaign will ensure that the experience can be extended beyond the campaign to other marketing materials and that sales can ramp up to take advantage of a successful campaign that is producing a lot of interest. In my research, about 35 percent of B2B marketers were not tracking the impact of their social campaigns, yet the objective of B2B marketers is to provide the sales team with qualified leads. That misalignment is costing these companies revenue. Remember to measure the success of your campaign, because it will enable the organization to adapt to new trends and to guide marketing spend toward things that have the biggest impact on the bottom line.

The Mobile Revolution

With six billion global mobile subscribers and more than forty billion apps downloaded to those devices as of June 2012, one begins to imagine how large the opportunities are for business in the mobile arena.

Welcome to the mobile business revolution.

The first time I can remember realizing how critical mobile phones were to people was back in 2006, while I was working in India. It was a blistering summer, and I'd heard the news that rural farmers were waiting in mile-long lines to bring their produce to market; most had to spend the night catching what sleep they could on their bullock carts. Sadly, the heat of the summer spoiled nearly all the produce that didn't make it to market that week, and many farmers were distraught.

A few farmers, I later learned, had used their mobile phones to find out about prices and wait times at different markets. Armed with that information, they sold their produce in the markets that had the shortest lines and highest prices. They had, in fact, saved their produce and their financial livelihood from certain ruin.

Situations like this one highlight crucial progress occurring in some of the most remote places on earth. People living in the most disadvantaged societies are utilizing twenty-first-century mobile technologies to help solve problems that have been around since the nineteenth century, if not before. That's a period of at least two hundred years bridged by a single device that can be carried in your pocket.

If Mobile Technologies Are Changing Today's Least Advanced Societies, Imagine What They'll Do to the Most Advanced

There's no other technology in the world that 87 percent of the world's population owns. And yet, despite mobile devices' ubiquity and connectivity, we are only beginning to realize what's possible. But most organizations, in fact most people, aren't ready for the massive cultural, health, business, and government impacts that these mobile devices are about to deliver.

I believe mobile technologies will displace many of the fixed-location technologies that keep people and businesses chained to physical places. Who needs a store when you can point, click, and buy a product from Amazon.com? Indeed, who needs to visit a bank branch when you can transfer money anywhere using services like PayPal or Square?

According to Price Waterhouse Coopers' latest Digital IQ survey,

66 percent of organizations are investing in mobile technologies for their employees. But these businesses *are reacting* to the "Bring Your Own Device" (BYOD) phenomenon, most are not preparing for it.

The smarter organizations are quickly adapting mobile technologies to their businesses by designing for mobile as an integral part of their future workplace. Andrew Dixon, vice president of marketing and operations at Igloo Software, characterizes the future workplace as "The blurring between work life and home life, the emergence of new mobile platforms, the shifting expectations of IT, and the rise of social as a transformative force in collaboration.... The future workplace is actually not a place. It's just what you do. That means business will happen wherever, whenever, and on whatever device it needs to happen, 24–7."

If you subscribe to Dixon's view, as I do, you can anticipate that work as we know it will change dramatically. Yet as David Swan, CTO of the actuarial and consulting firm Milliman, illustrates, there are some reservations about the shift. "The truth of the matter is that with mobile technologies, you could build an entire consulting company in the cloud and nobody would ever have to come to work. Is that okay? Is it okay if people don't have walls? Some Milliman practices virtualize that way. Everybody works from their home office."

Swan raises an interesting point, and I expect new businesses will emerge "without walls" and be based entirely on mobile devices connected to the cloud. In that situation, the economics are unbeatable. In this scenario, companies will need to understand mobile computing's potential impact on their competitive position in the market, and they'll need to figure out what they can do now to stay ahead of the curve. But before we explore that, let's review a few companies that missed the mobile call.

In her book *Kill the Company,* Lisa Bodell, founder and CEO of future-**think**, explains why it's imperative for organizations to change and notes that companies can be their own worst enemy: "The very structures put in place to help businesses grow are now holding us back." These structures have blocked companies from innovating and creating new shareholder value, condemning them instead to a type of sterile dogmatism. Ask yourself:

• **Why didn't Kodak invent Instagram?** Kodak's internal DNA defined itself as a traditional organization built on cameras and film. And, as happens in most command-and-control companies, Kodak's culture suffered from a case of innovator's dilemma, where entrenched employees and demanding customers prevented the company from disrupting its own profitable markets. Kodak's core business and the people who controlled it would surely have killed any attempt to create a non-revenue-generating mobile application. And that's a shame, considering that Facebook's Zuckerberg decided to purchase Instagram, with its thirty million users, for $1 billion.

• **Why didn't Zagat invent Yelp?** For nearly twenty-eight years, Zagat was the undisputed powerhouse in local advertising and reviews. But like the executives at many print publications, Zagat's founders never understood the shift to mobile computing, despite the fact that everyone is armed with smartphones or tablets. That mistake led Zagat to sell out last year to Google for a reported $100 million, while eight-year-old Yelp is today worth $1 billion.

• **Why didn't a music label invent iTunes?** While recording artists relied upon record labels to promote them on TV, radio, and online, the music labels were run by traditionalists who didn't understand the move first to the Internet and then to mobile devices. Worse, the top labels are run by legions of lawyers who would rather fight their fate in court than embrace the move to mobile technologies. Note to everyone: unless your primary business is law, allowing attorneys to run your business is a certain sign of decline. In fact, just last year EMI filed for bankruptcy protection, perhaps an indication that more are coming.

• **Why didn't Rand McNally invent Waze?** Established in 1868, the famous mapmaker was the undisputed leader in road maps for decades. But it too was led by people who resisted veering off the cash cow highway. The company missed the digital mapping trends on CDs and the Internet, then filed for bankruptcy in 2003. Restructured, it failed again to capitalize on social and mobile trends that could have fueled its revival.

Meanwhile, Waze just passed the ten million–user mark in January 2012, and its free GPS navigation application appears to be accelerating.

If I were to consolidate each of these examples into one lesson, it is that if there's a way to disrupt your industry with mobile technologies, it is either happening now or it will happen within a few years.

In the next five years, we'll see mobile technologies disrupt traditional business at scale. Those who leverage mobile technologies will be more adaptive and responsive and ultimately more competitive by enabling push and pull access to contextual information from anywhere in the world.

Mike Edwards, director of digital and experiential marketing at Amway, describes the direct sales organization's urgency to equip its distribution channel with on-the-go computing: "I've never seen any [IT initiative] with that level of speed in our organization. What we're trying to do now is focus on how we build an enterprise organization around digital and mobile technologies. In fact, for our distributors, we take a mobile-first approach, and then adapt that to our Internet experience."

Most organizations are still trying to figure out how to best utilize social media to get closer to customers, employees, and partners, and few, like Amway, are thinking about using mobile technologies to do it. It's a critical missed call.

But who can blame them? Change is occurring so quickly now that only the companies built to be immediately responsive to customer changes will remain competitive. When most everyone in the world can be reached instantly, and when anyone anywhere can purchase a product, view a video, and create content, there are immeasurable opportunities to listen and engage with a global audience.

Yet the most significant opportunities for leveraging mobile technologies in business lie in the hands of your employees. They lie in the use of mobile devices to capture innovations seen outside the workplace; they lie in sharing documents and content with each other whether traveling or at home; and they lie in creating new mobile applications that quickly and efficiently allow on-the-go workers to complete tasks that are integrated into the organization's front- and back-end systems.

In the past, knowledge workers spent days doing what we can now do with mobile devices in mere seconds. Just twenty years ago, if you wanted to take a picture, develop it, and send it around to your coworkers, the process took weeks. Just ten years ago, while some mobile devices included rudimentary cameras, most pictures were taken with digital cameras, then downloaded to a computer, then sent out via e-mail in hours. Today, the process of taking and uploading a picture to hundreds of sites can be done in seconds.

In order to stay competitive, your organization must learn to harness connected mobile computing devices to do things faster, more efficiently, and within context. To view mobile technologies as tactical devices to place calls, receive e-mails, and launch Angry Birds is a form of mobile malpractice. The convergence of mobile technologies, cloud computing, data analytics, and social media has established an innovation platform with unprecedented potential. There has never been a better time for that instinctive, human creative impulse to design, to build, and to ship.

That driving force is the reason it's imperative that you prepare and adapt mobile computing to your workplace. Your workforce needs solutions that connect them to the organization, no matter where they are, no matter what the time.

Here are five different ways to connect with your digital network using mobile devices:

1. **Create apps that connect your existing product lines to mobile**. At harmon.ie we developed mobile apps as an extension of our desktop software. This allowed our customers to use the software whether they were on the road or in the office. Because of mobile, we were viewed much more strategically. Create new apps that complement your product or service. Nike created the Nike Training Club app for users to download and use on their phones to help them with their workouts. While not directly related to Nike's products, the app kept the brand top of mind with the user. It's the new logo pen. If your company has a smaller budget, make sure you have a well-thought-out plan before creating a mobile app. Remember, your ultimate goal is revenue or cost reduction. I recommend that organizations develop apps that are either directly related to purchasing the product (for example, to enable

one-click flower orders) or that the user needs to stay productive (for example, the Nike app), which keeps your brand highly visible to users.

2. **Use an existing mobile app platform provider.** For most businesses, it's better to use a general purpose app created by an app developer to maintain the platform. Shopkick is one company that allows brands to give points to users for walking in that company's door or making in-store purchases. After accumulating enough points, users earn rewards. This gamification technique can be a very powerful motivator for many people.

3. **Develop a variable-product-price mobile program.** Whether your inventory is high or you just want to keep your customers guessing, creating a mobile campaign that changes product (or service) prices depending on some X factor can be extremely effective because it causes people to check in regularly. A great example is the Bud Ice Index campaign, which used the motto "The hotter the day, the less you pay." When users downloaded the app from Budweiser, they were given the temperature and how much they could save on beer that day. As the day's temperature rose, the price of the beer declined. Although the original intent of the campaign was to drive people to try Budweiser's new beer, it astonishingly led quite a few people to switch from their current beer to Bud Ice. It was reported that the average consumer tried Bud Ice four times, which was enough product exposure for the user to make the switch.

4. **Develop mobile campaigns to collect data from your users.** I admit, some of you may find this controversial, but if done with full disclosure it's a powerful method of collecting data about your customers or prospective customers. Let's imagine you've entered a market with an incumbent that owns more than 50 percent market share. You know it's going to be difficult to break in so you decide to create an app that intercepts the customer before he makes a purchase. The user finds the app valuable because, after a quick bar code scan, it tells him if the price for a product he's about to buy can be found cheaper online or in another store.

In this scenario, users find your app extremely valuable (you're saving them money) and at the same time, you're collecting data about their purchase activity. Furthermore, you can insert your own product at the top of the list whenever a product similar to the one you sell is scanned. Shazam's music listening app is a powerful example of a company that intercepts users and directs them for the company's gain. The Shazam app identifies songs being played, then asks users if they want to purchase the song or buy tickets for the artist's upcoming tour.

Again, the key to success for your mobile campaigns is to measure, measure, and measure again. Use mobile analytics to understand what's working and what's not. Without analytics, you don't know what's really moving the business forward. Make analytics a priority.

Mobile technologies offer the greatest economic opportunity of the last twenty-five years. New companies will emerge without walls, and smart companies will utilize mobile technologies to become more effective. Other companies won't be able to get out of their own way, and won't survive.

Keep in mind that Apple sold more iOS (iPads and iPhones) in 2011 (156 million) than all the Macs *ever* sold (122 million). So instead of ignoring or fighting the trend, let's learn how to better adapt our businesses to mobile technologies.

And we're just scratching the surface. Today and in the near future, we'll have apps that speak to other apps that automatically create new information (through a type of artificial intelligence) formed for a temporary purpose. These super apps will recognize your location, look at your calendar, examine your e-mail, and suggest items of interest based on your particular context (more on this in chapter 10).

Monitor, Measure, Adapt, Repeat

Professional American football is an incredibly strategic game. It also resembles the way an effective external social business should be run. Before every play, both the offense and defense huddle up to call the next play. Most of the time, a play is chosen by how much yardage is needed for a first down, but also giving special attention to how much time is on the clock. As the game goes on, both teams learn about the other and take advantage of any weaknesses. For this to happen, there needs to be people observing from the sidelines and taking detailed notes from coaches in skyboxes, as well as players reporting how things are working on the field. This information is consolidated and given to the coach so that he can modify the game's strategy, if necessary.

On the field, and before the ball is snapped, players are communicating back and forth as the offensive or defensive formations are seen by the opposing side. Sometimes the player captains call an audible (a verbal call) to change the play, in order to adapt to the perceived threat. After the ball is snapped and the play is in motion, offensive players are running the play while the defensive team is reacting to it. When the play is over, both sides study the impact of the play while planning their adjustments for the next play.

Though this is, of course, a simplistic example of in-game football strategy, it's meant to demonstrate how almost everything is monitored, measured, and adapted depending on multiple competing factors. That's also the way you should set up to monitor the success of your external social business within your digital network. But this example is only meant to highlight what's needed from day to day. As in football, the most important strategic work is done before and after the game.

If you ask ten National Football League coaches how they develop a game strategy, they'll give you ten different answers. Football is a sophisticated sport with several ways to win. But all will scout out upcoming teams, have strategy sessions with their assistant coaches, watch game tape, and use the information they gather to make a playbook and to prepare their players for the next game. It's all about the data.

The job of the people responsible for external social business is to create the infrastructure for the business so that they can receive market and competitive information in real time and on an ongoing basis. This is critical to a sustainable, adaptable business. If you want to remain competitive, you simply must have the best information available so that you can develop a suitable strategy. As in NFL games, there are several ways to "win": you must build the infrastructure, but first you need to map it out to make sure you are able to monitor and measure everything you do. Also remember that your strategy will change and so will the map. Develop an adaptive approach to building the analytical infrastructure.

Continuing with our football analogy, the digital network represents a brand's fans, governing league, thought leaders and industry media, competitors, suppliers, and partners. In short, it's the external market and market players for which you are competing. The more you monitor and measure your organization's impact on the digital network (and it on you), the better you will be able to adapt to its changes in tastes, competitive forces, and disruptions.

The Digital Network and Your External Social Business

According to the executives we interviewed, people need to see, on average, information from six different sources before they accept it as fact. What happens, then, when over half of the world's population is producing and consuming content? Will that figure change?

Old organizational models based on the broadcast model are hitting the end of their lives. People are behaving differently because they have the tools to talk back. In response, companies behave differently because what worked in the past doesn't work now.

What is changing is that customers are setting the rules and complaining loudly when those rules are violated by business. Business used to be about command and control, where you were told as a consumer what to buy and as an employee what to do. That's still the primary operating model worldwide. But all of that is going to change—and faster than you expect. We are entering the social age of business, in which business as usual will be the leading cause of decreased sales or, worse, bankruptcy. Our focus as business leaders should be on innovation, marketing, and profits while creating an adaptive infrastructure to support those goals.

The most powerful businesses today are mastering how to build adaptive organizations with huge communities, millions of committed followers, and a feedback system that gives them real-time information about how well they are performing in the digital network. When we create an internal and external infrastructure to support such a business, we multiply our capacity to be competitive.

This is what an effective social business looks like. This is an adaptive organization that is ready to compete in the next decade.

Survey

With all strategic plans, it's important to understand where you are before you decide on where to go. Here are some survey questions that will help prepare you before you launch an external social business program:

- What social media channels are you using at your enterprise to engage with customers? Are you communicating with your customers on your own branded sites? On third-party channels? Both?
- What type of listening and monitoring of conversations are you doing? Are the conversations around your brand, your products and services, your solution, your key staff, your vendors, your competitors?
- What are the conversations currently going on around your enterprise? What is the sentiment?
- Are you responding to relevant customer questions in a timely manner via your social media channels? Do you allow them to be public, so others can share?
- Do you have a listening and communication plan?
- What are the social media channels your employees are already most active on? How much time do they spend? What is their technical skill level? How many followers do they already have? How often do they offer feedback to their community?
- Which people have strong connections both within the organization and outside the organization, so they can be in a good position to provide timely and helpful feedback on social media channels to your customers (including answers to their questions that may be outside of the organization's general knowledge)?

Your Digital Network Is Both a Map and a Garden

We were surprised by how many companies lacked a map that clearly identified key influencers, thought leaders, suppliers, partners, and customers. Without a map, how do you properly engage those that can best help you or buy your products? These companies are flying blindly, hoping to land in the right places but more often than not getting caught in numerous storms. To make matters worse, the map is constantly changing, disrupted by competitors, market forces, and unforeseen political dynamics. The rules change again and again and those organizations without the tools to properly chart a new course eventually get lost.

The digital network is also like a garden. Successful companies will plant seeds and nurture the right people while removing a few weeds. The garden is a place for the forces of curiosity, knowledge sharing, global connectedness, and commerce; those are powerful forces in the new social world. It takes time to build a strong digital network, but in doing so will keep the organization nourished for years to come.

Let's take a look at the key concepts and ideas in this chapter in the form of takeaways:

• External social business speaks to the activities your business conducts that directly affect people outside of your workforce. It is much more strategic than social media; it is about empowering the community and the consumer toward cocreating value and achieving your business goals.

• External social business is no longer an option; it is an imperative for business success.

• The enterprises that are most successful with external social business manage to implement and train people on social technologies that simplify and improve communication, collaboration, and customer care.

• Always have your mission and strategy clearly defined for task members, so they don't become distracted and overwhelmed by information overflow.

• Have a plan that clearly explains to the C-suite and other decision makers how to integrate the social technology for managing and leading customer relationships

• Before you plan to add a new platform or tool, plan for what internal resources you'll need for implantation, training, and upkeep. Also put together a listening and communication plan that will have all participants keen on what to pay attention to and how to respond.

• Include an activity calendar for your external social business programs—have a master calendar for everything, and have individual calendars based on department, media, and/or social channel.

• Use social media insights across the whole organization—Product Development, Marketing, Sales, Customer Service, PR, HR, and so on. Your social media efforts shouldn't be limited to just the Marketing Department; it requires engagement by the entire organization.

6

Introducing the New Social Business Playbook

Failing to plan is the single largest reason organizations trying to become social businesses falter in their efforts. Not having a playbook is the single largest reason existing social efforts collapse. The playbook is your organization's strategic guide to starting, launching, and executing on plays that will help make your organization more effective.

Strategy is completely useless unless it is well understood throughout the organization. And based on a recent study by Chris Zook of Bain, only 40 percent of the global workforce was informed about their corporation's goals, strategies, and tactics. Imagine if you had a football team and only four in ten players knew what the game plan was. It doesn't work for a football team, and it doesn't work in a social business either. In this chapter, we'll look at why the new playbook is superior to the old playbook (and what's in that old playbook) and details about the playbook that have worked for the companies I interviewed as well for me in my work as chief social strategist at harmon.ie.

A playbook that's constantly updated and refined based on feedback allows you to constantly ask: "What's really important here?" and "Is our current plan effective?" The number one purpose of strategy is alignment: getting everyone in the organization to understand how his job impacts the overall goal. There is no better way to align all of the employees with the company's core goals than to create an adaptive, transparent social business.

One of the primary goals of the playbook is to get everyone to make good choices and to provide feedback on the choices from a broad selection of employees, partners, suppliers, and customers. From my research, a playbook is also an effective way of gaining a competitive advantage because it allows everyone to be involved in both creating and vetting ideas. Instead of information silos and closed conversations, open discussions about how to improve predominate, and they involve all the relevant people.

Because your company and its partners are pursuing a common value proposition, every stakeholder needs to know and contribute to your strategy—it shouldn't be kept secret anymore. I know you're thinking that you don't want Joe Shmoe from the mailroom chiming in on your strategic efforts, but the team can and will filter out the bad ideas from the good ones, and you might be surprised at the varied sources of great ideas.

Between departments, a friendly rivalry will push everyone to be more thorough; but don't get dragged into mindless debates about insignificant details. Start executing, learn from your experiments, then adjust as needed. In essence, be agile.

What Do You Mean by a Social Business Playbook?

A "playbook" is a book or other document that contains a sports team's strategies and plays. The playbook that outlines your company's social strategies and plays serves as an ideal tool for social business leadership and management.

A playbook, in the traditional sense, deals with sports teams' strategies and tactics for *winning* a game. Winning people over in business, both inside and outside the company, is the goal of the plays in your social business playbook. In social business, the first play is to *win* over your staff, your management, and your decision makers and mesh them together into a team; and your next play can be to win over your partners; and *then* the plays can be about winning over your audience and key influencers. When you are working with a strong and solid team, just as in sports, you are in a much better position to win over fans and influencers.

In both sports and business, team members execute plays based on their positions, which they are assigned based on their skills and performance. (One team member might be great at video, another at Facebook, another at Twitter.) Players also cross-train and have more than one skillset so they can serve as backup or support another player when needed. (This is about encouraging employees beyond their current job responsibilities and preparing them for other roles.)

The Old Playbook: The Bankruptcy of Lehman Brothers

For a classic example of command-and-control failure in corporate culture, for a culture in which executives are removed from their knowledge workers, you don't need to look any further than Lehman Brothers and its former CEO, Richard Fuld.

Fuld would arrive at work every day in a limo, and he'd call ahead and tell the doorman to push the "32" elevator button for him. Fuld was chaperoned into the elevator and went straight to the thirty-second floor. The company programmed the elevator for express service. They spent $100,000 to program the elevator to not stop at any floor so Fuld wouldn't have to interact with employees. He went up in his ivory tower where he worked every day, and he followed the same procedure when he left.

According to insider and author Lawrence G. McDonald, in *A Colossal Failure of Common Sense*, in the twenty years that Fuld worked at Lehman Brothers, he never once set foot on the trader's floor, and he never once engaged in any kind of company meeting. Most people within Lehman had never met the executive.

Thus Lehman Brothers provides a classic example of how the old playbook for doing business no longer works. The old playbook says, "If I'm hidden, I appear more commanding, I appear more ominous, I appear to be more important." As a result, according to McDonald, Lehman

Brothers, which held over $600 billion in assets, constituted the largest bankruptcy filing in U.S. history.

If Lehman Had Been a "Social Business" Could It Have Been Saved?

What most people don't realize is that information that may have prevented Lehman's collapse existed within the firm. But that information was trapped in people's minds, hallway conversations, and a culture of secrecy. You might argue that if the information had been given to Fuld he would have ignored it. But I'd counter, if the information was available in a digital village (this assumes it had become a social business), that information would have been extremely difficult to ignore given the pressure of transparency.

In a social business, information would have surfaced a lot earlier about what was happening with mortgages and with real estate, and earlier intervention could have saved the organization.

How many other big business collapses could have been averted if they had applied social business methodologies?

Comparing the Old with the New Game Plan

There are some distinct differences in the way businesses were run in previous ages and the way businesses need to be run in the social age. It's still about shareholder value, but the game is different now and the playbooks need to reflect the change. There are new rules, new strategies, and new ways of leveraging talent.

Old Way: Corporate Politics = Climbing the Corporate Ladder
New Way: Corporate Politics = Less Trust

Now, there will still be politics; we all understand that. But there will be a much more transparent system where *people will be able to see that someone is playing politics instead of working for the betterment of the organization.* Once a person knows she's being observed her behavior changes, and that's a key thing to bring up.

Today, with an internal social network (our digital village), executives are being observed, and they're being called out for corrupt political behavior. Moreover, employees who leave their firms often write about their experience and submit their reports to influential media outlets. Remember what happened to Goldman Sachs after a disgruntled employee, Greg Smith, told the *New York Times* that executives were calling their clients "muppets" and that the culture was toxic?[1]

Today's employees need to learn that in the new playbook, trust and authenticity will get you further than playing politics.

Old Way: Public Relations Agencies = *Get the Brand's Message Out*
New Way: Thought Leaders + Influencers + Employees = Get the Brand's Message Out

While traditional public relations agencies still have a role in today's businesses, they will become less effective at delivering a brand's message over time. The social customers, the media, and your industry's thought leaders are all tuning these one-way broadcasts out. They are no longer effective in today's social age. The new playbook calls for employees, thought leaders, and an organization's social team to provide quality content that attracts the right target audience and engages them in discussion. Those interactions over time will produce new customers who are eager to work with you.

Old Way: Information = Stored in Silos
New Way: Information = Stored in a Central Repository

As we discussed in chapter 4, organizations must provide an internal social network (digital village) that includes a social software platform which allows anyone in the organization to store and retrieve relevant information that helps them complete their work.

It's no longer acceptable to hoard information in silos. That's a page from the old playbook that isn't acceptable anymore.

Old Way: Workplace = Fixed Location/Fixed Time
New Way: Workplace = Anywhere/Anytime

Until just recently, most employees (including knowledge workers) were required to be at their desk working on the highest-priority projects and tasks. The company's culture would dictate the work hours, but the hours were fixed and everyone knew them. In the new workplace, because of mobile technologies and the cloud, work is being done from home, from the road, and even from vacation. The expectations have shifted from "Don't worry, you can get me that when you return to work in the morning," to "Hey, why didn't you reply to the e-mail I sent you last night?"

Like it or not, the new playbook doesn't have a fixed schedule or location.

The New Playbook Starts with CAST

The new playbook is built around culture, analytics, social media, and technology (CAST). CAST is the foundation for the playbook. Every strategy in the playbook is built around CAST, which helps to give shape and power to each of the plays. The CAST foundation applies to both external and internal strategic plays.

Let's take at a look at each element:

Culture: Culture Is King

Where the old playbook preaches control by the commanding executive and obedience by the employee, the new playbook stresses a culture of openness and experimentation, and highlights the necessity of community. To stay relevant, organizations need to move toward a new business culture, one informed by purpose, mission, objectives, and the business environment, both economic and social. Take the survey in chapter 3, in the section "How Do I Know If My Company's Culture Is Ready?," to determine whether your organization is prepared to become a social business.

Analytics: Monitor, Measure, Adapt

The primary aim of a social business is to make customer acquisition superfluous. Its aim is to know and understand the customer so well that your content and discussions create loyalty. The same can be achieved for employees—instead of customer acquisition, you're looking for projects, people, and information that help your organization become more adaptive and agile.

Think of analytics as a constant feedback system that is taking the pulse of an organization's employees, customers, suppliers, and partners. You'll need to deploy an analytical program to monitor nearly every social interaction the company is having in order to gain a complete picture of the health of the organization. That way, you'll have a better feel for what's working and what's not, and you'll be able to make decisions based on trends, failures, and successes.

Social Media: Part of the Tactical Execution

A lot has been written about social media in books, blogs, and even in the mainstream media, and *Socialized!* is about much more than how to use it more effectively. But social media, by which I mean tactical social initiatives, is a critical piece of social business infrastructure and it's a communication vehicle that needs to be in place for your playbook to be effective. Your organization must have a good understanding of social media and how to best use it in order to become a social business.

For our purposes, social media is part of the tactical execution of an organization's strategy to become more adaptive and competitive. In other words, it's a primary actor in the playbook, but not the playbook itself.

Technology: "The Supporting Infrastucture"

In order to sustain a social business, the organization must choose an all-encompassing social platform that supports its digital village and that allows workers to connect, communicate, collaborate, and share information. You can't create a social business without the technologies to support it. Imagine trying to launch into outer space without a rocket. It's not going to happen.

After you've determined your strategic objectives, evaluated your current technologies, and determined the gap between where you want to go and where you are now, you can move to implement the right technologies to support your plan. Don't skip this step. It's critical.

Summarizing CAST

Culture and tools can each influence the success of the other, and can make or break a company's social business transformation. Without the right culture, the tools may not be used. Without widespread adoption of the right tools, the organization will not have the means to be more collaborative, open, and transparent.

Social media and analytics are tools for fostering, testing, measuring, and refining engagement with employees, customers, suppliers, and partners. Your culture needs to support an environment where failure is an option so your employees can experiment without fear of retribution (following the social media policy guidelines, of course). Analytics tell the story of social media effectiveness. They will tell you what's working and what's not so that you can adapt to the needs of your target audience.

Again, this is the foundation of an adaptive organization. This is how you become hypercompetitive and quickly take market share from competitors. Although it may sound easy, it's not. There are a lot of command-and-control thinkers in today's organization who will resist the move toward becoming a social organization because they feel threatened.

The New Social Business Playbook

I've created the strategic playbook to help you build on the foundation of CAST and to accelerate your move toward becoming an adaptive organization. It's a strategic playbook that will call into question some traditional practices, throw out others, and prepare your organization for whatever is next. Because none of us has a crystal ball, I want to help prepare you to respond to the next opportunities and challenges. Let's get started.

The Genesis of Social Business

The start of any social business begins with a set of social media guidelines. I recommend you create them collaboratively with input from every stakeholder in the organization. How? Most organizations I spoke to used a wiki or a solution like PB Works that allows simultaneous editing and commenting. According to John Rooney, who heads the technology innovation team in IBM's office of the CIO, IBM didn't just push the guidelines out: "We didn't write them in a back room, negotiate them with HR, and then tell the world, 'This is what they are.' We published them in a wiki and we promoted them on our internal social platform. We asked people if they had an opinion, to please weigh in. Once we had them drafted, we asked the individuals who were actively blogging to review them and asked if they could abide by them."

Afterward, the team reviewed IBM's completed guidelines with Legal and Human Resources and shortly thereafter they became official. "It was important for us to publish those guidelines. A lot of people will look at corporate guidelines as being a control mechanism. Perhaps that's true to an extent. But they're also a way you give permission and you create confidence in people," Rooney pointed out.

Social media guidelines are also a proven method to gain participation—not just to send out rules, but to help people learn and be better participants in social media. Think about it. When you're involved in creating something, you're more likely to support and use it, even if you don't agree with everything in the final output.

IBM has since gone through two additional iterations of their social media guidelines, and both times the guidelines have been created publicly inside IBM. Everyone was free to comment on the new guidelines and suggest additions or deletions, and that's another important point. Social media guidelines need to be reviewed often and updated frequently, because the social landscape is changing fast. You can find IBM's current version on their website.

Most leaders forget that employees become cynical over time. Policies come and go. Some die; some are ignored. Start with a social media policy that your employees comment on publicly. This gives ownership of the policy to everyone in the organization.

A no-retribution clause enforced by the executives of the organization is a must (confidential data aside). If employees follow the policy, then they cannot be punished. In fact, hold up the employees' controversial actions publicly as if to say, "See, we're serious about recognizing your rights."

Some companies, like the *New York Times*, have policies that read: "Don't be stupid." They leave it at that.

Executive Sponsorship and Support

Most of the social business professionals my team and I interviewed for this book cited executive support as key to a successful social business transformation. We couldn't agree more. Executives set the cultural tone for an organization. Through their participation, they implicitly promote the use of social technologies.

The 2012 *IBM Global CEO Study* concluded, "As CEOs ratchet up the level of openness within their organizations, they are developing collaborative environments where employees are encouraged to speak up, exercise personal initiative, connect with fellow collaborators, and innovate." If your executives are not participating, they are subtly telling the organization that they don't value the program. We cover how to get executives on board with social business in chapter 7.

Other key findings of the IBM study include:

• More than half of CEOs (53 percent) are planning to use technology to facilitate greater partnering and collaboration with outside organizations, while 52 percent are shifting their attention to promoting great internal collaboration.

• Championing collaborative innovation is not something CEOs are delegating to their HR leaders. According to the findings, business executives are interested in leading by example.

- CEOs are most focused on gaining insights into their customers. Seventy-three percent of CEOs are making significant investments in their organizations' ability to draw meaningful customer insights from available data.

The IBM study shows that CEOs and the companies they manage must constantly evolve to stay competitive. Partners, suppliers, and employees want CEOs to communicate with them on a personal level to build trust and to help align them to the organization's strategy. Customers of these businesses like to see CEOs who are open, engaging, and transparent. This makes them and their businesses more trustworthy. There is a lot at stake here. So executives can't continue to hide, shielded by some old command-and-control mentality. They must lead by example and create an atmosphere in which there's a high tolerance for failure, an atmosphere that encourages employees to rapidly learn and adapt.

Invest in Social Media Training and Certification

"We've got ten thousand people trained and certified in social media that can engage Dell customers," explains Susan Beebe, Dell's chief listener, "but that's not enough. We want to arm all of our employees with the information they need to have relevant conversations with customers."

The days of PR and Legal controlling conversations with customers are coming to an end. Social business executives recognize that in order to stay engaged and be responsive to customers, the old rules need to be thrown out. Social media policies supplemented with training and certification programs will replace today's antiquated, corporate communication rules in which PR dictates when employees can engage with people outside the organization.

In our research, we found most companies deployed a multi-tiered certification program in which curriculum was created for each tier. Some companies deployed the certification program online using a series of scenarios and tests, while others conducted in-person, day-long training courses with a quiz at the end. Each tier permitted the employee an increased flexibility to engage customers, media, and partners. Most organizations designed their programs with the blessing of their legal team.

Create a Technology Adoption Program

As Peter Drucker famously espoused, "Neither technology nor people determine the other, but each shapes the other." Technology and people have a symbiotic relationship, and when new technology is introduced, people tend to find remarkable ways to use it.

Your organization must develop a program for bringing in and testing new technology on an ongoing basis; sometimes a particular technology is not a good organizational fit, and then you must have a process for removing it from the enterprise. In most companies, employees are already sneaking in digital technologies, whether they are on the web (SaaS solutions), on mobile devices (via apps), or on their laptops (via software). The issue, of course, is that these employees are introducing security and governance concerns, as these digital technologies may put the corporate network at risk.

By developing a technology adoption program (TAP), companies can mitigate the security risk while giving employees the opportunity to explore new methods for communicating, sharing, and creating. The goal of a TAP program is to create serendipitous opportunities for employees to discover ways to do their jobs better. Then, if these employees' experiments with the new technology are successful, it can be adopted more widely by employees with similar needs.

For example, let's say an employee of a company called "Alpha" is having trouble using SharePoint (a social software platform from Microsoft). That user does a search on the web and finds a company called harmon. ie that facilitates the sharing of documents and social activity between e-mail and SharePoint. Because the solution is free for single users, the employee submits it to the TAP committee for approval to use online. The TAP committee checks out harmon.ie, finds it safe, and allows the employee to use it.

After a few weeks of using harmon.ie, the employee loves the tool and suggests the CIO adopt it organization-wide. The CIO works with the TAP committee to create a larger pilot program so that they can obtain more results. If successful, the IT team rolls it out company-wide. If not, the company phases it out or perhaps allows the employee to use it on his own.

This example illustrates a key aspect of the playbook. Building and maintaining a social business requires technologies that support it. Having one without the other is not competitively sustainable. Companies must stay on top of the latest technologies by having a process that quickly evaluates them, then either adopts or removes them.

A final word about TAP programs: the TAP committee can help the IT Department understand how these technologies overlap or function together. I've seen too many circumstances where teams of employees bring in new technologies, only to find later that there are forty different versions of it floating around the enterprise or that Team A is using an IBM solution while Team B is using a Microsoft solution. Use TAP to help coordinate the company's use of technology and eliminate those redundancies.

The Playbook Initiatives

To be sure, management, like anything else, has its own set of opportunities and challenges. But just as the coach is not expected to play on the field (although some certainly have the ability), the goal for management in a social business is to support the team and to make knowledge more productive. Social business management, in other words, is a support function. In practice, management should provide the right atmosphere, guidelines, technologies, and opportunities for employees to thrive.

Social business managers must create environments that best leverage the knowledge of their employees, customers, and partners. Our playbook initiatives are designed to take advantage of that knowledge and connect people to people and information to people, and—through the power of social networks—expand the impact of that knowledge for a particular goal.

Your playbook will be refined and added to over time. Below are some key plays to include in your social business playbook. I've separated the list into internal and external initiatives to make it easier for you to follow (although some might cross over). You'll refine and add to your playbook over time, but start with this core of time-tested best practices:

1. Connect and Empower Thought Leaders

This initiative is about extending the reach of your organization through people your customers trust. You need to identify who your industry's thought leaders are and build quality relationships with them. The public relations soapbox doesn't cut it anymore; communications are now a two-way street. I can't say enough about the importance of working with the thought leaders in your industry. Your customers don't trust your advertising as much as they do the individuals they have been following for years. Make it a priority to build a relationship with these influencers.

Once you've connected with thought leaders using my very powerful and effective methodology (I'll cover how to find and engage thought leaders in chapter 7), it's time to work with them to educate your target customer about the pain they are experiencing, pain that your product can solve.

You'll soon find that some thought leaders are more receptive to working with you than others. That's okay. It may take a while to win some of them over. The key is to show that you really are interested in helping their audience and your target customers with helpful advice. That means no selling. Yes, you heard me correctly. Don't try to get thought leaders to promote your products through product pitches. They'll feel more comfortable if you can help them promote their books, content, or some other initiative they are pushing. Then, like magic, watch how most of them will reciprocate by including your product or brand in blog posts, videos, or presentations. After all, they didn't get to be thought leaders by being moochers. Most became thought leaders because other people helped them become popular through a process of mutual reciprocation.

2. Build or Join an External Community

We are moving toward a business environment of commercialized social communities. A business organization, or any organization for that matter, is as much a social organization (consisting of internal and external collaborative communities) as it is an economic organ. Today, companies are erecting the scaffolding for employee and customer communities so that the organization can better understand and connect with them. These social support networks provide the organization with far less expensive resources (the crowd of employees, customers, and partners) to execute on the objectives of the organization.

Building an external community around your brand is one of the most powerful things you can do to positively impact sales, create goodwill, and generate ideas. It's also an effective feedback vehicle. Imagine a community of thousands of people discussing topics related (and sometime unrelated) to your products every day. Your community is answering support questions, helping other members with career aspirations, or just networking.

A good example of a robust and powerful external community is SAP's two-million-strong customer community. One of the keys to SAP's success is the thousands of subject matter experts moderating SAP customer community topics and answering developer and business-related questions. Mark Yolton, senior vice president of SAP communities and social media, sees these happy customers becoming SAP evangelists—basically unpaid advocates who are promoting SAP within their companies. This is why SAP is promoting and investing in social technologies everywhere.

If your brand or product does not yet have enough authority to build a community around it, and if there is already a robust and thriving community where your customers are hanging out, then by all means join it. If your competitor is running it, you'll need to create a community around another subject related to your product.

Matt Michelsen, CEO of Backplane, likes to say that any company can build a community around subject matter related to its brand. He often cites Exxon Mobil as an example of a company unlikely to create a community. But, as Michelsen explains, there's even a community for Exxon Mobil. "Exxon can start a car club community. By setting up a community around the love of cars, Exxon will engender a lot of good-will toward their brand."

So where do you start an online community? Most use Facebook today, but I don't recommend that strategy for the long term unless Facebook makes significant changes to its fan pages. When you use Facebook, you don't control the changes made to your community. Also, the site is updated frequently, and customizations you've made to your fan page often break during those upgrades. Finally, you don't control the advertising on the site and you lose many opportunities to monetize the community.

To build a long-term sustainable community that you control, I recommend solutions from Michelsen's company, Backplane, or from Jive Software, Microsoft's SharePoint, Lithium for support communities, ThinkPassenger for research communities, NewsGator, or Telligent.

3. Build Internal Online Communities

To support an adaptive organization, employees need to connect, share, and expand on ideas. Most, but certainly not all, of the companies I surveyed use their social technology platform or social intranet as their internal community.

The goal of the internal community is to provide a place for all employees to go in order to share information, post updates, and connect with other employees. This is a critical part of becoming a more social, adaptive organization. Your company's employees must have the ability to share insight with each other easily and visibly. Imagine a professional football team that doesn't practice or share information about the opposing team. Indeed, imagine a football team that doesn't review its game tape. How effective would they be long term?

For an example of an effective internal community I like to point out the employee portal of Booz Allen Hamilton (BAH), which is called Hello. Hello is one of the best internal SharePoint communities I've seen. In fact, it is has become a tremendous sales tool for the BAH business development team.

When I asked about the competitive advantage of Hello, BAH's Walton Smith told me, "We have 480 communities up there for everything from parenting to cybersecurity to SharePoint. And for us, the fact that we can connect the dots with people who are around the country or around the world is a huge benefit."

Why is this important to BAH? Imagine the ability to leverage your organization's collective knowledge to complete projects faster, find the right experts, and close more business because you have the right information and people at your fingertips. I'd bet you'd say Hello to that.

The companies we surveyed were primarily using solutions from IBM (Connections), Salesforce Chatter, Microsoft (SharePoint with News-Gator), Yammer (now part of Microsoft), Jive Software, ThoughtFarmer, and PBworks. But do your research to learn which community software is best for your organization. My colleagues and I cover a lot of these companies on Forbes.com, you can also find more information on Information Week, CMS Wire, and ReadWriteEnterprise.

4. Make Heroes of Your Subject Matter Experts

Every company has at least a few of them. They are the people you look at and say, "Wow, how do they do it?" Social businesses must promote their subject matter experts (SME) both internally and externally. Making SMEs into industry celebrities attracts fans (customers), which attracts revenue.

The easiest way to find SMEs is to monitor your social platform (or examine the analytical data) for clues about who is producing high-quality content that other people tend to share or comment on a lot. Often, these SMEs don't need a lot of convincing to create content for external consumption. Occasionally, more introverted experts will need help from your social team, who can interview the expert or create quality content from the material produced by the expert.

The key for this play is to heavily promote the SME internally and externally. While many executives will find excuses not to because of fear, uncertainty, and doubt, this play has several benefits for the organization. Here are just a few. First, most employees appreciate being recognized and they are more enthusiastic about the company if they feel they are valued. Second, by promoting the SME externally, you'll find potential customers, partners, and suppliers gravitating to the SMEs content. Over time, the SME will be seen as a thought leader, which helps to humanize the company she works for. Third, all of that educational content is great for SEO purposes. You'll find more and more seach traffic arriving on your website because of the amount of content your SMEs are producing. Fourth, having multidisciplinary SMEs will show potential customers the depth of your organization. Your prospects will see that your efforts are not just about marketing and PR, they're about helping your customers solve problems.

5. Recruit a Chief Social Evangelist or Strategist

In early 2011, as part of a projection for 2012, I wrote a well-received article on *Business Insider* titled: "Why Every Company Needs a Robert Scoble." Scoble personifies the type of individual every company should have on staff. His formula is simple. Produce or share quality content with your legions of followers in order to create what psychologists call the *herd effect* (the ability to excite large numbers of people and direct them to your brand).

The chief social evangelist is the quarterback of the playbook. He directs all the plays and is almost always at the center of them. Admittedly, some of the businesses we spoke to are having trouble finding the right mix of social evangelist and industry expert to serve as their chief social evangelist. Some companies are solving this problem by training current staff to take on the responsibilities of social business, while others are bringing in outside experts on social and training them on the particulars of the industry.

Interestingly, once the evangelist is on board, the company's visionaries often realize they need to strip the Public Relations Department of its censorship duties. Social evangelists can't be effective if, every time they speak into the virtual microphone, they're met with PR interference and insistence on a diluted message. "It's all about a rapid response to customers and getting content out there, and not, we got to get PR or Legal to review this and wait twenty-four hours to move forward," Dell's chief blogger, Lionel Menchaca, tells me.

Pay close attention to the legal aspects of responding quickly, but recognize that not responding is a lot worse than ignoring the customer or waiting for the PR team to deliver a meaningless boilerplate response.

Over time, your social evangelist will be far more effective than your individual marketing efforts. If you've hired the right person, your social evangelist and her team will easily push content through their networks—and their networks will do the same. This "word-of-mouth" phenomenon is far more powerful than a press release or one-way marketing message/advertisement.

The keys for this play are, first, to create compelling, quality content. The debate between quantity and quality content is over: quality rules. Why? Because people want to subscribe and follow people who create quality content. They don't want to be on the receiving end of a fire hose of substandard material. We're all too busy for that.

The second key is to nurture and engage your company's followers. Here again, it's about the quality of your followers and not the quantity. It might be nice to have a hundred thousand followers for your Twitter or Facebook or Google+ account, but if they are people who are far outside your target audience or, worse, are spammers, you'll be wasting a lot of time nurturing people who have zero impact on your brand. Instead, take the time to attract quality followers. They'll be more engaging and passionate about helping you. Third, work with marketing to create a social wrapper around every marketing initiative. For example, if you're presenting at a conference about the "Future of Work," your social strategist could set up a page on Pinterest to post pictures and create a contest for the most futuristic workplace. After people from around the world submitted their photos, the crowd could vote for the best picture and the winner would be praised on the company's blog. Furthermore, the presentation can be posted to sites like SlideShare.net for global visibility. Check out some of the presentations I did offline, but later posted online (http:www.slideshare.net/Fidelman) for even greater visibility.

6. Become Your Own Media Publisher

If the traditional marketing playbook consists of press releases and calls
to friendly journalists, the new one resembles a rich tapestry of company-
generated content designed to engage customers.

Social businesses are creating and self-publishing this tapestry of content, because it's viewed as a strategic asset. They now put as much thought
and design into their content as they do their products and services. And
visionary executives are assigning the chief social evangelist to anchor the
program, backed by a team of social reporters and a camera person.

That is why the visionaries are scaling back their traditional PR efforts
and investing in social content instead. Ostensibly, it's to save money, but
some whisper it's because they can't connect the dots to revenue like they
can with socialized content. Because social content is online and track-
able, it's much easier to trace it to revenue (we cover this more thoroughly
in chapter 8). Instead, visionaries are enlisting industry thought leaders
to tell their brand's story.

Businesses must take control of at least part of the story about their
products and brand identity. You'll never regain full control over your
brand—customers' and others' opinions have been unleashed and will
never be quieted—but you can have an impactful voice. You do that by
becoming a source for news not only about your own organization but
about the industry you work in.

There are a few things you need to do to execute on this play well.
The first key to this play is building up at least one corporate blog (some
have hundreds) that focuses on a specific theme or topic. Your social team
should be posting quality articles and content at least once a week. They
should also be responding to comments from readers. Most companies
are doing this today, but they are missing the addition of product information on their blog sidebar or header. This commercial content replaces
the banner ad that most of us are used to seeing on commercial news sites.
This commercial content is usually a video, white paper, presentation, or
web page that explains your products or services. The best companies
automatically rotate this content and A/B test the results (A = content
test #1 and B = content test #2).

For example, let's assume I want to promote my new mobile application, which tracks corporate projects and how they are progressing. A blog review about the product is not something most people want to read, but if you write a story about how people are losing track of their project updates because they are on the road most of the time, you can bet the article will be shared among those who have that problem. Of course, surrounding the article, you post further information that explains how your company solves the project tracking issue.

The second equally important key to this play is to place your best communicators in tier 1 and 2 online media sites for your industry. Do media sites like the *Wall Street Journal, Forbes,* the *Huffington Post,* and the *New York Times* allow contributing authors? As of this writing, they do. Most organizations will need to aim a little lower at first, but over time, as the reputation of the contributor grows, your experts will either be invited to write or you can request guest posts to show how marketable your content is.

Recognize that as both an employee and a contributor to a tier 1 or 2 media site, you'll rarely have the opportunity to write about your company. However, most media sites allow contributing authors to include their bio and to provide links to their social networks and corporate home page. Over time, as I have witnessed firsthand, you will become more popular and your readers will begin to research your company and its products because they like your content. There are several IBM employees who write for tier 1 and 2 publications. The advantages for IBM are several, but the ability to add their voice to the mainstream media discussion is invaluable.

The third key, which we mention in chapter 7, is to regularly engage thought leaders to help promote your content. It's getting so noisy today, with all the content being produced, that many people will never view your content unless they've seen at least seven people mention, tweet, or link to it. I've also worked with my industry's thought leaders in advance of a story to help ensure that the content rises above the noise. This works really well, but you'll need to have built up a strong reciprocal relationship with thought leaders first.

7. Replace Traditional Marketing with Content Marketing

As we well know, traditional marketing via TV, radio, and print is slowly disappearing. It's failing because consumers are tired of the one-way broadcast. Instead, people want interaction and the chance to develop a relationship with the brand. Enter content marketing. Content created on SlideShare, YouTube, Flickr, and corporate blogs is all easily shareable and interactive. Your TV is not. Online content is portable, traceable, findable, and can be more effective in the long tail of context. Print media is not. Most of the social businesses we interviewed are publishing high-value content directly to their database of customers and in turn their social networks.

The key for this play is to really understand what your target customer wants and to deliver it to them in an engaging, shareable way. Then, as always, monitor, measure, and change your content depending on the reaction you get. For example, I've created several infographics that summarize and visually present information in highly effective ways. People love simplicity, so most of my infographics are shared widely. Of course, every time the content is shared, it leaves a brand impression and about 5 percent of the time it develops into an actionable lead for our sales team. This can't be done using traditional marketing methods, and it has the advantage of being far less expensive.

8. Build Mobile Apps for Your Mobile Workforce

One thing Apple, Google, and, to some extent, Microsoft have all shown is that mobile devices are powerful consumer tools. Apps can be downloaded to do just about anything. They help organize our day, keep us connected to friends and family, and help us find new places.

To date however, little has been created for employees to stay connected to the business. Information is still locked in Enterprise Resource Planning (ERP), Customer Relationship Management (CRM), and Human Resource (HR) systems and only a few social platforms permit mobile access. Yet mobile apps for business are the future.

We know from our research that mobile apps from companies like

Yammer, harmon.ie, and Chatter (Salesforce.com tool) that connect employees to their businesses and customers increase productivity, reduce miscommunication, and increase revenue because the employee is constantly connected to the business whether at the workplace or away from it.

In order to support a mobile workforce for your business, first study the key activities of your mobile workers. What are the specific areas upon which the employee relies upon for the success of his job? Most of the activities will be on every mobile worker's list. But if there are divergences and outliers (and there should be on a question as important as this) then list and prioritize them. Every activity that is discovered should be on the list.

Then, work with your IT department or an outside development firm to develop the mobile apps you need for your business. Rather than build them from scratch, you may want to start with a templatized approach like the ones Tiggzi provides. You may also want to build on top of location-based GPS technologies like Gimbal from Qualcomm that automatically provide situational context. The key in this play is to understand your mobile worker needs, then find or develop apps that support them.

9. Leverage Employees, Suppliers, and Partners As Sources of Innovation

It is the responsibility of business to convert information into new ideas, that is, into new solutions. And it is the responsibility of executives to provide frictionless platforms that allow employees to aggregate, discuss, and then bring these ideas to market.

Excuses don't cut it anymore, as there are social technology solutions that facilitate the idea-development process. Passenger (thinkpassenger.com), Spigit, and Brightidea are just a few of the organizations that provide good idea-to-market software. The executives we talked with stressed repeatedly that the key to remaining competitive in a social business world is to nurture the innovation process, from idea generation to idea refinement and implementation.

For example, the major innovations of the last twenty years were, to a large extent, the result of converting the new social environment—the Internet—into myriad business opportunities. This resulted from a new platform that enabled the sharing of ideas (forums, blogs, wikis) and greater transparency regarding the success (or lack thereof) of these ideas (after all, most everything on the web is visible to everyone else on the web). This gave rise to even better business ideas as business leaders and entrepreneurs learned from the mistakes of the previous generation.

A similar system can be cultivated and made more efficient within a business. To do that, companies need to focus on the right formula for success: software infrastructure, idea transparency, the right incentives, and internal funding to bring ideas to market.

The key to the success of this play is to invite your partners and suppliers to a secure area of your social technology platform. This is an area that IT has roped off from the outside world but which is accessible to your key partners and suppliers, allowing them to exchange ideas, keep track of project progress, and ask questions. It's also, according to our research, a great source of micro-innovations, or minor innovations that occur along every step of a product's lifecycle. For example, one company we spoke to told us that a supplier had recently cut $0.20 from the price of every part it made for them because the supplier was able to ask the company if using a new, less expensive material would work. After a debate among the company's employees (all done on the social technology platform), the company agreed that the new material would work even better than the old. Thus, they were able to save millions of dollars from a single micro-innovation.

10. Let Customer Support Be Your Strength

An analyst friend and fellow *Forbes* writer Ray Wang is constantly criticizing the United Airlines customer support team on Twitter. He's done the research and feels United isn't living up to its promise of improved customer relations.

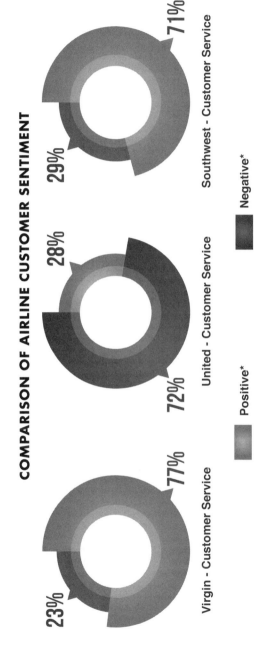

COMPARISON OF AIRLINE CUSTOMER SENTIMENT

23%   77%
Virgin - Customer Service

28%   72%
United - Customer Service

29%   71%
Southwest - Customer Service

Positive*   Negative*

Source: Ray Wang 2012 http://blog.softwareinsider.org/2012/05/18/fridays-features-using-attensity-analyze-6-0-to-compare-customer-sentiment-for-united-southwestair-virginamerica/

FIGURE 6–1

Viewing Attensity's Analyze 6.0, we can see that the sentiment analysis around the airline seems to suggest that United does a poor job of serving its customers. I believe United is making a huge mistake by not quickly addressing the issue. As Wang summarizes:

> In this shift from transactions to engagement, social business and customer experience shift the priorities of major organizations. Organizations must staff, train, and enhance the way their front office employees work with prospects and customers in multiple channels. Social media makes everything transparent and any competitor can monitor your company's social presence. Hoping that folks will ignore you if you ignore social media is a sure way to drive negative sentiment for your customer base.

Unless you're a monopoly, ignoring your customers is a model that's not sustainable. Today, your customer support is visible and in the near future your brand will be measured by what customers see (or don't see) online. There will be myriad companies that, similar to *Consumer Reports,* will measure your brand's customer support record and publish it for everyone to see. Would you be satisfied if yours looked like United's, above?

11. Listen Before You Engage

When you approach any new social situation for the first time, whether you're at a cocktail party, on a first date, or even attending a business mixer, do you just start talking or do you listen first to get the lay of the land? Hopefully, you listen first, because in this play that's what you need to do. Although this has been repeated widely, it's worth saying again: *you must understand your prospective customers, partners, and influencers before engaging in conversation with them.* Too many companies like to jump right in and engage without really understanding the language, attitude, and norms of a community. A few missteps can spell doom for your engagement efforts.

As an example, Toyota ran a campaign during the Super Bowl meant to promote and give away a free 2012 Camry. Toyota created nine new

Twitter accounts starting with @CamryEffect1 and ending with @Cam ryEffect9 to engage directly with prospective customers. But instead of creating their own hashtag, the Camry Twitter accounts started tweeting at anyone using the #Giants or #Patriots hashtags. As you may have guessed, even with a potential prize in play, not everyone cheering for a team wanted to be spammed by a Toyota Camry Twitter account. Shortly thereafter, Toyota apologized to "anyone in the Twitterverse who received an unwanted @reply over the past few days," and, in a show of adaptability, "learned from this experience and have suspended the accounts effective immediately to avoid any additional issues."

The point is, as in any social situation, you should seek to understand the community before engaging with it. So always start by listening before engaging.

12. Use Analytics to Refine Engagement Programs

Since you've set up CAST as a foundation for the playbook, you are already measuring and monitoring the success of your plays. As a reminder, all social business initiatives need to start with an analytics strategy. This critical aspect of any play involves measuring its success, so you have the information you need to determine whether you should drop the play or make it better by changing some key variables.

The following represents a summary of best practices about analytics strategy, gleaned from our extensive set of interviews with social business executives:

A. **If you can't measure it, skip it.** If there's no way to measure the impact of a campaign, social initiatives, or project, don't do it. Let's assume your organization is trying to influence a group of CIOs in San Diego, California. The team decides to create what it hopes will be a viral video targeting the trials and tribulations of an average CIO. Team members create the video using internal video experts, set up analytics on the landing page, and promote it via social channels (Twitter, LinkedIn, Google+, YouTube, Facebook, etc.). The video receives a lot of views, but the team quickly realizes that it can't parse out whether San Diego CIOs have seen it. Was the campaign successful? No one knows.

B. **Discover new sales opportunities by stalking your competitors.** You can learn a lot just by observing the interactions between your competitor and its customers. As Tristan Bishop, senior manager of digital strategy at Symantec, told me, "If someone complains about our competitors, I'm sending that right to Sales." Bishop uses analytics from Radian6 (a Salesforce.com company) to "measure share of voice within the industry for each product. We're measuring volume versus our competitors. We're measuring competitive sentiment over time. We are tracking the amount of product suggestions and we're looking at opportunities for social customer service that may help give us an advantage over our competitors."

C. **Combine analytical inputs from many sources to get the big picture.** There was a time when each department controlled its own data. Sales ran the CRM system. Marketing controlled the campaign result spreadsheets. The CFO owned the organization's financial data. This is no longer true. The information everywhere mind-set has set in for social businesses that want to use that information to be more effective. By combining analytical data across departments, organizations get a more vivid picture of their overall operational effectiveness. Patterns soon emerge that can act as early warning systems or that signal success in areas outside and inside the company. As a result, the company can more quickly prepare and respond to imminent challenges or opportunities.

D. **Once you understand the patterns, take action.** If the data indicate that a particular activity is impacting the bottom line negatively or positively, you need to have a team ready to act on it. Most organizations operate in an ad hoc fashion, assembling teams after the fact. Often, those teams are filled with employees who have more time than experience. Don't make this mistake. If the data suggest you need to take advantage of sales opportunities in Brazil, by all means take action before your competitor does.

Review, research, refine, remix, and repeat. This oft-cited phrase is a critical aspect in maintaining an effective analytics program. The top social businesses are constantly tinkering with the analytics to learn about everything from their customers to whether an employee is going to be successful. Walton Smith, principal at Booz Allen Hamilton, told me, "We're starting to see more companies leverage the cloud to do data analytics around employee success. For example, Deloitte's Australia had a 26 percent employee turnover rate but they found that for employees who made at least ten posts on Yammer (their social technology platform), the turnaround was only 3 percent. What that revealed to Deloitte is that once people feel connected to the community, they stick around. The key takeaway? Use analytics strategically (measure, monitor, adjust, and repeat)."

13. Use Selective Gamification to Drive Strategic Behaviors

According to Michael Wu, Lithium's Principal Scientist, and author of *The Science of Social,* work needs to be more like a video game. Most video games give the player enough autonomy to select her own path. From a business perspective, there's no single linear path to success, but a series of choices the employee makes to reach a goal. Sure, the goals and objectives need to be defined by the company, but a gamification approach gives people real choice and feedback along the way.

Wu expands on the importance of feedback:

> You need to show an employee's progress and give them rapid feedback. Typically this requires tracking and analytics. You need to track everything they do that's relevant to their job. For an engineering organization, you may want to track how many lines of codes they submitted, then compare it to their colleagues. You need to provide specific, rapid feedback every time they check in. There's also some long return performance metrics. Over a long period of time, a quarter or a year, you also want to be able to track their performance.

Most people like video games because they are receiving rapid feedback (usually a score) about their performance. Even better, the score increases when the player is closer to the goal, and may even decrease if she strays too far from it.

Wu emphasizes the point, "I can't imagine playing a video game and not receiving a score until the game was over. That would be kind of a weird feeling."

14. Create the Potential for Serendipitous Relationships

In 2012, Tim Clarke, a graphic designer for the Arizona-based Thunderbird School of Global Management, developed a social program called StaffUnity that randomly matches employees in different departments for small group lunch dates.

Clarke suggests that if just 10 percent of a 250-person company participates in two-person lunches for a full year, they'll make 650 new connections over that time. (Person A has lunch with person B, then B with C, then A with C...) This is a great example of using digital technologies to help foster better communication, more collaboration, and increased productivity.

Companies need to think about creating innovative ways to make these connections possible. Don't force it, just create an environment inside and outside the company to facilitate the possibility.

15. Set Up a Corporate Blogging Strategy That Works

Much has been written about starting a corporate blog. Not much has been written about how to do it effectively. We've captured the proven methods and secrets for success from the companies we interviewed. I can summarize this way: quality, rather than quantity, is far more effective at driving the right traffic. The smaller social businesses that do content well report that their blog is either their number-one or number-two customer acquisition vehicle. This finding was further underscored by a 2012 HubSpot *State of Inbound Marketing* study, in which 57 percent of the respondents reported that they have acquired a customer through

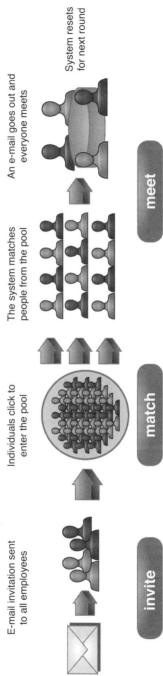

CREATIVE MEETUPS

E-mail invitation sent
to all employees

Individuals click to
enter the pool

The system matches
people from the pool

An e-mail goes out and
everyone meets

System resets
for next round

invite

match

meet

SOURCE: Tim Clarke, Thunderbird School of Global Management.

FIGURE 6–2

their company blog. Larger social enterprises find that their blogs (large companies almost always have many) are one of the best tools for keeping current customers engaged and interested in their brand. It's also one of the best methods for establishing thought leadership for your industry.

But how does a company do it better than anyone else?

• **Be creative.** Instead of a text-only blog entry, use rich infographics to further illustrate the point you are trying to make. On average, I've seen more than a 300 percent increase in traffic as a result of adding infographics to my articles and blog posts. Don't skimp on the graphics: use your best design team or hire a professional to do them.

• **Use video.** Always carry a video camera at trade shows. Why? Because you need to be interviewing people on camera to get their perspective on your industry's hot topics. People love to see themselves on camera and on your blog (especially if you're a well-known brand). Video is a fantastic tool for telling your brand's story. Keep it short, but don't skimp on the production quality.

• **Make your customers heroes.** If I haven't emphasized it enough already in this book, I'll say it again: a lot of being a smart social business is maintaining a hyperfocus on the customer. Don't just examine the customer, however; use your blog as an opportunity to make your customers heroes. Larger brands have the advantage here. Imagine if, instead of featuring art in Google Doodles, Google were to take a similar approach with their best customers. Surely anyone featured on the Google blog would be very appreciative and feel a closer kinship with the Google brand. This pays off in unexpected ways in the future, because most people feel a need to reciprocate.

• **Hire fantastic writers and a content creation team.** Would you hire a carpenter to write about the benefits of your latest microprocessing chip? Would you hire someone who can't string two sentences together to be your website copywriter? Of course not. Then why do most organizations use their least experienced employees to manage their blogs? It would be like Hollywood television studios using inexperienced writers to create scripts for today's hottest shows. It doesn't work. You need to treat your blog as if you were running an award-winning TV show. That means providing content that resonates with your targeted audience. To do that you need the highest-quality bloggers, content producers, and designers you can find. Don't skimp here. Their ability to shape the organization's story has never been greater.

• **Learn from the best.** Search out examples of fantastic blogs and see what they do right. When I'm asked which companies best represent a world-class blogging strategy, I like to cite ExactTarget, Marketo, and HubSpot for smaller companies and My Starbucks Idea, Coca-Cola Conversations, and Marriott on the Move for larger companies. Incidentally, you may want some hard return on investment facts to bolster the case for a remarkable corporate blog. Marriott Hotels reported that they make about $4 million in sales and get 12 million visitors per year from readers clicking through to book rooms. While that may not represent a lot of money in terms of the hotel's overall revenue stream, remember that Marriott gets a huge benefit by building a closer relationship with its customers. That loyalty pays off in many other ways. The point is, study and learn from the best. They'll give you some great ideas to try for your own blog.

Note: Once you've established a high-traffic blog, you'll be amazed how easy it is to use that platform to secure customer interviews, guest posts from key thought leaders, reciprocal links from other high-traffic sites, and many other hidden benefits. Having a high-traffic blog is like owning a popular news show. Everyone will want to be on it.

The Social Business Playbook at Work

A social business playbook contains the strategic initiatives that help you compete in a rapidly changing world. Every organization should create its own social business playbook to keep everyone on the same page and get all employees executing on the same plan. The playbook is your organization's guide to creating a more adaptive organization.

But you must provide the right work environment for your employees to use it. So create environments where desired behavior is supported by the infrastructure, governance, people, and initiatives.

And please don't buy into the myth of a tactical social media plan. There are far too many companies that are executing tactics without understanding how they align to the company's goals. Instead, start with the systematic framework of a playbook to create your own reality, a reality that infuses the organization with the vision, strategy, and tactics of a more collaborative, communicative, and open organization. That is, make yours a more social organization.

Here are some questions you should answer before you start putting together your social business playbook:

- Do you already have your social business team or teams in place? If not, how do you plan to scout who will make up your team?
- Can you create plays for every aspect of your social business, internally and externally?
- Who will be the key playmakers?
- Which plays will you be able to execute continuously? Which ones will you execute once a year? Which plays should closely follow others?
- How will you put together a training program for your players? Who needs all-purpose training and who needs specialty training?
- What technologies—platforms, software, and other tools—will your team need?
- How will you incorporate your "fans" into the plays?

7

The Rise of the Social Employee

He was a new man in an old enterprise. It was so easy to laugh at Edward Johnson. It was something he himself often did. But he was a recovering alcoholic that had lost his two kids, wife, and career just ten years earlier. He had suffered great hardship, but was able to heal his wounds through humor. There was astuteness in the man, and great intelligence. And he was known not to suffer fools gladly.

When I first joined the company, the CFO pulled me aside to relate an account that had occurred before Johnson became CEO:

> At the time Johnson was still attending AA classes and felt pretty lucky to have a job. So one afternoon he approached our previous CEO after a strategic planning meeting and let his guard down. "Mike, if there's anything I can do, anything the company needs, I want to offer my services to you. All you need to do is call. I'll do whatever it takes to be of assistance to you. I'm here for you."
>
> The CEO smirked and inquired, "Do you think Jeff Wagner (a business rival) is more charismatic than me?"
>
> Appalled at the self-centered response, Johnson turned away, sighed heavily, and left the building. He quit hours later. News of this interaction between the CEO and Johnson, and Johnson's subsequent resignation, reached the board. And the board, apparently

looking for a reason to fire the CEO, decided that they had had enough and fired the CEO a few weeks later. Johnson's boss at the time, an older but astute business man—in fact a product of the 1950s, called Johnson back into his office to offer him his old job back. It seems Johnson was the only person in the company that understood how the Internet was going to transform their industry, and knew what to do about it. You see, in reinventing himself, Johnson spent every waking hour learning about the Internet. He learned html, how to design user interfaces, how to create applications, how networks worked; in fact, his skills were so profound, that he was virtually unemployment-proof. Johnson, not realizing how big the Internet was to become, happily accepted his old job back and after a few years became CEO.

Johnson had an uncanny perception of the trends that were going to impact the future. Once a vendor approached the company, introduced by one of our board members, no less, with a multimillion dollar proposal to put an advanced contact and opportunity management system (an early CRM solution) on every salesperson's desktop computer. At the end of the day, each salesperson would send a file via e-mail to a systems administrator, and all of the salespeople's deals would be tracked in a central location. This situation would then provide an unprecedented executive view of all the deals in the pipeline. The board and the rest of the executives were thrilled. They'd finally have a comprehensive picture of expected revenue, which meant they would be able to plan better. But Johnson said, "We're not going to do that deal." He was firm, even though the board warned that they could fire him—they thought the CEO didn't want transparency.

But nine months later that CRM vendor went out of business. It had overinvested in an expensive technology that was about to be flattened by Internet software as a service (SaaS, then called ASPs) solution. Our company had narrowly averted an expensive disaster. "How did you know not to invest in their CRM solution?" we asked Johnson. "The Internet is the most efficient solution for connecting salespeople and management.

I'm not going to spend a few million dollars this year only to have the technology outdated next year." Johnson was right.

A few years went by and the Internet age was in full swing. I was playing around with some early social networks like Friendster, LinkedIn, and a company I was advising at the time called ZeroDegrees. Each offered a lot of promise, but none had figured out the right business model. I asked Johnson what he thought of the technologies. "It's intriguing," he said, "let's call in our sales team and ask them." "But, Mr. Johnson," I exclaimed, "you know our sales team doesn't like to share their contacts and leads and they are certainly not going to share them with the people in their network—some of whom may be competitors." "Precisely right," said Johnson, "but if they can't figure out that there's even greater benefit to networking with their potential customers, I don't want them here. Because the future belongs to those who understand how to grow and influence their own networks."

Executives Who Aren't Social Will Lose Their Jobs Within Five Years

The most troubling thing about becoming a social business today is that employees don't need executives the way they used to. In the past, executives were typically the most informed and adept at solving company issues or engaging with partners, suppliers, and customers. This worked because information was typically sourced for the executives by outside analysts or employees paid by the company to do research for them. But now, because of the ubiquity of useful information from industry thought leaders, analysts, bloggers, etc. on social networks, any employee can be as knowledgeable as the smartest executive in the company.

In fact, in our research we found that most of the executives from high-performing social organizations are learning as much or more from employees and thought leaders than they are from industry analysts and traditional sources. In this new world, the celebrated "super executive" is no longer the company's chief intelligence source. Employees, partners, and suppliers are often way ahead of them because of their extensive, real-time use of social media to gather and share intelligence. Today's executives need to realize that one of their chief concerns is making sense of all the information and working with their stakeholders to create the most effective strategy for the organization.

The other chief concern involves building a social presence both internally and externally. Let's imagine a scenario five years from now in which two company vice presidents are competing for an executive position. The first VP has years of experience but lacks any social presence either internally or externally. She was "too busy" to deal with social networking or building an internal following. The second VP, although less experienced, has taken the time to build an internal following. Whenever he communicates on the organization's internal social platform, thousands of people read and respond to his messages. Externally, he has built a huge following on Twitter and Google+. He regularly puts out content that is considered valuable to the company's customers and partners. In fact, he has attained a thought leader status in the industry. Which VP do you think the company will promote?

For me, the answer is obvious. The vice president who has taken the time to build a community around himself will be more influential and will be able to more easily accomplish his objectives both inside and outside the organization. His large networks will wield tremendous power, collective intelligence, and the ability to influence both employees and customers.

Since late 2010, executive resistance to being more social has been significantly reduced as executives start to see real results from their own efforts or from the efforts of their peers. Almost 80 percent of the executives we interviewed who had some engagement in social media told us that it added to both their own personal brand and, more importantly, to the organization's. Only 30 percent of the executives told us that they had any internal followers, citing the lack of a robust social platform as the primary reason. But more than 60 percent of them believed that participating in social networks both internally and externally would improve their effectiveness as leaders.

So as you can see, ignoring the social trend is equivalent to career suicide. I'll take it a step further and predict that executives will soon be unemployable (as executives) if they don't have a social presence. There will simply be too many other executive contenders with larger, more influential markets. Sure, there will always be exceptions; monopolies, law enforcement, and government officials may not need to become social anytime soon. But for those in positions where communication and influence are key ingredients to success, having a large network will be a significant advantage and eventually an executive requirement.

The Social Executive's Playbook

The new model for executives is one in which trust and respect are cultivated rather than one that relies on traditional authority. It's more idea driven than command driven. It's more consensus driven than rooted in ivory tower decision making. But it's still about great leadership. It's about smarter leadership that harnesses the power of networks and the wisdom of crowds.

So how do aspiring and existing executives create their own personal community? What skills must they learn? How do they convince their peers that it's an endeavor worth pursuing?

Executives like SAP's Oliver Bussmann already realize that being a social executive (or any employee, for that matter) is the best form of unemployment insurance. In fact, most of the social executives we interviewed regularly receive offers of employment, opportunities to connect with other thought leaders, paid speaking engagements, and offers to start new businesses or endeavors. They aren't as worried about finding something to do—it's finding them. Here's what every executive must do to remain relevant in the next five years.

Define Your Personal Brand

What are you most interested in? How do you want to be perceived? What's best for your long-term aspirations? What's best for your current company? I advise executives to take all of those questions into account and create a Zen diagram (a play on Venn) that passes these three tests: sustainability, legitimacy, and authority.

- **Is your brand sustainable?** Choose an area of focus that will have sustainable appeal. No short-term fads or trends.
- **Are you legitimate?** Can you communicate about your chosen area with legitimacy? Are you an expert or are you at least knowledgeable about the subject?
- **Are you an authority?** Do other people view you as an authority on the subject? Do you have the right experience or background?

EXAMPLE OF A ZEN DIAGRAM

FIGURE 7–1

If you feel comfortable that you've chosen the right area of focus for your personal brand, then proceed to the next step.

Create Your Personal Community

It's not enough, of course, to simply declare that you've decided to focus on a specific area, you need the right strategy and tools to support that mission. The right strategy and tools are dependent on your area of focus, but there are a few you should work on first.

- **Use a blog as your home base.** Use one blog as a central place to post all of your long-form (over a hundred words) content. My preference is Wordpress or Tumblr.com, which both offer easy templates and hosted options that can be set up in minutes. But as you begin to build a following, pay a skilled designer to make the blog look professional. Also, purchase a domain name (an Internet URL like www.myname.com) so that you have more flexibility when deciding where to host your blog in the future. You may decide that using your corporate blog is the best home base for you and your organization. Only you can make that call. Recognize however, that after you leave the organization, that content remains the property of the organization (unless you stipulate otherwise in your employment contracts). For a great example of an executive blog, read michaelhyatt.com.

- **Build a proactive presence on LinkedIn.** Most executives use LinkedIn as their preferred social network, but they don't use it wisely. They may connect with a few colleagues and upload their current resume, but most treat it like a static profile. That's a mistake. Use LinkedIn as a proactive tool. Use it to display your latest blog posts and presentations on Slideshare.com, status updates that show up in your peers' activity streams. But there's much more. Join or create industry groups to connect with like-minded people, answer questions on LinkedIn Q&A, and follow companies that you're interested in tracking. LinkedIn is also one of the best tools to connect with people who can help your business.

- **Master one social network.** For my area of focus, social and mobile business, Twitter provides a large community of people who are consuming and delivering relevant social and mobile content. For my interests, there's simply no better place to connect and learn from like-minded individuals. It's also one of the best places to promote content from my organization as well as my own content. For you, it may not be the best place to build a following and to connect with people in your industry. Take the time to discover whether Facebook, Google+, You-Tube, or a niche social network includes the people you want to engage with. Start with one social network, build up a following, then move to another social network if there's a good reason to do so. Remember, though, to focus your time and become well known on one network first. It's important not to be too spread out.

• **Connect with thought leaders.** One of the most powerful yet underutilized strategies for building a personal brand is to let others build it for you. Find the thought leaders, analysts, and influencers in your industry and connect with them. To them, you're a potential source of information to help them create better stories or to help make sense out of industry trends. Most will want to connect with you, so introduce yourself. Over time, as you develop mutually beneficial relationships, they will enhance your brand and may also promote your organization's products. The key here is to have a transparent and honest relationship with them; be helpful and they will in return help you. I cover in detail how to find and get the instant attention of influencers later in this chapter.

• **Participate in your industry's communities.** Find the top digital community in your industry and build an influential presence in it. If there isn't one, consider working with your organization to start one. In the community, build a friendly reputation as someone who asks intelligent questions and who provides relevant answers. Connect with community leaders and build strong connections with people—both can help you with your company and personal objectives. Imagine the power of testing and launching a product in a community where you've earned a lot of respect. You'll get honest answers and new customers.

• **Create original content.** Let's face it, most of us don't have the ability to write like Thomas Friedman. That's okay. Start by choosing a communication channel that plays to your strengths. Are you a writer?

A talker? Are you good on video? Start with one channel and start putting out content. Ask some close friends or peers for feedback and improve your communication abilities over time. This is a marathon, not a race. The key is to create content that makes people think, react, and share. Observe what the thought leaders and influencers are creating—then, do it better. Hire designers to create infographics out of data, use an editor to improve your writing, work with a video producer to create better videos. The key is, as Seth Godin says, to "be remarkable."

• **Share content and engage with people.** One of the quickest ways to establish connections is to actively engage in meaningful conversations with people. That means commenting on their blogs, asking them questions on social networks, leaving positive remarks for people who have created great content. In effect, becoming a cheerleader for the industry and for the people who are helping to shape it.

• **Monitor, listen, and respond.** Make listening a core competency. You can learn so much by just paying attention to how customers, thought leaders, and influencers are reacting to current events or long-term trends. I use Hootsuite (others use Tweetdeck), to monitor conversations on Twitter, Facebook, LinkedIn, and Google+. These social media dashboards are an inexpensive solution to manage all of your social networks in one place.

I'm often asked how much time I spend engaging on social channels, writing articles, and connecting with like-minded individuals. The answer won't satisfy you because it depends on your goals. I have replaced reading the paper and water cooler discussions with digital engagement. I use those small breaks between work to engage on social networks and I spend a few evenings a week writing articles and creating visual content (presentations, infographics, images, etc.).

I hear a lot of skepticism from executives about becoming more social. They either don't believe they have the time or they don't see the value. For them, it looks like a lot of work, and it is, but many other executives have told us that being social will make you ten times more effective as an executive in the mid- to long term.

Preparing for the New Workforce's "Digital Natives"

Years ago, when young people got out of college they often took the first job they could get. Those with options went after the big companies. "Making it" was about salary and status. For me, the chief goal was getting that first job that was going to launch my career; I didn't stop and say to myself, "What's the culture of that company like?" Your work life and your personal life were mutually exclusive, and you were expected to show up to work at a certain time and a certain place so your bosses had "proof" you were actually working.

The workforce today is not fixated on salary or logos or a fixed workplace or work–life separation. Their personal values play a much greater role in their choice of where, how, and when to work. They are driven more by a sense of purpose and fulfillment and by personal happiness and flexibility, and they demand that social media be integrated into their professional roles (and respected in their personal and private lives). They also demand opportunities to network with those outside their company and to be part of a culture that encourages communication, collaboration, sharing, openness, and transparency, no matter which rung of the corporate ladder they happen to be standing on.

But this is no disadvantage for recruiters at enterprises. Rather, it is a wonderful benefit. Technology has given us the freedom to hire based on skills, talent, and passion instead of being limited by geography. It lets us better select the top talent from a much larger pool of applicants, and allows us to see active measurements of their abilities to produce engaging content and establish strong relationships with their own social networks. There is no better time than the present for recruiters to truly assess who is right for the job, just as for applicants there is no better time to see if a company is right for *them*.

Why Recruiters Can No Longer Settle for "Business-As-Usual"

Thought leaders in the area of the new workforce include Michelle Manafy, coeditor and author of *Dancing with Digital Natives: Staying in Step with the Generation That's Transforming the Way Business Is Done*. "I berate executives that aren't starting to take their organization more to a social organization. Part of the cost is not attracting the best young talent that come in and replace individuals that are retiring," says Manafy.

The new workforce wants, even demands, to work for a social business. If you want to hire the best talent (especially the best young talent), you must demonstrate that you *are* a social business. (Or, at the very least, are willing to make the transformation to become one.)

The Rise of Social Media Has Led to an Increase in Personal Branding

"Personal branding is becoming a core part of our culture," says Dan Schawbel, a leading personal branding expert for Gen-Y. Schawbel is the bestselling author of *Me 2.0: Build a Powerful Brand to Achieve Career Success* and the publisher of both the Personal Branding Blog and *Personal Branding Magazine*. Schawbel explained in his book that we now live in a "Web 2.0 culture—which amplifies how we network, placing increased emphasis on first impressions, personal visibility, self-promotion."

According to Schawbel:

Digital natives live their lives online. The smartest of them strive to create a constructive personal brand that will help them achieve their career objectives…Understanding how digital natives create a personal brand…can also help hiring managers staff their organizations with employees who bring these skills with them and who can apply them toward the company's objectives.

Of course, most of us realize and accept that personal branding is not just for our personal lives; it now extends into our work lives, into the enterprise.

Says Schawbel:

If you work for a company, and enjoy doing so, then personal branding becomes the cornerstone for moving up the hierarchy and gaining recognition as a leader within your organization. If you are considering moving on or seeking growth opportunities elsewhere, your personal brand will likely be how other organizations discover and recruit you, or your network will be the way in which you identify the best opportunities in the marketplace.

Comparing the Traditional and the Digital Workforce

I've spent the last year traveling around the United States and Europe visiting executives from large and small organizations, and I saw a dramatic rise in the attention given to social employees in the workplace. These executives understand that social and mobile transformations are changing the game, but few know how to prepare for it properly. Here are a few of the observations and trends that I saw.

Old Way: Information Is Stuck in Silos
New Way: Information Sharing Is Pervasive

There's one big takeaway about information and the new workforce, and that is: sharing is the new currency. Those who create and share content are more likely to be seen as influencers, authority figures, and experts. People are rejecting and calling out those who hoard information in silos.

Old Way: Senior Managers Hide from Their Employees and Customers
New Way: Senior Managers Engage with Their Employees and Customers

Part of the old playbook is the idea that, "If I'm hidden, then I appear to have more gravitas, I appear more ominous, I appear more important."

Now leadership is about making yourself available, present, and accessible, and about engaging with the public and your employees. With the new workforce, trust and transparency equal respect.

Old Way: Working in Analog
New Way: Working in Digital

Why is it that we still can't capture and interact with notes produced in our physical environments? Sure we can snap a picture of a whiteboard, but the picture doesn't understand the contents of the whiteboard. That's going to change. Harald Becker, who leads business strategy for Microsoft Office Labs, showed me how mobile devices are interacting with smart boards and screens placed around a room. The technology enables bidirectional content sharing from screen to mobile devices with the press of a button. This will enable far greater collaboration and information capture for both manager and employee.

Old Way: Hierarchical Command-and-
Control Management Structure
New Way: Flatter Management Structure

The social employee wants a reporting structure that is flatter than the hierarchy-driven, command-and-control model that some executives prefer. Supervisors and executives are certainly essential to the enterprise for their ability to manage employees, especially with the new social workforce, but social employees expect to work in an environment where *everyone* gets a voice, no matter what her title or time with the company.

Old Way: Working for a Paycheck
New Way: A Sense of Purpose

"Beyond being paid fairly, people need a sense of purpose," say Amber Naslund and Jay Baer in their book *The NOW Revolution*. "Employers should focus on giving people far greater amounts of autonomy, helping them improve and make a contribution, and infuse what people do with a greater sense of purpose." I saw this sense of purpose in most of the social businesses I visited. These organizations provide clear information on their organization's mission and culture, and they outline their expectations of their workforce. These messages are also continuously reinforced in the organization's digital village.

Keeping the Workforce Engaged

Isaac Getz, who in 2012 gave an inspiring, thought-provoking TEDx talk on the new workforce, believes that today's knowledge workers must be "free and responsible to take any actions he/she decides are the best for the company." Or else, as he explains, more and more employees will become disengaged from the company and its mission. During his TEDx talk, Getz cites the research he and his team conducted over five years in which he found that only 27 percent of the workforce are actively engaged (he called these engaged workers *roosters*). A shocking 59 percent of employees are not engaged (he called them *tired dogs*). And an alarming 14 percent of employees are *actively disengaged* (these he called *foxes*). For most companies, Getz's findings are troubling. If, presumably, 100 percent of new employees are actively engaged when they arrive, what happens to them between their first day of work and now? How do we reverse the situation and convert the 73 percent of disengaged employees to engaged employees? And most importantly, how can every company avoid the phenomenon altogether?

For me, the solution involves a combination of social business principles, along with some of Getz's suggestions.

1. Intrinsic solution discovery. Companies must let employees take ownership of the problem and be responsible for sourcing the solution to the problem. Otherwise, you are creating a dependency relationship, which is demoralizing in the long term. Do teach your employees to engage their digital village and digital network for ideas and insights. Coach them toward finding answers to the solution, but don't do it for them.

2. Personal growth through digital education. Create a learning environment within the digital village, where employees are encouraged to take online classes provided by internal or external sources. Award certificates, points, or bonuses for every class the employee passes that aligns with the mission of the organization. That way, the employee is always challenged by what interests him most and views the organization as essential to his career development.

3. Self-direction equals buy-in. Is having an HR Department an acknowledgement of failure in the organization's leadership? Getz seems to think so, though I'm not sure. But having smart employees decide on the best course of action for a given circumstance is a great way to give responsibility and authority, which build employee loyalty and engagement.

Developing the Core Social Teams

In chapter 2, I outlined the seven key people needed to build the case for a social business; here I will show how to develop the core team that sustains the social business.

Building a top social team is one of the most important steps toward becoming a social business. As the organization develops and becomes more social, the importance of a social team becomes critical. If executives refuse or delay the addition of the team, they will inhibit the social business transformation and may even cause it to fail.

But what does a social media team look like? Who needs to be on board?

An Ideal Social Business Team

Let's first examine an ideal social business team for a midsize company (1,000–5,000) employees.

The size of the team should scale depending on need. The diagram that follows is only a guide that I've used when advising companies of this size.

You'll first notice that the distance between the CEO and the chief

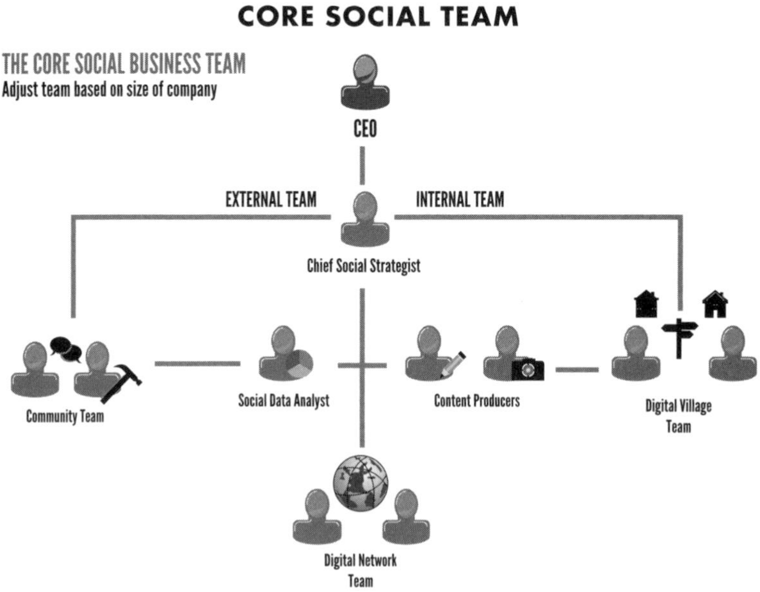

CORE SOCIAL TEAM

FIGURE 7–2

social officer is one degree. I am a big proponent of giving the chief social officer a seat at the table. And while conflict between marketing executives and social executives is sure to exist, there's greater risk in allowing the marketing executive to set the agenda. It may, however, be acceptable for the head of social to be placed directly under the most senior marketing executive (and the reverse is certainly true). But keep in mind that, over time, social principles will trump traditional marketing approaches for branding, awareness, and lead generation. It's going to happen within the next five years.

The Six Major Roles of a Social Business Team

Through our research and my own personal experience, my team and I have identified five key roles that effective social business teams must play.

1. **Chief social officer (CSO or head of social).** This person's chief concerns are to create the vision and strategy for the team while

ensuring that the proper resources are in place to execute on it. The CSO is also responsible for socializing the strategy with key executive stakeholders so that the organization is in alignment.

2. **The digital village.** These employees are responsible for building and maintaining the health of the digital village. We found some were broken into product groups or by region (for localization and language reasons). These inward business–focused team members can be found encouraging people to participate on the social platform, supporting key internal initiatives involving the digital village, or helping employees to be more effective (onboarding, adoption of platform, etc.).

3. **The digital network.** These employees are responsible for engaging customers, prospects, and partners on external social networks, blogs, and other social media. They are charged with identifying potential sales opportunities and responding to customer support issues. These people represent your brand to the world and can be considered the official voice of the company. Special care and extensive training are recommended.

4. **Community managers.** These employees are the farmers. They are responsible for nurturing and developing the digital communities organized by the brand (e.g., on Facebook, Backplane, Lithium, LinkedIn, Google+). They also support digital communities not controlled by the brand by engaging in them with helpful content and answers.

5. **Analyticals.** These data jocks are responsible for making sense of the social data created internally and externally in order to draw insights for the organization. For example, my team quickly identified some key demographics about software solution buyers on Twitter that we never had engaged before. Internally, companies like IBM identify the key influencers or experts and ensure they are made more visible for other employees to leverage. This role is critical for identifying key opportunities and challenges for the company.

6. **Content producers.** Unless everyone on the social team possesses all of the qualities of expert content designer, extraordinary writer,

and Hollywood video producer, you'll need a team to create quality content for them. Some organizations use marketing team
resources, but what we witnessed was that marketing prioritized
their projects first, then turned to social initiatives only after the
marketing projects were complete.

Social Command Centers

United Airlines is in a tough industry. Flights are canceled or delayed
due to weather, mechanical issues, unruly passengers—the list goes
on. Most of the time, these issues are outside the control of United. Yet,
according to a Crimson Hexagon study in which the company monitored
social networks, United finished last among its peers in customer sentiment about the brand, with a 78 percent dissatisfaction rate. Why was
United's customer sentiment much lower than JetBlue, which had only a
40 percent dissatisfaction rate? And how could United change the situation? (See figure 7–3.)

Let's examine a typical experience with a commercial airline. After
deciding to travel, we first look at prices on our preferred airline to our
intended destination. Then we compare those with prices from competing airlines (well, most of us do). After purchasing a ticket from United
Airlines, we wait until travel day and print out a boarding pass (or check
in via a mobile device). We then drive to the airport, park, and enter the
terminal. We stand in line to check our bags. Then we stand in another
line where we need to remove our jackets, shoes, computers, belts, and
toiletry items. By now, most of us are really annoyed at the process
and are in an agitated state.

But then it gets worse. The flight has been delayed due to weather
and we realize that we are going to miss our connection. We then stand
in line at an under-manned counter so that we can be rerouted. As a
result, we take out our frustration by tweeting: "I hate United Airlines
because they suck." The airline takes the brunt of the damage, but had
little responsibility for our circumstances. But people don't care about

JETBLUE POSITIVES VERSUS NEGATIVES

Negative Topics of Conversation

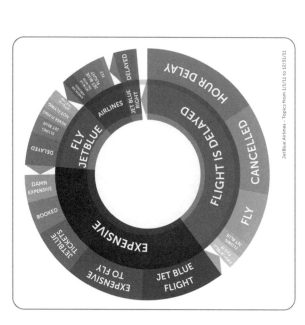

Positive Topics of Conversation

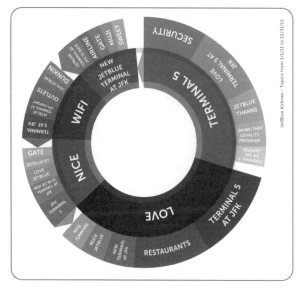

FIGURE 7–3

UNITED AIRLINES POSITIVES VERSUS NEGATIVES

Negative Topics of Conversation

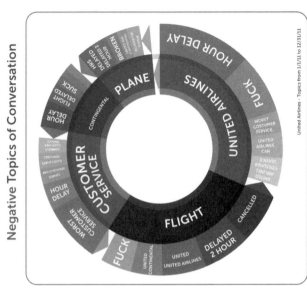

Positive Topics of Conversation

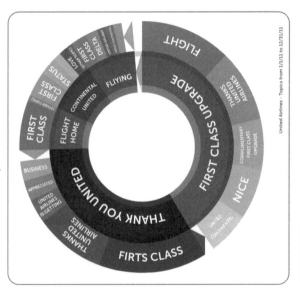

FIGURE 7–4

fault, they are upset by the entire experience. United receives the criticism because it's the most visible target.

But what if United tailored the way it engaged customers according to the information it possesses about its customers? We've not conducted serious research on United's current social media approach or infrastructure, but just from observing its customers' social behavior online, it seems to me that most of the animosity could be avoided.

Let's rewind the situation and begin again at the point where a customer decides to travel. In this case our customer is an average user of social media and updates his status on Twitter to say that he is looking to traveling from San Diego to Chicago. Seeing this, a United employee tweets back that United is offering some special prices on the routing and includes a link to the "specials" page. The customer clicks on the link and decides to purchase the flight. For the next few weeks, United reaches out to the customers using automated tweets to update the customer on special events in Chicago and savings on hotels and cars. Twenty-four hours before departure, United sends the customer an SMS text message alerting him to check in and receive a mobile boarding pass. Two hours before departure, United updates the customer on Chicago weather conditions and potential traffic delays in San Diego en route to the airport. United may also include a map showing where the plane is located so that the customer has a better understanding of any potential flight delays. The customer notices that his plane appears stuck in San Francisco due to a weather delay.

He then sends a tweet to United and a United social team member confirms that the plane is still in San Francisco and updates the customer with a new estimated departure time. Later, United sends a tweet to the customer telling him to start the drive to the airport, because traffic is building on the highway and the plane is taxiing to the runway in San Francisco.

Before the customer arrives at the airport, United automatically sends a coupon for a parking lot located just outside the airport. If the customer acts now, the parking lot owner will include a free car wash. The customer accepts. At the airport, United sends a tweet to the customer

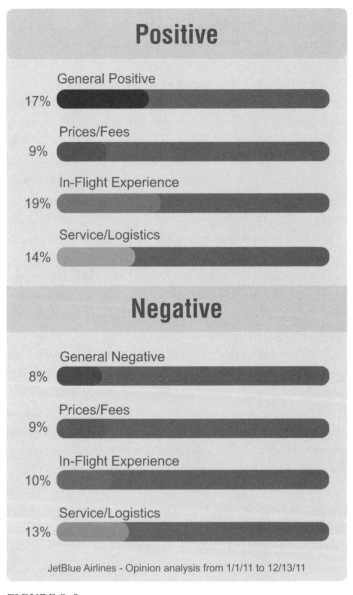

FIGURE 7–5

UNITED AIRLINES SENTIMENT ANALYSIS

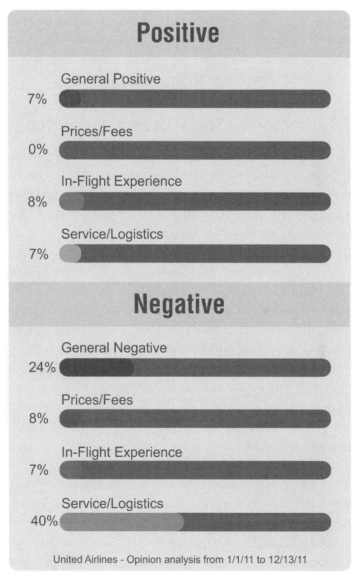

FIGURE 7–6

with new departure instructions, the movie that is playing, and the food options available on the plane.

It's hard to imagine in this hypothetical situation that any reasonable customer would take to the social airwaves to complain about United. And all of the technology in our hypothetical situation is available now and at very low price points. So why doesn't United build it? Because, they are not yet a social business.

Building the Social Command Center

Dell's been tuning in to its prospective and current customers' social media conversations about them for the past five years. Initially, the monitoring started as a small project, but Michael Dell quickly ramped up the program by asking the team, "Why aren't we monitoring everything in the realm about us?"

Today, Dell uses sentiment analysis to identify issues with its brand and products in order to *proactively* solve customer support issues. The company monitors consumer trends for potential R&D benefits. And it analyzes the industry's social stream to stay informed of competitor impact and activities, all from a highly visible social media command center located right in the middle of the customer support floor.

The results are higher "demoter to promoter" scores (basically the ratio of negative to positive advocates), increased customer loyalty, and higher first-touch resolution *rates* (did Dell solve the problem immediately). And Dell believes it's more competitive.

Technologies used: Radian6, custom Radian6 dashboards, Bazaarvoice, and Salesforce.com.

So what is a social command center (SCC)? It's a space filled with people, computers, and screens that are monitoring the social activity surrounding a business, industry, or event. It's a purpose-driven command center architected to discover, engage, and support its social objectives. But most importantly, it's a social media war room that provides real-time social media analytics to help identify and engage your target audience and to help them with solutions to their problems.

The SCC is architected for several different jobs its owners need

DELL'S SOCIAL COMMAND CENTER

FIGURE 7–7

done. This architecture facilitates the discovery of new disruptive insights while strengthening the organization's ties to thought leaders, prospects, and partners through timely engagement. The SCC is a must-have for organizations with hundreds of thousands of prospective customers or those that are in highly competitive situations, and it's critical for organizers of well-attended events like the Olympics or the Super Bowl.

Seven Steps to Creating an Effective Command Center for Your Organization

We've seen the social command center (SCC) be used for two specific reasons. The first is temporary and set up for events. For example, the SCC for the 2012 Republican National Convention held in Tampa was set up to answer questions about the convention and to help people navigate the city. The second use of an SCC is to monitor and respond to a brand's digital network in real time. These command centers are built for the long run and designed to give the brand a competitive advantage by responding to people in real time.

Increasingly, these command centers will be used for other purposes. For example, in 2016 one may find a Democrat group operating their own SCC in order to respond to Republican policies and to direct people to websites run by Democrats. In fact, there will be many such cases where SCCs will become increasingly common as engaging in social channels becomes more prevalent.

Here's how you set them up:

1. Define a purpose and target audience. It should be obvious, but it's best to reiterate that you need a business purpose before building an SCC. This purpose usually starts with identifying sales opportunities and customer support challenges, but an SCC can also be used to support innovation initiatives and to test new ideas. For Taulbee Jackson of Raidious, who ran the 2012 Super Bowl social media command center, the purpose was to ensure a safe environment and to be helpful to the fans. "They don't even need to ask; we see 'we can't find a place to park' on Twitter and our team jumps all over it to guide the spectator to the closest garage," Jackson explained.

2. *Create the SCC space.* Today, because of digital technology and social media, we can effectively build a space that monitors key trends and opportunities in real time. And because the social team is in one place, they can more effectively conduct social initiatives that further the purpose of the SCC. The SCC space should be large enough to accommodate the key people necessary to fulfill the purpose, and should be designed so that team members can collaborate effectively.

Use the right tools. What are the best tools to fulfill your SCC's purpose? That depends on many factors. Here are a few: Where does your target audience reside online? If it's on Facebook, then find a solution that effectively monitors Facebook conversations. Does your target audience use many different community sites, social networks, and forums?

Then you may need a robust customer relationship management (CRM) and marketing automation system like Salesforce.com (with Radian6) and Marketo to track and target that audience as they move from your website to your community and on to social networks.

The most effective SCCs I've seen have a few whiteboards, a large screen for "hot" opportunities, and dual small screens for team members to effectively context switch from tool to tool.

3. You'll learn a lot by listening. If properly set up, the first thing you will realize is how quickly the SCC helps define the profiles of customers most willing to buy your product. First, structure your listening by keyword, then segment and characterize the conversations by attributes (needs, pains, ideas). You'll receive clear inputs on what your prospective customers want. Most surprisingly, we also ascertained what customers wanted to get done for themselves when they bought the product. This real-time feedback provided us with the insights that traditional market research missed.

4. Engage but don't sell. Engagement is all about intelligently and opportunistically connecting people with great content. You accomplish that by listening to conversations about your industry, brand, or product, then providing messages and links to content that is seen as helpful. In your digital network, you want to be seen as a good and helpful global citizen. Some organizations are assembling virtual focus groups to explore whether their own products' faster, more feature-rich, less expensive options would better satisfy some customers. The most surprising results from this online research are how these organizations are uncovering product ideas and use cases they had never anticipated.

5. Always be measuring. Think of all the data insights and intelligence these companies are generating in their SCCs. What happens to that data beyond the tactical execution of an initiative? Most of the organizations with SCCs are using the aggregated data to determine trends and new opportunities, and to nurture key relationships with influencers. In

the future, this data will be used to deliver context-sensitive automated alerts and messages according to scenarios defined by the organization. A security and networking company called Enterasys has already done this; follow Vala Afshar, Enterasys's chief customer officer, to see how the idea develops.

6. Adapt and improve. The key to becoming a world-class social business is to learn to adapt to changes. The experimentation and resulting data will help you improve your engagement with people over time. You will also be seen as an organization that is highly responsive and thus more likely to attract customers.

The SCC Is the Intelligence Core of an Adaptive Enterprise

Before the social and digital age, and while I was working at a managerial consulting company, my company created a war room so that Unilever could monitor its supply chain. It was basically a conference room with hundreds of paper-based graphs and tables taped to the walls, which gave the team a holistic view of where the company's products were at any given point in time. It was effective because it was updated twice a day, but it lacked the real-time digital feedback that the team craved. We also could not query the data, or do much, if any, scenario planning without persuading a large group of data analysts to crunch the numbers.

I believe the SCC is the genesis of a new infrastructure designed to listen, engage, and analyze interactions between people. It's the social version of the telecommunications call center, but instead of large rooms filled with people making outbound calls, the SCC contains the analysts, the data gatherers, the content providers, the community managers—in fact, it's somewhat analogous to the advanced traffic control hubs in most major cities. Over time, SCCs will replace the traditional methods of reaching people (phone, e-mail, TV, radio, postal mail) with more modern approaches that mirror how people are communicating.

I believe that the SCC will provide a set of new lenses through which you can gain insights into the probability of success for a product or service. The SCC provides a new information architecture that will get you as close as possible to your target audience without having to observe them in person. Most advantageous, according to our research, is developing a set of hypotheses by listening carefully to what people are saying about their needs and then testing and measuring them with a variety of social initiatives. Because the SCC has been designed to monitor reactions in real time, in the places where your target audience is likely to be, you will find quick and accurate answers to your hypotheses.

Dell Computers[1] has become a master listener, attuned especially to things people are trying to get done. Dell marries the insights they gain through social listening with solutions that help prospective customers get their work done effectively. And although the company's traditional marketing research will still uncover some underserved opportunities, I maintain that that approach is weak at synthesizing these ideas in a real-world context. When matching prospects with your products, you'll find that listening and questioning customers about their needs, combined with community-sourced information, will significantly improve your products' chances for success and perhaps gain customers' and thought leaders' attention at the same time. This will vastly improve your chances for success.

Why Digital Network Influence Is So Critical

People need to communicate solutions to customers in need. The impersonal brand can't do it as effectively. People want to communicate with other people, not with logos. If employees are allowed to build relationships with customers and prospects, when a customer finds herself in a pain/need circumstance, she will instinctively think of the employee with whom she already has a relationship. Enabling and encouraging employees to be thought leaders will humanize the brand and replace the brand's logo or product as the primary focus point for customers wanting to solve that pain.

I realize this is a huge shift in thinking for most branding experts. And for some retail products, this may not seem tenable. But I like to point to fictional and real-life examples to make my point. Richard Branson, Donald Trump, Betty Crocker, the Maytag Repairman, and Mr. Whipple ("Please don't squeeze the Charmin") are all company spokespeople who, over many years, replaced the logo as the first thing people thought of when dealing with need or pain. Is it possible to do the same in a smaller way using employees? I believe the answer is a resounding yes, and our research shows that this trend is just emerging.

Some executives worry that having employees replace the company as a customer's first thought when experiencing the need/pain will lessen the brand's appeal. But they can solve this issue by always having the employee append their company name to the correspondence. For example, do you think less of the Boston Red Sox because Adrian Gonzalez is one of the primary reasons the team is attracting additional fans around the world? Of course not. In fact, Gonzalez enhances perceptions about the Red Sox just by representing the team. Even when Gonzalez retires or leaves the Red Sox, the team will find new stars (from the farm league or through trades) to replace him.

From my viewpoint, most brands are vessels into which traditional marketers try to stuff meaning. If a brand's messaging is targeted toward customer pain, it's usually perceived by the customer as biased or subjective. Conversely, if an influential human delivers the message, customers will better relate to the message and it will be viewed as more objective. So when need/pain arises in a customer's life, he will remember the human influencer and buy the product. Customers will pay significant premiums for brands that engage them through employee influencers and not through hollow marketing broadcasts.

Increasingly, brands will not have a choice whether to participate. It will soon become necessary for companies to connect influential employees with customers. As competitors begin to realize that people are discussing their pains and needs on social channels, their employees will step in to become part of the discussion. The brands that don't participate will soon find that their traditional marketing approach of "logo to customer" will lose to the "employee to customer" approach.

Most brands already have potential employee influencers (some people call them advocates) in their midst. At a South by Southwest panel discussion titled "Slaying the Four Horsemen of the Social-Media Apocalypse" in Austin, Texas, Greg Matthews, the former director of social media at Humana, a health-care company, related that out of thirty thousand Humana employees, nearly one thousand of them were bloggers. When Matthews surveyed them, he found that 10 percent blogged about health-related subjects. Each, in my view, is a potential employee brand influencer.

To relate the concept to an offline example, simply visit any Apple Store. Digital and social strategist Cheryl Burgess explains in her article "Brands Under Pressure" how Apple's Genius Bar is the ultimate in employee branding for retail. Each of Apple's retail employees is trained to provide a remarkable experience for the customer. She notes that the genius bar is "…a lynchpin of the most successful retail concepts and innovative employee brand relationships of our time. Apple simply gets it," she writes, "employee branding matters." However, for most organizations, employees as influencers (or employee advocates) are not enough. They need external influencers and evangelists to help create the halo effect that most well-established companies enjoy. The best way to do that is by creating truly remarkable products worth talking about; the next best way is to get influential people talking about your products so that more prospective customers can find them.

Great Content + Influential People + Sales Messages = Growth

In 2011, healthier chip maker Popchips and Ashton Kutcher, its official "President of Pop Culture," teamed up with Monster.com to find a "Vice President of Pop Culture"[2] for a one-year, paid position earning a $50,000 salary. All candidates had to do was submit a short application video on the Popchips Facebook page, showing their ability to creatively connect social media and pop culture.

The response was tremendous. Just months later, Popchips received 236 contest entrants, 783,803 contestant YouTube views, 1,193 new channel subscribers, and 112,708 new Facebook fans.

We recognize that not all brands can afford celebrities like Kutcher (who happens to also be a mega-influencer online), but we believe that you can replicate a similar effect by enlisting your industry's celebrities. Or, as we call them, the thought leader influencers for your industry. Let's return to Popchips for an example of its impact.

In another campaign in 2011, Popchips teamed up with Klout, a company that attempts to measure a person's influence across a variety of subjects. Klout provided Popchips with the three hundred most influential people in the healthy food category and Popchips sent each of them a free sample of Popchips in the hope that they would write, tweet, or talk about it.

Again, the response was impressive. Popchips reported that three hundred healthy food influencers generated 14,819 tweets, which produced 46.7 million product impressions.

So what's going on here? Does this really work?

Think about the dynamics of both campaigns. In the first, Popchips used Kutcher's celebrity to promote a social campaign to drive awareness and followers. For those goals, the campaign clearly worked. In the second campaign, Popchips leveraged the industry's top influencers to build relationships and to get them to help create buzz and awareness. This campaign also appears to have been effective. Importantly, though, the difference between the two is that the second campaign was far less expensive to run than the first.

I'll explain. In the first campaign, the cost of Kutcher's salary, the $50,000-a-year job, and the infrastructure and people to support the campaign had to exceed $500,000 (this is only an estimate). In the second campaign, the costs were minimal. Klout charges an estimated $5,000 to run a campaign. Then, we'll estimate that the three hundred influencers receiving free samples cost $3,000 ($10 per influencer); most of the people and infrastructure needed to run the campaign are provided by the influencer and social networks. It's clear from this comparison that, while both are effective, the second campaign is the most attainable for the majority of organizations.

That's what the following sections are about: identifying the influencers in your industry who can best help connect your company to your target customers and strategic partners. I've developed a methodology never before published that is far superior to Klout's (but which is more difficult to execute) that identifies key influencers in your industry or category. We've experienced, after executing on this methodology, a dramatic increase in brand awareness and sales. This section alone is worth ten times the price you paid for the book.

It's critical to connect with your industry's thought leaders because they are in effect shaping the discussions about your industry, customers, and at times your product. Not having a relationship with your industry's thought leaders is like flying a large plane in crowded airspace without air traffic control. You need a relationship with thought leaders to understand where and how to land your message safely. Let's look further at the importance of thought leaders.

What Do We Mean by a "Thought Leader?"

"A thought-leader is someone who is willing to step into the
spotlight and voice their points of view, innovative ideas,
and potentially controversial opinions. He drives conversation
and peppers the Internet and other outlets with his insights,
ideas, and expertise. She inspires others to follow their
dreams and teaches them to think big, solve problems,
and face their fears."
—*Marla Tabaka, Inc. Magazine*

The obvious definition of a thought leader is someone who leads others by sharing his thoughts. The earliest public record of the term *thought leader* originated in 1994 with Joel Kurtzman, then the editor-in-chief of Booz Allen Hamilton's magazine, *Strategy + Business*. "Thought leader" was the label applied to the magazine's interview subjects, people the editors selected because they had business ideas that merited attention.

Thought leaders are widely recognized for sharing insightful ideas with an audience that is significantly influenced by them. In business, thought leadership influences this audience—particularly target consumers and clients—highlighting the benefits of a new product, service, or approach. Thought leaders can also create interest and demand indirectly for something that hasn't existed before.

You can also view thought leadership as a kind of social capital earned by thought leaders from their target audiences through a combination of shared content, expertise, experience, access, trust, authenticity, consistency, conversations, and a sense of community. In the modern area of social business, while content is still king, the feeling of kinship—a personal connection—is a mighty queen.

How Thought Leadership and "Influence" Are Connected

In social business, the term thought leader is used interchangeably with *influencer.* Social business thought leader Brian Solis describes influence as "the ability to cause effect, change behavior, and drive measurable outcomes online."

- "Influence" is the effect of one person or thing on another and the ability to persuade or cause someone to take specific action.
- An "influencer" is someone who can move other people to action.
- A "center of influence" is someone who has a large community, and who serves as a hub connected to other centers of influence to which they reach out.

Haydn Shaughnessy, a fellow *Forbes* columnist on leadership, points out that thought leadership is not without tangible goals. It is "real leadership, concrete business objectives for new markets, real sales." Shaughnessy emphasizes leadership as the essential component in thought leadership; while it seems obvious, he says this point is often overlooked: "Thought leadership must contain ideas that are in some sense leading a conversation, a market segment, a professional group."

How to Connect Product to Influencers and Influencers to Customers

Social media is the most effective method for facilitating word-of-mouth recommendations. According to almost every study we've seen, about 90 percent of consumers trust a peer recommendation, compared with the 33 percent who trust traditional advertising.

So how does an organization get its prospective customers' peers to refer them more business? There are two primary methods. First, create a remarkable product that excites people, and, second, create a community of influencers, employee advocates, and customer advocates around your brand. Because the first method is outside the scope of this book, we will focus on the second.

Creating a Top Twenty-Five Influencers List

We've learned that finding, ranking, and promoting a list of the top twenty-five influencers for a given topic relevant to your organization's objectives is the most powerful method for engaging all topic influencers. While at first you may be skeptical, follow along as I outline the process and explain why this powerful social initiative will transform your industry's most influential people into brand advocates.

Step 1: Finding Industry Influencers

There are a number of different methods for finding and connecting with online influencers. As is often the case, the easiest are the least effective. Using Klout or Kred (another social profile ranking tool) can help identify influencers by topic, but I've found that these tools only capture a small subset of influencers and do little to reveal the true impact of those individuals. For example, after a comprehensive influencer search for a client of mine, we discovered nearly one thousand influencers on the subject. That same search on Klout yielded sixty-two. Moreover,

Klout only provides one score for an individual and doesn't (yet) break influence scores down by topic. Therefore, many of the high Klout score individuals were simply not that influential in my client's industry.

The best method of finding influencers for a topic, industry, or category is to use a variety of tools that gather potential influencer candidates into a funnel. Why a funnel? Because you'll be performing a variety of tests to determine whether the prospective influencers meet your specific criteria to help you with your objectives. Each of those tests will cause some of the prospective influencers to fall out, thus reducing the number of them at each stage of the funnel.

For example, if I am trying to identify influencers to help evaluate a new social software solution, I may not want software influencers, I may want *software and social* influencers. Once I apply the social and software filter to the funnel, many of the influencers will drop out.

But first we must define the topic, industry, or category where we want to engage with influencers. Let's continue with the hypothetical example of a new social software solution. This new solution helps companies build communities around their brands by providing a stunning visual interface and a mobile solution that encourages people to interact with one other in innovative ways. Now, we could focus on influencers who are influential in the B2B community space or we could focus on influencers who are influential in building mobile communities. Let's assume that for this business, building mobile communities is more important for the target audience.

Now that we have the topic selected—mobile communities—we will use a variety of tools to find influencers for this topic. Let's begin with Twitter. It's easy to find influencers on Twitter if there is a common hashtag (symbol: **#subject**) used to connect a tweet to a subject. For mobile communities, there is a ***#mobilecommunity*** hashtag but it's rarely used. Therefore, it's best to use the Twitter search tool to start collecting profiles of people who often discuss mobile communities. Start adding these people to an "influencer spreadsheet" and record their names, number of followers, and Twitter handles because you'll need these later, during the scoring step.

Then do a Google blog search for "mobile community" and record in your spreadsheet relevant blogger names for that subject, Alexa or Compete scores (these sites tell you how much traffic the blog is receiving), Twitter handles, Google+ handles, and any other social network handles that are important to your digital network. Pay special attention to people the bloggers have on their honor rolls or blogrolls (these are lists of blogs the blogger finds interesting, with links) and visit their blogs as well. You may find some additional people to include in your spreadsheet.

Next visit Klout, Kred, and PeerIndex.com and search by the topic "mobile community" as well as other search variations like "mobile marketing" and "mobile innovation," and record those names, their Klout, Kred, and PeerIndex scores, and their social network handles. Start clicking on the Twitter handles you see (user names) and look through lists to find people to investigate further. Remember, you're just trying to fill the funnel; you'll filter the list later.

Other sites that help find influencers:

- Brandinfluencers.com: Helps identify influencers who bring traffic to your website by examining Google Analytics
- Appinions: Finds influencers with opinions
- WeFollow: Provides a list of influencers by topic
- Twellow: Provides a list of Twitter users by topic, category, and subcategory
- *Listorious*: Helps you find lists of influencers broken down by hashtag or topic
- TwitterLocal, TwellowHood, Localtweeps: Find Twitter users based on geography

Step 2: Filter the List

Once you've accumulated an exhaustive list of influencers, it's time to narrow it down by applying a set of filters. If you have a long list (more than five hundred names), then I recommend skipping to the next step now, then returning to this one. You'll want to do that so you can narrow down your list by influence rank (a top one hundred) so that this step becomes easier.

Each of the filters you apply to the list must be checked by an individual to determine whether the influencer passes each of them. It's important that you take the time to understand the influencer holistically. Also, don't use subjective criterion; use objective criteria that will remain credible to anyone who views the final results.

Here are some of the filters I have used in the past.

- Does the influencer's content match your topic at least 50 percent of the time?
- Does the influencer post articles or use social networks regularly?
- Are his social network interactions relevant to your chosen topic?
- Does she describe herself as a subject matter expert on the topic?

The key in this step is to create the right profile for the ideal set of influencers you want to connect with in order to expose them to your products and brand.

Step 3: Rank the Influencers

I've had a lot of debates with some really smart people about this step. In 2010, Mark Miller, founder and editor of EndUserSharePoint.com, created a list of influential people in the SharePoint community and published it on his site. He received a lot of attention inside and outside the SharePoint community, and the list was well received. But he didn't rank the influencers, he only broke them into categories like media, technical, and bloggers.

The following year, in 2011, my team decided to conduct our own research, and we ranked the influencers based on a scoring methodology that I'll cover below. I know Mark will agree that our top twenty-five ranked list was considerably more popular due to the friendly debate that ensued over who was on the list and who wasn't—and who was at the top of the list and who was not. Traditional media and new media got into the action and republished the top twenty-five influencers list several times, generating even more awareness.

So how do you rank the influencers? The unsatisfactory answer is, it depends. It depends on several factors, but let's continue with our hypothetical mobile community example to illustrate. To provide a rank for a set of influencers, we need to devise a formula and apply it evenly across the field of influencers. Our formula consists of several metrics that are weighted and added together to create a score. That score determines the rank of the influencer.

Let's return for a moment to the spreadsheet from step 1, which we used to gather information on influencers. By now your spreadsheet has several rows of names and several columns of data points that you gathered. It should look something like this:

TABLE 7–1 INFLUENCER LIST AND DATA

	Twitter Followers	Klout Score	Kred Score	Alexa Blog Traffic Score	Facebook Subscribers + Friends	PeerIndex Score
Name #1						
Name #2						
Name #3						
Name #4						
Name #5						

Each of the columns contains a number or metric that will be used as part of the formula to arrive at an influence score. But first, we need to determine whether the current set of metrics is relevant to our topic and whether we have enough data to determine how influential the person might be.

Here are some other sites I've used to add additional metrics.

- Proskore.com: Gives a score to influencers
- Traackr: Tracks key influencers by topic
- Radian6: Sentiment analysis and much more
- Lithium Scout: Sentiment analysis
- Twitalyzer: Analytical tool for Twitter
- TwitterGrader: Measures impact on Twitter

- SocialMention: Measures mentions on social media
- Google+: Number of people who have circled the influencer
- Google Search: Number of search results about an influencer

In determining whether a metric is appropriate for your formula or not, answer the following questions:

- Is the metric important to the outcome? For example, if the topic is about Google+, then number of Twitter followers may not be an important metric.
- Is the metric a fair representation of influence for my topic? For example, if one of the influencers writes for Forbes.com, which has an Alexa score of 221 (which means it's the 221st most visited site in the world), should that influencer benefit from the work of hundreds of other writers?
- Is every influencer being scored or calculated by the metric provider? For example, although wefollow.com provides a ranking score, you need to have signed up for the service to be measured. Most likely, some of the influencers haven't signed up for the service, so it's best to leave that metric out of the formula.

The key to determining the appropriate metrics for the formula is to think of it in terms of fairness. Does the metric provide a fair representation of influence for the topic?

Once you've determined the appropriate metrics, you need to create a weighted average score for each of them. Most of the time, the metrics should be weighted according to importance of the metric for your topic. For example, in our hypothetical scenario, if most of the target audience is interested in enterprise software solutions, then they probably get most of their information from bloggers and media sources. Therefore, you may want to weight the Alexa or Compete score higher than the Klout or Kred score. The process of weighting the metrics is subjective and requires a lot of debate amongst team members before finalizing the formula.

Once the team agrees on the right metrics and the right weightings of the metrics, it's time to create the formula. Our preferred method is to do it in two steps. The first step is to rank the metrics relative to the other influencers. Allow me to illustrate with a list of five names:

TABLE 7–2

Metric	Twitter Followers	Twitter Followers Rank
Name #1	1000	4
Name #2	2000	2
Name #3	1500	3
Name #4	3000	1
Name #5	500	5

Once every influencer metric has been ranked relative to every other influencer, you multiple by the assigned weighted percentages.

TABLE 7–3

Metric	Twitter Followers	Twitter Followers Rank	Twitter Followers Weight (20 %)
Name #1	1000	4	0.8
Name #2	2000	2	0.4
Name #3	1500	3	0.6
Name #4	3000	1	0.2
Name #5	500	5	1

You do this for every metric, so that every influencer metric has a weighted average rank. Once all of the weighted metrics have been tabulated, you add them up for each influencer and rank the list according to lowest score. Following is a basic example of what it might look like.

The reason we chose this method over a straightforward weighted average formula based on raw scores was to minimize the high likelihood that some metrics will overpower the others. For example, if influencer 1 had ten thousand Twitter followers and a Klout score of thirty while influencer 2 had one thousand Twitter followers and a Klout score of eighty, the impact on a straight weighted average score would bury the significant difference in Klout score for influencer 2.

TABLE 7-4

	Twitter Follower Rank	X Weight 20%	Klout Rank	X Weight 15%	Kred Rank	X Weight 15%	Alexa Rank	X Weight 30%	Facebook Subscrib-ers +	X Weight 10%	PeerIndex Rank	X Weight 10%	Sum of weighted ranks	Weighted Rank
Name #1	4	0.8	1	0.15	5	0.75	5	1.5	2	0.2	3	0.3	3.7	4
Name #2	2	0.4	2	0.3	4	0.6	1	0.3	1	0.1	2	0.2	1.9	1
Name #3	3	0.6	3	0.45	3	0.45	3	0.9	4	0.4	1	0.1	2.9	3
Name #4	1	0.2	5	0.75	1	0.15	2	0.6	5	0.5	4	0.4	2.6	2
Name #5	5	1	4	0.6	2	0.3	4	1.2	3	0.3	5	0.5	3.9	5

This step alone is why our method for determining influence is far superior to PeerIndex, Klout, and Kred, and it's why, after numerous ranked lists, we've rarely had any complaints about the process or the resulting ranked list. When measuring influence, an individual needs to look at each individual holistically. There's no machine algorithm that has been invented yet that can do that.

Step 4: Promote the List and the Influencers

This step separates an average response to your top twenty-five influencers list from one that will cause it to be the talk of the industry. Because you'll be featuring the story on your blog, you'll welcome the increased traffic.

Once the top twenty-five list has been determined, collect photographs of all the influencers—these can always be found online by doing a quick Google image search. Then, get your content producers to produce a top twenty-five infographic. Spare no expense on the design: you want to create a design that everyone will share.[3] Also create an embeddable top twenty-five badge that influencers can embed on their blogs. Of course, the badge links back to your blog, which displays the top twenty-five influencers list.

Next, contact the top-tier media outlets for your industry. These could be *Forbes*, the *Wall Street Journal*, Mashable, the Huffington Post, *Fortune*, *INC.*, or niche publications like the *Automotive Times*. Have your public relations team call and e-mail all of them to let them know that you have a story they will want to cover. Make sure you give them an angle for the story; for our example, you might say, "We're going to recognize all of the top mobile community influencers in the industry, and there's a great story in how these communities are flourishing." You even have an infographic that you're willing to provide. Get some commitments from the media, call in some favors, make this happen.

Then, reach out to the top twenty-five influencers to notify them that they are on the list. If you have media commitments, let them know that they'll be featured in them. Ask them to promote the articles that will appear on your blog and other media sources. The reason for contacting the media and the influencers prior to the publication of the top twenty-five influencers article is to increase the probability that the article will become popular. In our experience, by doing the pre-article outreach, you'll increase viewership by 500 percent.

Now that you've reached out to the media, the influencers, and anyone else who can help promote the article, publish it on your blog. Be sure to write about some of the influencers and what makes them special. Also comment on why you created the list and why you feel it's important. Embed the infographic and badges directly into the article—make it the focal point and be sure to publish it under a creative commons license so that otheres can republish it on their own sites.

Step 5: Influencer Reciprocation

Influencers love attention, and since you've just given it to them in a big way, all but the most stubborn will reciprocate. But wait a while before asking for their help. You'll find that a few will take the initiative to comment on your influencer campaign or will take it a step further and write about your product or company. A good first step after the influencer article is to ask each person on the list to participate in a TweetJam about your chosen topic, with your organization as the moderator. That will further connect you to the influencers, as you work together to promote each other's interests.

Over time, as you're building relationships with the influencers, ask them if you can show them how your product solves an industry pain point. Get them comfortable with you and your products.

If your organization crisply defines its purpose and guides the influencers to promote your various products and the products actually fulfill their promise, everyone wins. Both brand and thought leader benefit from this relationship, thereby strengthening the overall brand appeal of each.

This is but one of the thought leader strategies that helps customers connect their need to a brand's product, which makes the brand's ability to sell those products easier. In our experience, it's one of the most effective.

It's quite stunning when you think about how much easier it is today to become an influencer and to connect with influencers in meaningful ways. These new, more effective methods will strike most executives as a dream come true. What more could they want than a situation in which customers are easily reached, formidable competitors are swept aside, and you are lifted by a group of industry influencers to new heights?

We will explore in the next chapter why this dream can end up being a nightmare instead, and we'll recommend strategies and tactics for how to prepare for it.

8

Darwin's Funnel: Measuring ROI

"In business you are responsible for some expected outcomes, as well as for determining the strategy for driving those outcomes. This is also true for social [business] initiatives."

—Natalie Petouhoff, Professor and Director of the UCLA Executive Education Program for Social Media

P.F. Chang's is an American national restaurant chain that has been using Twitter to sponsor fun, promotional parties. The restaurant found success with Twitter and has built a following of 44,500 people as of July 2012. While P.F. Chang's was satisfied with Twitter, it wasn't until the restaurant combined Twitter with a mobile advertising campaign during the lunar new year that it discovered what P.F. Chang's digital content and community manager Jason Miller called "staggering" results.

The restaurant spent $25,000 to display sponsored tweets on Twitter to people searching for terms like "Chinese New Year" on their mobile phone, tablet, or personal computer. By the fourth day of the campaign, almost one million prospective diners had clicked, shared, or engaged with the Twitter promotion. And because P.F. Chang's saw that 70 percent of those prospects were mobile device users, it quickly shifted the entire budget to target mobile users.

In April 2012, P.F. Chang's launched another mobile Twitter campaign to offer lunch promotions, but Miller told the *Wall Street Journal* that the campaign wasn't as effective because, he speculated, the Twitter ads may have been better for "time-sensitive events rather than for awareness-building efforts."

Miller's speculation may be accurate, but does the company really know which social activities are working and which are not? How do companies set up systems to measure the performance of their social activities?

Social business is still "business"—you need to measure its performance and its value to your organization. Without these measures, executives may not have the fortitude to invest further or may significantly underinvest in the transformation. I understand that a social business transformation is an investment of your company's resources—people, time, money, all of it. So you have to be prepared to show how that investment will pay off for the organization. After all, how can you articulate and justify a business case for social if you can't show or project the positive effect it will have on the bottom line, which is what management is responsible for?

Throughout this book, I have argued that creating a digital village and participating in its surrounding digital network will make your organization far more competitive and adaptive to changes that will impact it in the future. This chapter demonstrates how, when, and why to measure your social initiatives and explains how to make changes to your programs depending on the results.

Social Business Benefits: What You Measure = What You Get

A 2012 study by MIT in collaboration with Deloitte revealed that most organizations are not measuring the benefits of their social business initiatives. The survey did reveal, however, that most participants believed social software was important or somewhat important to managing customer relationships, product innovation, acquiring and retaining employees, and growing revenue, among many other benefits.

MIT AND DELOITTE STUDY

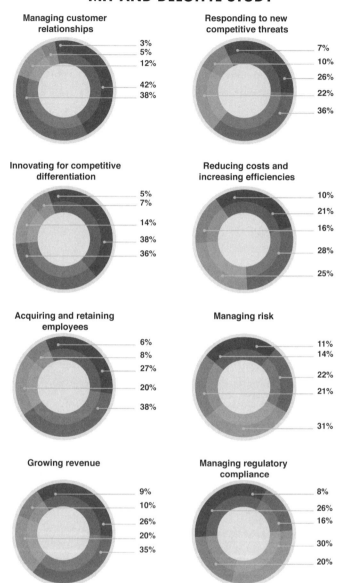

Source: 2012 study by MIT in collaboration with Deloitte

FIGURE 8–1

While perception is important, actual measurement of results is far better. But before you start any of your social initiatives, you must first identify your objectives. Following are some common company objectives our research has identified, together with a few of my own:

- Increased brand visibility
- Increased "social proof"—mentions, shares, likes, tweets and retweets, reviews, comments, etc.
- Increased product awareness
- Positive sentiment change
- Increased engagement with audiences, key individuals, and target markets
- Improved responsiveness with target audiences (consumers, customers, prospects, and influencers)
- Increased quantity and quality of contributions, collaboration, correspondence, and connections
- Increased efficiency (time savings)
- Increased productivity
- Increased quantity and quality of leads (that convert)
- Increased revenue from specific products and services
- Decreased costs from cost avoidance or cost reduction

It's important to outline your objectives because you need to clearly articulate why you're engaging with customers, suppliers, and partners in a social context. Once your objectives are clear, you can put the proper analytics in place to measure the progress toward each goal. Don't tackle an objective unless the outcome can be measured. How else will you know if you should continue to invest in it? Before you launch any social initiative—before you send one tweet or respond to a community member—have the proper analytics and measurement systems in place to be able to gauge its effectiveness.

For example, if your goal is to launch a new product using social channels like Twitter, Facebook, and Google+, you need to be able to track the path of users from first contact to actual purchase. You'll need to know what action (or inaction) the user took at each step in the process.

You'll need to know if the user shared the product information with her friends and what those friends did with the information.

The point is, you need to have listening posts in place at each step in the buying process. It's much like hiring an expert to watch a buyer receive the message, follow the buyer into the store, track her as she wanders through different departments, figure out which displays hold her attention and which do not, and chronicle what she buys.

The same model applies to B2B companies. Track which social channels are driving prospective customers to your website, follow the paths they are taking through it, determine which content they are consuming, look at the frequency of their visits over time, and assess which web pages are most likely to signal an interested buyer. From our research, we know that one of the most valuable web pages for any organization is the "how to buy now" page. Whether a prospective customer actually took the next step and bought the product or service at that time didn't matter; once a prospect hit that page, he self-identified as an interested buyer.

Note: Most organizations used Marketo, Eloqua, or HubSpot to track users online and Lithium's Scout or Radian6 to measure social impact in social channels, along with a robust CRM solution like Salesforce.com.

Bottom line: you need to observe both behavior and demographics in order to develop a profile of your ideal customer for a particular product.

Measuring ROI (Return on Investment)

"Many people mistake social media data, metrics, and key performance indicators (KPIs) for ROI," says Natalie Petouhoff, professor and director of the UCLA Executive Education Program for Social Media. Petouhoff is a former Forrester analyst and also author of the Radian6 white paper, *ROI of Social Media: Myths, Truths, and How to Measure.* But metrics and data are not the same as ROI, according to Petouhoff:

> Metrics are how you show a positive or negative change in your business. Some things go up, some things go down. Metrics are numbers that describe which business indicators go up or down.

But metrics alone won't show your company's return on its investment. To get to ROI, you have to take the metrics and turn them into business benefits.

To measure the ROI of a social initiative, you need to determine how much you are spending on *that specific initiative.* Then you must understand the KPIs that are important to the outcomes of that initiative. At that point you can determine the ratio of cost to gain for *that* initiative.

The standard ROI equation goes like this:

ROI FORMULA

$$ROI = \frac{Benefits - Costs}{Costs} \times 100 = \text{Percentage Return on the Investment}$$

FIGURE 8–2

Social business ROI calculations are similar to any other ROI calculations: they're based on numbers that have either a direct or implied *benefit* for the social business initiative minus the *costs* of the investment associated with that program. Multiply that by 100 and we have our percentage return on investment.

Once you have set up a system to measure social initiatives, you are already far ahead of most organizations. Taking the next step of calculating ROI on those initiatives moves you into an even rarer group. To scale the model and determine ROI across the entire organization's social initiatives, simply add up the value across all of the initiatives and divide by the costs. It won't be easy, and in some cases measuring social initiatives are more expensive than the benefits they bring. In my opinion, if you can't connect the dots to revenue or some other measurable objective, you should pass on the social initiative. There are too many other things you can be doing that demonstrate ROI.

I could simply end here and say it's all about measuring and determining ROI on social initiatives—but this book is for those organizations that want to be far ahead of their competitors, and I aim to please.

Darwin's Social Funnel

You've probably seen a traditional marketing or sales funnel where leads sources appear at the top of the funnel and customers are at the bottom. In between, the funnel has been segmented into linear steps, and at each stage a percentage of leads makes it through to the next stage. This process continues through each stage until a small percentage of the leads become customers

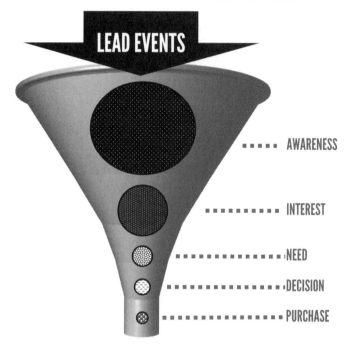

FIGURE 8–3

This traditional marketing approach presupposes a solution for customers without ever understanding their problem. As the prospective leads advance down the funnel, some mysteriously make it through while others do not. Smart companies compensate for this by A/B split testing content (testing one idea versus another) and messaging to gauge whether the content has a positive impact on moving prospects through the funnel. While this linear approach can have a measurable impact, it does not properly engage prospects and show them what the new information means for their decision-making process.

Think about purchasing a new car. Most people go through a decision-making process in which their opinions change as they learn new information. For example, let's imagine a prospective car buyer named Bill is in the market for a new electric vehicle. Bill has heard about how these cars help protect the environment and save on fuel, but he doesn't know many people who have experience with them. So he decides to ask his friends and contacts on his social networks for feedback by sending a request on Twitter and Google+.

A few people on Twitter respond and give their opinions about how great it is that Bill is going green. But one current owner of an electric car on Google+ claims that owning an electric vehicle is extremely difficult because there are too few recharging stations and recharging the vehicle at home is not practical. The owner also claims the car lacks acceleration and doesn't climb hills well.

Those possibilities obviously raise some new questions about the efficacy of electric vehicles for a potential buyer, so Bill visits the car manufacturer's website hoping for some more information. The website has some high-level content about recharging options and a six-month-old map of vehicle recharging stations, but nothing about acceleration or hill climbing. So, Bill decides to e-mail the car manufacturer to get more information. Luckily, the manufacturer responds, but gives him the phone number of a dealer located one hundred miles away. At this point Bill is ready to give up, but he decides to place the call anyway. After ten minutes on hold with the dealership, Bill is passed to a waiting salesperson. The salesperson seems knowledgeable but can't answer Bill's specific questions about fueling stations in his area or why his social network contact was having trouble accelerating and climbing hills. The salesperson asks him to drive a hundred miles to test drive the vehicle and see for himself. But Bill's had enough. He likes the idea of an all-electric car but he's already spent too much time trying to get basic information. As a result, he stops in the middle of the car manufacturer's traditional marketing funnel and doesn't become a customer.

If the electric car manufacturer's executive team learned about this experience, they'd be justifiably upset. Yet this scenario plays out every day across multiple products and services both in the B2C and B2B spaces. So what's the solution?

The traditional marketing funnel needs an upgrade to support the social era. And the approach I use is similar to the way top-ranked golfers play golf. At every hole (funnel stage) I study the landscape, choose the right club, ask for advice from the rest of the foursome, and finally swing away. Based on the results of the shot, I either continue and finish the hole (if successful) or examine what went wrong by asking the rest of the players what they saw. Viewing the segments of a traditional marketing funnel like a hole on a golf course emphasizes the importance of review and revision as conditions change, and shows the escalating benefits of many small improvements in continuous iterations. This adaptive, real-time feedback approach to the funnel is what I call Darwin's Social Funnel.

Think of Darwin's Social Funnel as a series of small improvements that make the organization more effective (a better golfer, in our analogy). Over time, the company develops a better understanding of the golf courses, the clubs needed at each hole, the people needed to make them successful, and how to handle their fans. Using this new approach, a company can be placed in any landscape anywhere in the world and can become successful faster because it has learned to be very efficient in adapting to its surroundings.

To further illustrate how this works, let's go back to the electric car example. Once Bill made his request for information about the car on Twitter and Google+, a company that is tuned in to certain keywords like "electric car" or "fuel economy" would be instantly alerted to a potential opportunity (stage 1). At this point, it may make sense for the company to test out a few short messages (using Twitter) or a lengthier response via Google+. The key is to follow and watch Bill's reaction. If he responds positively, then the company recognizes that this type of engagement was successful in moving Bill to the next stage. If he didn't respond positively, then the company can either reach out to him directly to ask him a question or try another approach. These small wins and losses become institutional knowledge and make the organization more effective over time. It also prepares the company for the next prospect who displays similar needs.

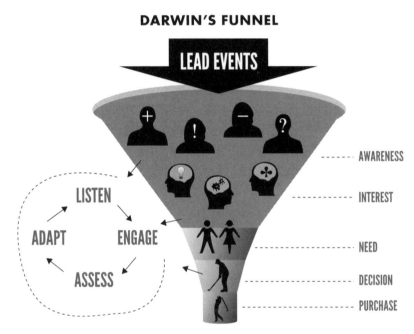

FIGURE 8–4

When Bill receives the bad news from one of his contacts on Google+, the company can decide if it makes sense to jump in and respond to the objection. Perhaps Bill's contact lives in a city that doesn't have a lot of recharging stations and has found owning a car in that city impractical. Furthermore, Bill's source may have bought a model that was underpowered for his needs and should have bought a more powerful electric car. The point is that the company is ready to respond to objections or engage in context with a personal message for the prospect. This creates trust and desirability.

Because the company is now engaging prospects through social channels and content, it can better affect potential customers' actions. I call this the "social impact effect." The benefit of this phenomenon is that you can learn right away how different methods of engagement affect your prospects. As a result, you acquire five benefits: First, you gain deeper insight into whether the prospect intends to buy your product. Second, by having short conversations with prospects on social networks, you will gain valuable knowledge that can help you modify your product messaging. Third, just engaging a prospect via social channels may be the deciding factor in whether or not he buys from you. Fourth, if the prospect is charmed by your organization, he most likely will refer you to a few of his friends or relatives, thus adding prequalified prospects to the funnel without the company spending large sums of money to do so. Fifth, because the most popular social networks (especially Twitter) are open, new potential prospects may begin to inquire about your products and services because they admire how you handle existing prospects.

Here's another example of how to use Darwin's Funnel. A few years ago I was having an issue in our B2B sales cycle because prospects for a particular product were entering our funnel and suddenly dropping off at stage three (our demonstration stage). Our conversion rate shrunk compared with our other products' performance at the same stage. We knew it could have been the product, but we suspected it was something else. Instead of simply throwing out more content after the demonstration to see what would move the prospect to the next stage, we decided to take a more immediate, strategic approach in an effort to understand the low conversion rates. We invited the next twenty-five stage-three prospects and five industry thought leaders to a tweet jam (a live, open conversation on Twitter) during our web demo. Imagine twenty-five targeted prospects all tweeting to one another, to us, and to the world about their experience with our web demo.

In a virtual room of twenty-five, people are not afraid to speak their minds. We soon learned from our stage-three prospects that our demo was too technical and product focused, and we learned from our thought leaders that the few benefits we did mention weren't resonating with the audience. Both sources gave us the immediate information we needed to modify our demo, product messaging, and content to improve the conversion rate. (One of the funniest tweets during the tweet jam: "Is it okay if I smoke in here?")

Let's look again at our example of P.F. Chang's mobile Twitter campaign, which we talked about at the beginning of this chapter. Let's say that instead of running the first promotion right before Chinese New Year, the restaurant ran it in April. If you remember, P.F. Chang's Digital Content and Community Manager Jason Miller told the *New York Times* that the April promotion wasn't as effective. In our hypothetical example, Miller has no knowledge of the Chinese New Year's promotion (which was extremely successful) and, based on experience with the April campaign, P.F. Chang's may have canceled its mobile Twitter program right then and there.

I'd argue that a functioning Darwin's Funnel would have significantly improved P.F. Chang's chances of discovering that a Chinese New Year promotion would work, because it would have drawn out small successes over time. To illustrate, in the less successful April campaign Miller would have learned that mobile users do respond to Twitter promotions. By listening and engaging with the respondents who clicked on the promotion, he'd learn that mobile users are more likely than Internet users to share these promotions with their friends. He'd also learn that some of these people share promotions with their friends so that they can meet as a group to celebrate birthdays, retirements, and, yes, even holidays. With all this information in hand, Miller would have the evidence he needed to see that a Chinese New Year mobile Twitter promotion would likely be successful.

Darwin's Funnel Automated and Machine Driven

Darwin's Funnel is an evolving, predictive model of your business. It can be used to better adapt your customers, partners, and suppliers to your vision of the future. It's a symbiotic relationship in which the parties change and impact each other over time.

To be most effective, however, your digital village and digital network must be ready to test concepts and content through social engagement, to learn from the results, and to adapt to the new reality. In essence, your organization must design its business to function at the highest possible level for a specific period of time until a new reality sets in. It must also design itself to be adaptive to changes in its digital network so that it can take advantage of new opportunities and better mitigate foreseen and unforeseen risks. Your organization must design itself to be innovative in order to create new opportunities based on its own understanding of its digital network.

But what if you could also automate parts of the funnel with machines and artificial intelligence? What if machines automatically participated in social network discussions based on a set of parameters outlined by the social media team? Better yet, what if the software analyzed the responses to determine the best response to an issue over time?

Think this is science fiction? It's being done today.

Darwin's Funnel: A Case Study

Enterasys Networks is an organization with twelve hundred employees and a small but growing 1 percent market share for its security and network management software solutions. The company has developed a highly automated and intelligent solution that's using social networking to communicate internally with employees and externally with prospective customers.

Using Salesforce.com, Radian6, and Chatter as its social software platform, Enterasys uses a set of complex filters and algorithms to automate social activity. Internally, the platform notifies key people about changes that impact their business. Externally, the platform is looking for leads on social networks that match an Enterasys solution. And it's all automated.

Internally, when one of the deals in the funnel changes status, people who are "subscribed" to that opportunity are notified. When a sales forecast trends downward or when there are ten days left at the end of a quarter and a forecasted opportunity hasn't closed, Enterasys executives are informed so that they can help close the deal. When an opportunity reaches a commit stage (95 percent probability of closing), an e-mail or chat (in Chatter) is automatically generated and sent to the customer, essentially saying: "(Name), we appreciate the fact that we are getting closer to earning your trust in our business. Here's my e-mail address if you have any questions."

Externally, the platform looks on social networks for phrases like, "I'm not happy with my wireless network" or "I'm not happy with my switching density" or "I'm not happy with port speed." They use the funnel in reverse to find all the discussions related to their business and then intelligently filter it by sentiment so that the sales team receives super-qualified leads. Over time, they fine-tune (or adapt) the search for these phrases to better understand the probabilities that certain key phrases will become deals. But they take it a step further. Not only do they search for key phrases, *they automatically respond to them.* Of course, the responses are measured and tracked and they too are fine-tuned over time to maximize effectiveness.

Vala Afshar, Enterasys's chief customer officer, explained the benefits to me:

Look, the 99 percent of the networks that are not Enterasys are communicating on social networks. We believe most of the larger organizations in our industry are not social, and don't necessarily care about their customers' success. We see that as an opportunity to earn new business. Because in every competitive opportunity, communicating on social media makes us look more human and approachable than our competitors.

Once you're a customer, Enterasys continues its remarkable use of automated, adaptive social media by enabling its machines to participate in social networks. I'm not kidding. Here's why and how they did it: The Universidad Complutense de Madrid, which has 110,000 undergrads and 20,000 graduate students, used to call Enterasys about wireless network problems occurring when students simply walked from the library to the dorm. "How does one begin to solve that issue? Is it the access point, the switch, the router, the applications running the network? They're all solution-oriented, very complex problems which one agent is expected to solve without much support from the hardware," Afshar told me while explaining why they developed the solution. Back then, the machines weren't talking.

But today, when Enterasys proactively detects that a user has sustained low signal strength for a period of time, it issues a command using Salesforce.com's Chatter to find out who the user is, what happened to the service, and where the user is and has been up to that point. It then takes that digital forensic information into Salesforce.com, parses it, and creates a case in their Services Cloud solution. "Our service cases have built-in automated workflow and notification services. Once a case is created, it then chats back to the user who's experiencing poor wireless connectivity letting them know that we know you have poor connectivity. We also issue a help desk ticket and we'll notify them once the situation is resolved," Afshar explained.

But here's the kicker: the entire lifecycle is machine to machine. There are no humans involved.

Not only does Enterasys give its customers and employees the ability to "friend" machines to get alerts and updates, Enterasys software can also send simple secured human language commands to machines via social networks to tell the machines to undertake an action. But Afshar has taken it many steps further. Within Salesforce.com, Enterasys has created private *machine* social networks where machines are collaborating with other machines. Humans are only there to observe and receive updates.

Even better, the Salesforce.com solution allows Afshar the ability to securely extend a connected yet private cloud to customers. Once connected, Enterasys can monitor the health of its network while Salesforce.com proactively alerts the customer to any issues on her social network of choice. Since it's a shared workspace, machines and humans work together to keep the network healthy.

Adaptive Modeling and the Social Vacuum

The adaptive methodology I recommend for each stage of the Darwin Funnel can also be applied to demographic and behavioral models so that, like Enterasys, you can turn the funnel into a vacuum of sorts. Once you've created models that identify where your prospective customers consume information—such as communities, social networks, blogs, etc.—and what messaging, content, and engagement works with them, you can optimize specific social programs for customer acquisition, up-sell, cross-sell, or some other objective through better targeting.

While most companies are still executing siloed social campaigns (if they're doing social campaigns at all), the most competitive organizations are creating an optimization journey. Using data-driven insights gleaned from Darwin's Funnel, these companies can easily identify their best prospective customers and those customers' social channel preferences; using that information, the companies can design a unified and multilayered social strategy while measuring interactions and optimizing campaigns based on real-time feedback. If you implement this methodology in your own organization, this optimization journey will, over time, make you an expert on converting your prospective customers to buyers effectively and efficiently.

Any learning journey of course requires some method of capturing its lessons. I've found that the best way to properly understand prospective customers and their movement through Darwin's Funnel is through a robust CRM platform that supports sales, social, marketing, and data analysis applications; these tools properly measure every digital interaction with a prospect, whether it's on your website, via e-mail, in community forums, or on social networks. This platform is a must-have in order to support Darwin's Funnel and to properly determine ROI.

How Does Darwin's Funnel Improve ROI?

Using Darwin's Funnel in combination with social campaigns will improve your ROI dramatically. Why? Because every message, every piece of content, and every action can be factored into the ROI calculation to determine a distinct efficacy-to-cost ratio over time. Want to know whether that white paper impacted a sale? Because you've set up the proper analytical systems for Darwin's Funnel, you can quickly determine the number of times the white paper impacted the sale. Because the nature of Darwin's Funnel is evolutionary, through a series of feedback loops, you can gain additional insight from white paper readers, and that information can help improve the white paper, potentially increasing ROI. Then, by factoring in the cost of the white paper, you can quickly derive a distinct ROI, which will guide you in future decisions about whether to create white papers (is the juice worth the squeeze?).

This may sound daunting to many organizations. Not surprisingly, a system that measures every social interaction and engages with every person as he flows through the funnel will cause some companies to pause. Perhaps they have a popular product that generates a lot of prospects (and tire kickers) or maybe they don't have a system in place to properly measure interactions. I like to challenge those companies to compare the cost of creating a Darwin's Funnel System with their current marketing expenses. Once they realize that they are potentially throwing away millions of dollars in unmeasured and unengaged marketing activities, they see that the benefits of this system far outweigh the costs.

Today, engaging prospects on Twitter, Google+, Facebook, YouTube, and other social media is one of the most effective and least expensive methods to push people through your funnel. Large companies like IBM, Dell, eBay, SAP, and Google, as well as thousands of small and medium-sized businesses, regularly engage people on social networks and report significant benefits. Social engagement adds the element of social listening, which allows these tweaks to the funnel to be faster and more fluid.

In terms of the costs for setting up a Darwin's Funnel System, let's look at typical setup for a large, medium-sized, and small business.

TABLE 8–1

Large organization: > 1,000 employees
• Prerequisites: A functioning digital village and digital network
• Tools: A robust CRM platform that supports sales, social, marketing, and data analysis applications; for example, Salesforce.com with Radian6, Marketo, and a social engagement application
• Technology investment: $100,000 to $300,000
• Team size: 10 to 20 people

Medium-sized organization: < 1,000 employees

- Prerequisites: a functioning digital village and digital network
- Tools: a robust CRM solution platform like Salesforce.com, Microsoft Dynamics, or SAP CRM, along with social listening and engagement tools
- Technology investment: $50,000 to $100,000
- Team size: 5 to 10 people

Small organization: < than 50 employees

- Prerequisites: a functioning digital village and digital network
- Tools: A CRM solution for smaller companies, like Nimble.com, along with Hubspot and Hootsuite
- Technology investment: $100 to $500 a month
- Team size: 1 or 2 people

Let's assume your large company wants to build a Darwin's Funnel. You'll need to hire the right team, ensure that the existing CRM solution will support engagement and measurement, and train the team on how the system works. If you're not ready to jump in full time, you can start with a smaller team that is engaging and recording successes manually. After a few weeks, tally the results and present them to your management team. I would bet that, if you've followed the advice in this book, you'll find ample ammunition to make your case.

The Economic Value of a Social Business

According to the PulsePoint Group study we discussed in the introduction, companies that fully support social engagement are experiencing four times the business impact that less engaged companies are. They understand how to properly use negative and positive sentiment about their brands to make changes and are more adaptable to the shifting tastes of their customers.

According to PulsePoint, these social enterprises also realized the following benefits:

- A 3 to 5 percent return: the average return on social engagement was calculated to be between 3 and 5 percent. The most engaged businesses are reporting a calculated 7.7 percent business impact. The lowest performers achieved a 1.9 percent estimated return.
- Improved marketing and sales effectiveness: the top two areas where executives thought social engagement had real value were improved marketing and sales effectiveness (84 percent) and increased sales and market share (81 percent).
- New ideas for products: big-return companies crowdsource new products (57 percent) or let customers know new products will be derived from social engagement insights in the future.

In addition, PulsePoint found that successful companies do the following to get beter engagement:

- Active executives: two-thirds of the organizations achieving the highest returns reported that their C-suites are active advocates of social engagement.
- Wide reach: the most successful companies extend social engagement beyond marketing and communications to sales, product development, and other functional areas to generate greater business impact.
- Top metrics: The research indicates that benchmarks (33 percent) and key performance indicators (30 percent) will be the top approaches for measuring social engagement in the next two years.

The Funnel Is the Business

As I've shown, measuring ROI is an important aspect (perhaps the most important) in the success of your social business. Realizing positive ROI is the outcome. Adding Darwin's Funnel allows an organization to measure micro-ROI (or how every move affects the bottom line) and make real-time adjustments based on real-time feedback. No longer do organizations need to wait months for the results to trickle in, they can take a proactive, social approach that enables them to fine-tune the funnel so that it is faster and more fluid.

Remember, social business is still business, so you need to measure its performance and its value to your organization. You need to prove the value of any initiative, especially an enterprise-wide transformation. Few executives will make such a move on faith.

9

Learning from Mistakes

Every time I hear about an organization that is oblivious to its poor customer service and employee morale, I'm reminded of a memorable *20/20* episode titled "A Life Without Pain." The episode is about a girl named Gabby who doesn't experience pain. She has a condition called congenital insensitivity to pain (CIPA), which allows her to feel touch, but prevents her brain from receiving signals that she's experiencing pain.

When Gabby was a toddler, she accidentally scraped her cornea and was given an eye gel by a doctor who prescribed the standard treatment for such cases. No one thought to ask other experts who were knowledgeable about Gabby's condition, and so no one was prepared for what happened next.

"The thick gel had a reflex reaction to rub your eye," Gabby's father, Steve Gingras, said. "When you don't feel pain, you don't know how hard you're rubbing, and pretty soon she had damaged both eyes."

Unfortunately, after a short struggle, she lost vision completely in one eye. "No parent should ever have to watch their child suffer through something like this," Gabby's mother said to *20/20*.

Most scientists believe that humans' sense of pain is an evolutionary necessity that helps them avoid injury and death, it's a protective feedback loop in which the brain learns to avoid things that hurt the body. Not having that protective feedback loop means that people who suffer from CIPA continue to hurt themselves.

In a lot of respects, many corporations have a form of CIPA, and untold damage is occurring inside and outside the organizations but the executives don't seem to feel it. They are not receiving the painful signals and thus they carry on as if nothing has happened. These companies don't have the ability to feel pain and certainly don't know how to respond to it. I hope by now (after reading the previous chapters) you've learned how to create protective feedback loops in your digital village and digital network, and your culture is such that it's acceptable to report them; but in case you're not yet convinced, I will cover in this chapter some of the hazards of not being a social business.

We'll begin with one long and two short case studies of companies that were negatively impacted by social media and then we'll synthesize a set of strategies that you can follow to avoid these organizations' mistakes, missteps, and malfeasance. Then, we'll close by suggesting takeaways for what to do about it.

First we begin with a case study that examines a social business lesson learned.

The Motorola Saga: How an Innovative Social Culture Became Toxic

Motorola Inc. is an American multinational telecommunications company based in Schaumburg, Illinois. It had been revered not only for its decades of growth, but for its happy employee culture. But after suffering record multibillion-dollar losses between 2007 and 2009, the company spun off into two independent public companies, killing off a major branch that supported most of its innovation and killing off its social culture as well.

"Jennifer" (not her real name) was a product manager for Motorola, and she worked for the company from 1996 to 2011; she saw the company at its height and during its collapse. She explained to me how Motorola had been a more social culture in earlier years, and speculated on what led to its downfall as an anti-social enterprise: "We used to go and have parties; we used to have volleyball, softball. Everyone got together from all the different locations and departments. If you worked at night or you worked weekends, it was okay because you were working with the people that you hung out with. It was great. That was the place you wanted to go. You invited your friends. Your friends came and joined. It was awesome."

According to Jennifer, because the company was family owned and run by CEO Chris Galvin, the culture in the beginning was much different from the way it would later evolve. The Galvins wanted to make money but they wanted to make money by treating people with respect. "They made a place where their family wanted to work, their employees wanted to work, and their friends wanted to work," Jennifer explained, "so we became fully invested in the company and therefore we did more for the company."

The Galvins were known for their mistakes, especially the project that nearly killed the company, a failed satellite phone venture called Iridium that cost the company a reported $7 billion dollars. But, according to Jennifer, the company learned from its mistakes and continued to be an innovator. "Even if some things felt like they were pie-in-the-sky, you always had people who wanted to work on new projects. It was cool. We were developing things that were going to be totally revolutionary."

Jennifer pointed to the poor market research and the lack of listening to dissenting employees on the Iridium program as the beginning of Motorola's downfall. By 2000, the company had sold off the Iridium technology for $35 million dollars, a huge loss.

A few years later, in January 2001, Chris Galvin was let go as CEO by Motorola's board of directors. According to Jennifer, that was the beginning of the end. The company quickly went from feeling like a family-run company to a corporate-run company. "You could almost feel the culture change. The whole ethos suddenly changed from 'take care of our customers and employees and the money will follow' to a fixation on the bottom line," Jennifer said.

Then, the trickle of layoffs due to Iridium became a torrent. "We were like, 'Okay, whatever. You have to make cuts. That's okay.' But the layoffs weren't short term. Over eight years the company just started shrinking, and shrinking, and shrinking, selling off businesses and assets and the company became really unstable."

For Jennifer, the layoffs were especially detrimental to corporate culture because management never communicated when they were supposed to stop. Her friends and coworkers stopped communicating with each other during work hours for fear that they'd be a part of the next round of layoffs, which never seemed to stop. For her and her coworkers, it became a kind of huge downward cultural death spiral.

Jennifer described it to me this way: "No one wanted to laugh at work, no one wanted to act like they're having fun at work because you might be the person that the big boss walks by and he doesn't know you and he says, 'Oh, that guy; I see him goofing off,' and then you're the next one tagged for a layoff."

Then the company stopped promoting people in a transparent way. "They'd promote some people, but in secret because they didn't want anyone to be mad," Jennifer said. Worse, they began to selectively pick winners and losers. "If you happened to be on a strategic project they would still have a party or something special for that group. But if you weren't on one, you got nothing."

They also stopped the incentive programs that employees felt were unique and special about Motorola. According to Jennifer, the executives defended their actions by reminding employees that they were still getting bonuses at the end of the year. But according to Jennifer the employees reacted negatively and management never got word. "Instead of giving everyone a $10,000 bonus at the end of the year you could have taken $1,000 and spread it out across—had little parties, had little pick-me-ups and it would have gone a lot farther—even a pizza party on Friday or something. In the engineering community those types of things go a long way."

Most demoralizing, the company would conduct surveys without any clear plan to learn from them. "They would just do nonstop surveys that clearly told them that everyone's unhappy, everyone's upset," Jennifer said. "And they didn't understand the results or were unwilling to take any productive action to correct them."

A natural response to any toxic culture, especially one without transparency and executive communication, is that employees start to hoard information. Jennifer explained that as they got farther and farther down the layoff list, people stopped putting all their stuff on the shared file system, wiki, and informational directory, "because information hoarding became a way of keeping your job. As long as no one could do your job then they had to keep you."

Internally, the company's employees stopped blogging and the only people Jennifer knew who continued to blog were a few corporate VPs. While employees still commented on blog posts, they'd do so anonymously. "I stopped reading them because all I saw were negative remarks. Even as they tried to turn the company around our employees were so pessimistic that they stopped caring," Jennifer told me.

After a while, the company's employees went into lockdown mode. Whereas employees in the earlier culture had felt rewarded for initiative and team building, employees in this new culture no longer wanted to get involved. Whereas employees had once shared their ideas with their coworkers and management, employees in this new culture became apathetic. Whereas employees had found it easy to locate experts on a particular topic, strangely, management in this new culture had removed the means for finding experts and projects.

By 2010, Motorola was still in a cycle of downsizing, and that year decided to break into two independent companies called Motorola Mobility and Motorola Solutions. In 2011, it sold a large part of Motorola Solutions to Nokia Siemens, which did another seventeen thousand layoffs. What's left of Motorola today is Motorola Solutions, a company geared primarily for public safety, and not given to a lot of innovation.

Motorola Lessons Learned

Motorola's ultimate demise occurred for two reasons. First, because of a poor decision to bet the company on a $7 billion-dollar project to put satellites in space so that customers could talk anywhere in the world (but only outdoors!), the company was forced into a defensive cost-reduction and containment program. According to Jennifer, the company's executives were warned by employees that the solution wasn't viable, but the CEO charged ahead anyway. Had the employees and partners been able to examine the strategy of a $7 billion investment (the technology wasn't available then), perhaps enough voices would have convinced the CEO to change course.

Second, because of the massive loss in the Iridium project, the board ultimately fired the "family run" CEO and brought in a new team to cut costs through multiple rounds of layoffs, benefits reductions, and hiring freezes. As a result, the employees became frustrated, then apathetic, and finally succumbed to Isaac Getz's "actively disengaged" stage (the foxes). This situation created a toxic environment where innovation and employee engagement (Getz's roosters) were suffocated. The mistake Motorola made when it understandably began to cut costs, was that it failed to properly create a new vision for the company and to engage its employees to rally around the cause and help with ideas. Put another way, it ignored the very same employees who had made the organization successful in the past and alienated them through a series of poorly formed policies.

Popchips: The Accidentally Racist Ad

So far, I've held Popchips up as a shining example of how to properly execute an influencer campaign. But one of its social media campaigns was a disaster.

In April 2012, Popchips released a video of Ashton Kutcher performing a variety of bachelor roles in a parody dating service commercial. In the commercial, one of the characters Kutcher played was an Indian guy named Raj, and Kutcher donned brownface as part of the act. The campaign had an estimated budget of $1.5 million, and included video, outdoor ads, and placement on social media sites like Facebook and YouTube.

Within hours Kutcher's portrayal of Raj set off a firestorm of protest, including charges of racism. Anil Dash, a popular tech influencer, called the video, "a hackneyed, unfunny advertisement featuring Kutcher in brownface talking about his romantic options, with the entire punchline being that he's doing it in a fake-Indian outfit and voice."

Now, no one (including Dash) really believes that Popchips would commit brand suicide by purposely creating a racist ad to sell healthy potato chips. But when people of Indian descent started to complain on Twitter and other social networks, the company didn't react right away. It continued to promote the ad.

Dash pressed on and took to Twitter with a series of critical tweets; here's one that was retweeted 113 times, "Hey, startups that are helping @aplusk (Ashton Kutcher Twitter handle) get richer, can you tell him that racist brownface ads aren't cool? Thanks!"

Finally, Popchips founder Keith Belling reached out to Dash to apologize and told him that the company was going to pull the campaign. Later, Belling took to social media himself to officially apologize on behalf of the company. "We received a lot feedback about the dating campaign parody we launched today and appreciate everyone who took the time to share their point of view," Belling wrote in the company's blog. "Our team worked hard to create a lighthearted parody featuring a variety of characters that was meant to provide a few laughs. We did not intend to offend anyone. I take full responsibility and apologize to anyone we offended."

But was that enough?

Popchips Lessons Learned

Whether or not you thought Dash and others were too sensitive about the portrayal of Raj in the dating video, it was clear that Popchips and Kutcher misunderstood that their core customers are health conscious, urban, and upper middle class, and are likely to be sensitive about racism. As the numbers of negative responses to the ad began to mount, Popchips was a little slow to react because they didn't believe the video was racist and they hoped the controversy would blow over. And it may have, had one influential blogger not taken to social media. You see, this is a case of an influencer having the power to damage your brand. Take note.

Credit, however, must be given to Belling for calling Dash to apologize and then issuing a formal apology on the Popchips blog with comments enabled. This showed that the brand was capable of apologizing for its unintended mistake; by allowing negative comments, Belling demonstrated that Popchips embraces transparency. Both of these actions engender trust and are signs of a company that understands how to be a social business.

Strangely, Kutcher never publicly tried to defend the ad or apologize for portraying Raj. That's a mistake. Although he probably had little to do creatively with developing the campaign, his reputation took a hit.

Shell Oil Is Drilled Online

In June 2012, a Shell Oil Company site called Arctic Ready was calling on people to create ads for the company and share them with their friends. Shell provided images of polar bears, whales, birds, and oil rigs, and visitors to the website were asked to create custom captions for each of the images. There was also a game for kids called "Angry Bergs," in which players were given points to keep the icebergs away from the oil rigs for fear they'd damage them. The site was an immediate hit, registering more than two million views in less than a week, but it wasn't a hit for Shell. The ads that visitors created were extremely embarrassing; for example, one ad read, "Turn the power on, it's time to melt some ice," and in another, "Birds are like sponges for oil."

Shell's social response team on Twitter @ShellIsPrepared made matters worse by tweeting, "Our team is working overtime to remove inappropriate ads. Please stop sharing them," and "PLEASE DO NOT RETWEET ANY OF OUR TWEETS. They are intended for our @ recipients only!" This only made more people want to explore the ads and retweet the content. That led influential journalist Marc Ambinder from *The Atlantic* to tweet, "Ain't the way it works guys." Meaning, this isn't how you stop a social media campaign that's spiraled out of control.

All told, ten thousand ads were generated (the majority of them negative), there were several hundred thousand social shares on Twitter, Facebook, and Google+, the Twitter hashtag #shellfail was trending, and the site received millions of page views. The social campaign was a complete disaster, leaving many to ask, "What was Shell Oil thinking?"

As disastrous as the campaign was, you can't blame Shell for it. For it was not led by them, it was created by Greenpeace and The Yes Lab.

Everything, from the site to the @ShellIsPrepared Twitter account, was fake; it was an elaborate ruse played on one of the most well-known brands in the world. Remember the days when Greenpeace activists used to smash into large ships or chain themselves to drilling equipment? The task was extremely dangerous and expensive. Nowadays, Greenpeace is using the power of social media to combat its foes, and it's working to devastating effect. The media, influencers, and several thousand people were duped by the campaign.

Which is odd, because a few weeks earlier an Arctic Party Fail video appeared on YouTube, purported to be shot by a visitor to a Shell Oil meeting held on top of Seattle's Space Needle. In the video, a drinking fountain shaped like an oil rig malfunctions and starts spraying the room uncontrollably, to the shock of many spectators. That, too, was believed to be real because of widespread media reports from Gizmodo, Boing-Boing, TreeHugger, the *Seattle Post Intelligencer*, and others who over-whelmingly believed the video to be authentic. But of course it wasn't. More than eight hundred thousand people watched the video on You-Tube, and several thousand more on media sites, blogs, and social media.

Despite the fact that the Arctic Party Fail video had repeatedly been reported as fake, as was its successor fake ad generator, visitors to the sites continue to be duped by them. This can't be good for Shell.

So why didn't Shell Oil respond with a lawsuit or on social media? Fearing even greater attention to the fake campaigns, the company apparently decided to take a pass on it, choosing to issue the following statement: "The advertising contest is not associated with Shell, and nei-ther is the site it's on. And Shell did not file legal action in this matter. Our focus is on safely executing our operations."

When asked about the fake campaigns, Greenpeace was brutally hon-est and claimed the moral high ground. It also boasted to Salon.com that the stunt only cost them "tens of thousands of dollars," and Greenpeace sees more uses for this kind of tactic. "It's fun rather than preachy," said James Turner, a media officer for Greenpeace, "We're mastering corpo-rate tools and using them effectively against corporate villains. It's quite new, it's fun to do, and it's very effective."

Shell Oil and Greenpeace Lessons Learned

Clearly, Greenpeace got the better of Shell, embarrassing the company and diminishing its brand. And with Shell choosing not to engage in the fight, Greenpeace will continue to hammer at the company and others as a way to influence public opinion. Make no mistake, this could happen to you. While it most likely won't be Greenpeace, it may be another activist group, a disgruntled customer, a competitor, or a super PAC (I'm teasing, but you get the point). The costs of doing these types of pranks online are minimal and they're available to most Internet users. Therefore, brands must be prepared for the inevitable attack, especially if they are involved in controversial business practices.

Brands can't rely on the media (which, as we've shown, is easily fooled) for protection; they must build a strong community around their brand that includes influencers and brand advocates. That way, when the brand is assailed there are legions of people who will step in to set the record straight. How does a company like Shell create an engaged community around its brand? Simply: because their product is oil, which many of us use but are not too excited about, the company needs to find a social cause that people can rally behind and support. One obvious type of community Shell could help sponsor or run is online car club communities.

How Do You Protect Your Organization? A Strategic Synthesis

We extract from these case studies five strategies managers can use to protect their companies from potential embarrassment, financial ruin, or cultural decay. They can use these strategies to build a powerful network that will help them mitigate potential disasters.

1. Companies must create a well-connected digital village and digital network to avoid the corporate equivalent of CIPA. When pain signals can easily reach people within the organization who can

act on them, that organization will be better able to adapt and avoid misfortune.

2. An organization's employees, customers, partners, and influencers must be trained in crisis management to mitigate any potential public relations threats to the company. Create Crisis Communication and Customer Support workflows so that when a crisis is identified, each of the stakeholders understands how to act. They must be equipped with tools that allow them to address the various situations they encounter.

3. As anticorporate and antigovernment activists become more knowledgeable about how to create the social media judo effect, using a brand's own reputation and a gullible media's desire for a controversial story against that brand, organizations must develop proactive, external communities to help counter such attacks.

4. The company must learn to proactively circulate gray area social media campaigns to its stakeholders to flush out any potential embarrassing messages. With a functioning digital village and digital network, this strategy becomes much easier.

5. Human Resources (HR) should be both the stewards and watchmen of the corporate culture. When a change in leadership occurs, HR should work with the new team to remind the new management of the parts of the culture that worked well for the organization, as well as the parts that didn't. A company that moves away from either innovative culture or community culture is especially at risk for internal strife and failure.

The external challenges of participating in social conversations with customers are only going to get more complicated. As new, sophisticated customers, activists, and competitors understand their ability to be disruptive to your company, your organization will become more vulnerable to its mistakes, apathetic snubs, and poor customer support. Many companies and personalities, from United to Qantas Airlines, from Kenneth Cole to Anthony Wiener, from Aflac to Lowe's, and from Toyota to Chrysler, are learning the hard way that poor behavior may have consequences. In the past, these organizations used agencies and other third parties to carefully vet each campaign and each communication. Today that's not practical.

More troubling, as more and more people become comfortable with social networks they will expect brands to communicate with them in minutes, not days. The organizations that are ill-prepared to deal with this new reality will be penalized by some and punished severely by others, for a well-connected influencer who is motivated by a cause can inflict significant damage to your brand.

Most organizations today believe that having a presence on social media channels like Facebook, Twitter, LinkedIn, and Google+ is all they need to mitigate potential public relations and customer support issues. But that is the wrong strategy. They must invest in building communities that include employees, partners, and customers to help support and motivate the rest of the community. In so doing, they create a shared sense of purpose that perpetuates and sustains itself even when challenged by unforeseen events.

It's quite extraordinary when you think about it. Building and supporting both internal and external communities where customers, partners, and employees are all working toward the same goals would strike most executives as business fiction. But as this book has shown, the technologies and communication channels now exist so that every company can develop and benefit from them effectively and inexpensively.

10

The Future: Why No Company Is Invincible Anymore

I have long admired Jim Collins and his book *Good to Great*. I once saw him speak about his "great" companies at a conference and was stunned by how he pulled everyone (including me) in the room into his gravitational force. Not many people can match Collins' charisma and ability to captivate a room, but his faith in the seven characteristics of companies that went "from good to great" were incomplete. His book's conclusion about what it takes for organizations to be "great," by today's standards, only takes you so far.

The world is much flatter now, so much faster, so much more connected. Perhaps that is why three of Collins' "great" companies have gotten into significant trouble since his book was published. Circuit City filed for bankruptcy in 2009, Wells Fargo received $25 billion in bailout funds from TARP, and Fannie Mae was involved in a colossal home mortgage scandal. According to *Freakonomics* coauthor Steven D. Levitt, only Nucor has dramatically outperformed the market, and he noted that books like *Good to Great* are mostly "backward-looking" and shouldn't be used as guides for the future. Levitt seems to suggest that Collins and his team were suffering from a form of cognitive bias, in which the past success of these "great" companies contaminated their judgment, and the correlations in the readily available data did not in fact indicate causation. I hope you've learned by now that we are not trying, as Collins did, to provide a strategic guide that offers the holy grail of "greatness." What we have done is offer a guide to make your business more adaptable and thus more competitive to the market forces and competitors that are working against it. Our goal is to increase your odds of being great, not to guarantee it. We've detailed how to navigate and succeed at making the case for a social business and how to build one. And because some executives have survived by maintaining shrouds of byzantine bureaucracy and tortuous policies impervious to even the most energetic employee, we've even suggested that the journey to become a social business may be an impossible one in certain companies; if that's truly the case, we've suggested you find a more forward-thinking company to work for.

What I do want to offer you in this conclusion is a perspective on what I can see today that may impact you tomorrow. I am not making predictions as much as connecting the dots on some key trends. But I do (cough, cough) reserve the right to update my thoughts on these insights on my *Forbes* column or on my personal website. So with that disclaimer, let's get started.

The Future of Business: Six Key Trends

1. **Successful businesses will operate more on principles of *Moneyball* (gaining a competitive edge by using analytics and evidence) and less by trial and error.** The adaptive business is, of course, one that hypothesizes outcomes then learns from the result. The most successful businesses will use new tools to make sense out of the vast reams of social data to make their hypotheses better, and thus find undervalued opportunities quickly. These organizations will stay ahead of the curve as other companies become social businesses, thus diminishing any competitive advantages, and they will become ruthlessly effective at outwitting challengers.

2. **Crowdsourcing strategies with close partners and allies will become essential.** Several studies have shown how the wisdom of crowds can be used to successfully evaluate certain business challenges and opportunities and to help uncover new business opportunities. The primary benefits of this are threefold. First, as

companies receive diverse and unforeseen perspectives from their closest and most knowledgeable business partners, executives who own the strategy can make the final plan better and less risky. Second, when strategic partners are engaged in suggesting new ideas for products and services, because of their unique perspective they may uncover new business opportunities that the company's employees could not possibly see. Third, as more stakeholders are involved in shaping the organization's strategy, those stakeholders become more engaged in executing it effectively and are better able to recognize threats that may derail it.

Context-sensitive pricing and adaptive engagement will become more critical. According to Mashable, in July 2012, a Spanish marketing agency called Momentum installed several soft drink vending machines filled with Coca-Cola's lemonade beverage Limón & Nada. These smart machines are able to read the outside temperature and provide incremental discounts as the temperature rises. The theory being, as it gets hotter, more people will be persuaded to buy Limon & Nada because the price makes it easy to say yes. Why run home for a glass of water when the price of lemonade is so low? We believe that this is just the start of a new business practice of context-sensitive pricing, not just in physical retail outlets, but online as well. As more intelligence is added to an increasingly digital supply chain, combined with context and A/B testing, computers will automatically adjust pricing according to several factors defined by the business.

For example, let's assume that you are in the market for a new car. As you're doing research from a mobile device, an ad pops up for a new car that a local dealer has in stock and is willing to sell for far below invoice. You click "No thanks," but before the ad closes it asks you why you didn't accept the offer. You choose an option that reads, "Because I am only in the market for a used car." Instantly, several new offers appear from local dealers that eerily match the exact cars you've been researching online. To make matters more interesting, all of the cars are in a price range that meets your budget requirements.

So what went on here? First, a computer determined your location and made some assumptions about your income based on a profile it automatically generated about you. Second, special software analytics on the website captured your research behavior and matched it to a profile in its database based on past user behavior. Third, supply-chain software checked the inventories and pricing of local car dealers and matched them to the profile it had for you. It may also have automatically contacted the car dealers to ask if they were willing to reduce their current prices for a hot prospect. Fourth, once it had the additional information it couldn't determine from your behavior or demographics (the used car answer), the system provided several real-time "take it or leave it" offers that were an exact match for the car you were in the market for.

3. **Employees will have to take responsibility for their own career growth.** The speed of business is moving at a velocity never before seen in human history. Knowledge workers can no longer accept that the business skills they acquired in high school and college will be enough of a foundation for the rest of their careers. In our research, even the best universities in the world fall far short on their undergraduate and MBA curricula for teaching modern social business principles. When we last checked, only a handful offered classes that taught even the most rudimentary social and mobile business strategies.

4. **Mobile, social, local, and commerce (SoLoMoCo) integrated technologies will offer unprecedented business opportunities.** In July 2012, mobile heavyweight Qualcomm released a powerful new mobile platform solution called Gimbal. Tech pundit Robert Scoble called it "the biggest thing in tech right now," but I believe he's underestimating its potential. Gimbal enables mobile software developers to add context-sensitive functionality to their applications. To put it simply, Gimbal will talk to the phone's hardware sensors: GPS, motion sensors, temperature sensors, the compass, and the camera, as well as look at software connected to Gimbal, such as a calendar, tasks, and other third-party applications, and make sense of it for you. I asked Roland Ligtenberg, product

developer at Qualcomm Labs, about the technology, and he told
me that Gimbal will also reduce the battery burden of powering
these technologies because it's leveraging the phone's chipset.
This means Gimbal-powered devices will become our intelligent
personal assistants at little expense to the phone's battery.

Here's an example from Ligtenberg on how the technology
might work: "In the future, my cell phone will know I ordered a
pizza. Will know when I get in my car. Will know who is in the
car with me. And will give me contextual data that will make my
life better. For instance, on my to-do list I might have put 'pick up
a hammer at the hardware store.' It will know that Round Table
Pizza is near the hardware store. It will know I have an extra fifteen minutes. It can use Waze to route me to the hardware store
first, tell me to pick up my hammer, and then head to Round Table
to pick up that pizza. All while measuring how many steps I took
(Nike Fuel points!) and telling me who has crossed my path."

5. **Our workplaces will go digital; they will have no choice.**
    Our work spaces will have to change from analog to digital work
    spaces. What we've seen in our research with executives and com-
    panies like Microsoft and IBM is that the world is moving faster
    and product cycles are shorter, yet the workplace is still built for
    slower-moving organizations. I can say with confidence that the
    workplace has to change dramatically in order to remain effec-
    tive. The effective workplaces of the future will find a way to
    integrate their organization's culture and mission. They will cre-
    ate adaptive workplaces where physical objectives and software
    adapt to the working style of the organization and not the other
    way around. Work in the workplace will become more human
    and more results oriented. In the end, the future workplace will
    be more of a digital and analytical environment that smartly
    enables more innovation, more collaboration, and more learning
    opportunities, all of which will increase competitiveness and the
    bottom line. The future workplace will remind employees that the
    business does not exist in a vacuum and it will help set organiza-
    tional priorities.

Becoming SOCIALIZED!

Situations demand that people adapt to new changes, new opportunities, and new challenges. Some people are better than others about recognizing and adjusting to them. Our central message in this book is that becoming adaptable through social means might seem daunting to some and opportunistic for others, but the necessity of it can't be ignored. General advances in technology, in economics, and in culture bring new rewards and new risks. There are winners and losers in their wake; the adaptable survive, while those who aren't become extinct. The once invincible Blockbuster, Lehman Brothers, Borders Group, Tribune Company, and Tower Records all went bankrupt because they could not adapt to changing market conditions or didn't have the social software systems in place to understand and react to Black Swan events.

I wish to propose, in closing, a new set of skills that we noticed participants in our research surveys possessed. These are people like Oliver Bussmann and Jon Becher from SAP, Vala Afshar from Enterasys, Matt Michelsen from Backplane, and Sandy Carter from IBM, most of whom are incredibly busy executives who have made becoming a social executive a priority. Being "connected" has afforded these executives greater opportunities and bigger platforms on which they can share their ideas. It's also given them a unique skill set, one that all employees will need in order to adapt to the future of business.

First, social business is about recognizing that the game has changed in business. No longer do the winners hoard information in silos, build ivory towers around themselves, or ignore the crowd's input. In the future, successful employees will readily share pertinent information, build reputations as subject matter experts, and source new ideas from people inside and outside the organization.

Second, business is becoming more mobile. Future employees will need to learn how to collaborate and develop work product remotely. You may even see new companies without walls, in which all employees are working virtually. Master the skill of working and managing remotely, and you're already ahead of the curve.

Third, those who can synthesize and act on social data will become tomorrow's Mary Meeker (a partner at Kleiner Perkins Caufield & Byers, who is known for her technology prognostication skills). It used to be that information was fed to you in the form of industry news, or perhaps the company's chief strategist would decipher key industry trends for everyone. That won't cut it in the future. Successful employees will learn how to tune in and interpret the streams of social information pertinent to their jobs and their careers.

Fourth, employees will need to be competent on emerging technologies. There are new mobile and social tools that are being developed every day that can change your business and career overnight. Successful knowledge workers will learn how to sift through all of the new technologies and mobilize around the ones that can give them a competitive advantage.

Fifth, successful workers will learn to develop a personal group of knowledgeable specialists that can help them synthesize ideas and put them into action. These specialists will be people with circles of knowledge that are outside the employee's expertise but related to it. Most knowledge workers have a deep understanding of how to accomplish the tasks in front of them, but as new challenges emerge from a hypercompetitive future, their sense of what to do may become fuzzier. The curve of knowledge, in those circumstances, can be extended by utilizing the strengths and knowledge of those within our circles.

Sixth, employees will need to learn how to be effective and influential on internal and external social networks. Remember how SAP's Oliver Bussmann used Twitter to connect with analysts and thought leaders? He discovered through his subsequent discussions with them that a new trend in mobile apps was emerging and that it was in SAP's best interest to capitalize on it. Bussmann then used his influence to mobilize the company internally to act on that information. Bussmann would not have discovered a new business opportunity without first utilizing his soft skills—that is, emotional intelligence to effectively connect with people inside and outside the organization.

In business, technology, and science we live in a remarkable time. So it is that truly outstanding performance in this new era requires a new skill set. Do not lament the skills you've developed in the past or decry the ones you'll need in the future. Celebrate instead the massive opportunities in front us. Do not lament the "traditional ways" of doing business. Celebrate instead the new tools that give us unprecedented means of connecting with anyone in the world. Do not lament the democratization of information in business today. Celebrate instead the ability to harness that knowledge to create something truly great.

Above all, remember that the new possibilities for each of us in this new world are truly extraordinary. Political borders are less relevant in business today and will be even less relevant in the future. Geographic constraints to participating in this new social era are irrelevant, and no longer will people be limited by class, politics, culture, or gender. We will all delight in the new innovations and businesses that start in the most remote areas of the world, because that is what true human progress means.

I, for one, am excited about our world's future.

Endnotes

Chapter 1

1. Steven W. Usselman, "Still Visible: Alfred D. Chandler's The Visible Hand," *Technology and Culture* Vol 47: 3 (2006): 584596

2. "Facebook S-1 Amendment: New Stats From Q1 2012 And More," Huffington Post, accessed April 23, 2012, http://www.huffingtonpost.com/2012/04/23/facebook-s-1-amendment_n_1446853.html

3. "48 Significant Social Media Facts, Figures and Statistics Plus 7 Infographics," JeffBullas.com, accessed April 23, 2012, http://www.jeffbullas.com/2012/04/23/48-significant-social-media-facts-figures-and-statistics-plus-7-infographics/

4. "Unleashing the Power of Social Media Within Your Organization" APCO Worldwide, Accessed May 20, 2012, http://www.apcoworldwide.com/content/services/ism.aspx.

5. "Infographic: Social Media Statistics For 2012," Digital Buzz Blog, accessed May 2, 2012, http://www.digitalbuzzblog.com/social-media-statistics-stats-2012-infographic/?goback=%2Egmp_2352580%2Egde_2352580_member_108306409.

6. Juan Enriquez, "The Data That Defines Us," *CIO Magazine* (Fall/Winter 2003). Accessed July 19, 2006.

7. "Cisco Visual Networking Index: Global Mobile Data Traffic Forecast Update, 2011–2016," Cisco Systems, accessed May 15, 2012, http://www.cisco.com/en/US/solutions/collateral/ns341/ns525/ns537/ns705/ns827/white_paper_c11-520862.html.

Chapter 2

1. "Staples' mobile strategy based on customer convenience, loyalty", BtoB Online, accessed April 16, 2012 http://www.btobonline.com/article/20120312/WEB02/303129949/staples-mobile-strategy-based-on-customer-convenience-loyalty#seenit

2. For an excellent book on the subject, buy Nancy Duarte's, *Resonate* (Wiley, 2010).

3. Interestingly, on July 10, 2012 I was alerted to a Global Social Marketing position on LinkedIn

4. Sources: GlassDoor.com and interviews conducted by author Mark Fidelman.

Chapter 6

1. http://www.nytimes.com/2012/03/14/opinion/why-i-am-leaving-goldman-sachs.html?pagewanted=all

Chapter 7

1. At the time of this writing, Dell seems to be struggling, but sources tell me the social listening made them aware of a significant market shift and they are executing on a plan to capitalize on it.

2. "Ashton Kutcher Seeks VP of Pop Culture," PR NewsWire, accessed May 2012, http://www.prnewswire.com/news-releases/ashton-kutcher-seeks-vp-of-op-culture-116309874.html

3. You can find a few of mine here: http://www.flickr.com/photos/fidelman

Acknowledgments

This book is the shared vision and mission of innumerable employees, executives, and consumers who believe that traditional business approaches are over. To my close friends and family who suffered through my late nights and lost weekends, my eternal appreciation for not giving up on me.

I am forever grateful to those that helped me with the book and took my call to learn about their success. People that helped me with the research, Grant Crowell, Jas Dhillon, and Kare Anderson. The more than one hundred people that took my call to be interviewed for the *Business Insider* or *Forbes*. People like my wife Kelly Fidelman, Gary Lane, Hal Wendel, and Jenna Dobkin who provided some much needed clarity around this book's concepts. To my publisher Bibliomotion who agreed to fast track this book given my desire to provide the most relevant content in a timely manner. To the social business community who has never stopped supporting me and promoting my best ideas. For PB Works, for agreeing to allow me to build this book on their platform. To Forbes.com's Bruce Upbin who took a chance on me with the *Forbes* column "Socialized and Mobilized" which allows me a huge platform to get my ideas out into the business community.

Grant Crowell—Researcher and Co-Editor

Grant Crowell is a trusted veteran content marketer, author, blogger, speaker and all-around Jack of many trades. He has worked in the online marketing industry since 1996 providing digital strategies and development to enterprises and entrepreneurs of all sizes, including video, search marketing/SEO, social media, usability, legal issues, and ethics.

Index